"HIV Is God's Blessing"

"HIV Is God's Blessing"

REHABILITATING MORALITY IN NEOLIBERAL RUSSIA

JARRETT ZIGON

UNIVERSITY OF CALIFORNIA PRESS
Berkeley   Los Angeles   London

University of California Press, one of the most distinguished university presses in the United States, enriches lives around the world by advancing scholarship in the humanities, social sciences, and natural sciences. Its activities are supported by the UC Press Foundation and by philanthropic contributions from individuals and institutions. For more information, visit www.ucpress.edu.

University of California Press
Berkeley and Los Angeles, California

University of California Press, Ltd.
London, England

Library of Congress Cataloging-in-Publication Data

Zigon, Jarrett.
    HIV is God's blessing : rehabilitating morality in neoliberal Russia / Jarrett Zigon.
        p.   cm.
    Includes bibliographical references and index.
    ISBN 978-0-520-26762-6 (cloth : alk. paper)
    ISBN 978-0-520-26764-0 (pbk. : alk. paper)
    1. Russia (Federation)—Moral conditions.   2. Russia (Federation)—Social conditions—21st century.   3. Church and social problems—Russia (Federation)   4. Social values—Russia (Federation)   5. Drug addicts—Rehabilitation—Russia (Federation)   6. AIDS (Disease)—Religious aspects—Orthodox Eastern Church.   7. Orthodox Eastern Church—Russia (Federation).   I. Title.
    HN530.2.Z9M6985   2011
    303.3′72094709051—dc22   2010039368

Manufactured in the United States of America

20   19   18   17   16   15   14   13   12   11
10   9   8   7   6   5   4   3   2   1

This book is printed on Cascades Enviro 100, a 100% post consumer waste, recycled, de-inked fiber. FSC recycled certified and processed chlorine free. It is acid free, Ecologo certified, and manufactured by BioGas energy.

Contents

Acknowledgments   vii

Introduction   1

PART I   BACKGROUNDS

1. HIV, Drug Use, and the Politics of Indifference   20

2. The Church's Rehabilitation Program   31

3. The Russian Orthodox Church, HIV, and
    Injecting Drug Use   54

4. Moral and Ethical Assemblages   62

5. *Synergeia* and *Simfoniia:* Orthodox Morality,
    Human Rights, and the State   73

6. Working on the Self   94

PART II   PRACTICES

7. Enchurchment   114

8. Cultivating a Normal Life   148

9. Normal Sociality: *Obshchenie* and
    Controlling Emotions   159

10. Disciplining Responsibility: Labor
    and Gender   201

    Some Closing Words   223

    Notes   235
    References   247

Acknowledgments

This book would not have been possible without the help and support of many people along the way. I would like to thank the following persons for important conversations around the topics explored in this book or for reading various versions of it, whether in part or in whole; all of them have been essential to its outcome: Matt Curtis, Daniel Wolfe, Nancy Ries, Catherine Wanner, Douglas Rogers, Melissa Caldwell, Chris Hann, Eugene Raikhel, Jason Throop, Alex Edmonds, Oskar Verkaaik, Michael Blim, Thomas Blom Hansen, Anita Hardon, Peter van Rooden, Patrick Neveling, Thomas Widlok, Talal Asad, and Joel Robbins. The research for this book would not have been successful without the tireless work, support, and friendship of my research assistant, Yaroslav Morozov. To a great extent the final version of this book took shape thanks to Reed Malcolm and the thoughtful and stimulating comments of the three anonymous reviewers. I would also like to thank all of those who have slipped beyond my memory at this moment.

Many thanks also go out to the following persons for their friendship throughout this long process: Johnny Phelan, Karin Zilliacus, Jimmy Weir, Dylan Turner, Esin Egit, Eric Werner, Natalie Frigo, Mark Francis, Friedrich Binder, Ida Harboe Knudsen, and Florian Mühlfried. Of course it goes without saying that none of this would have been possible without the love and support of my parents—Sandy, David, and Janelle. They have given me more than they will ever know. Finally, thanks to Sylvia, whose presence in my life has revealed to me the true joys of living.

In the end this book would not have been possible without the participation of all those in St. Petersburg who allowed me to become a part of the delicate and excruciating process of rehabilitation. Their lives, experiences, and struggles have allowed this book to come into being, and they have also forever altered my own outlook and approach to life. For that I am most thankful.

Research and writing for this project was made possible through funding provided by a Postdoctoral Research Fellowship from the Max Planck Institute for Social Anthropology. Parts of chapter 4 are drawn with modification from my previous book, *Morality: An Anthropological Perspective* (Berg Publishers, 2008), and from "Morality within a Range of Possibilities: A Dialogue with Joel Robbins," *Ethnos* 74(2), 2009. Parts of chapter 9 are drawn with modification from "A Disease of Frozen Feelings: Ethically Working on Emotional Worlds in a Russian Orthodox Church Drug Rehabilitation Program," *Medical Anthropology Quarterly* 24(3), 2010.

Introduction

Andrei was found by his mother lying on his back in the corner of the bedroom, his mouth and throat filled with his own vomit. He had been dead since the previous evening. I first met Andrei in the recreation room of The Mill, the Russian Orthodox Church's drug rehabilitation center near St. Petersburg, where he was using the exercise equipment one afternoon in November. He told me that he had started rehabilitation two weeks earlier to get off heroin and that he was doing so for his mother. "I am all she has, and I finally realized I was slowly killing her by using this stuff," he told me, slightly out of breath from the workout. He seemed determined to overcome his addiction. Three months later he returned to St. Petersburg and began using heroin again in less than a week. About a month later he returned to The Mill and told me that this time he would stop for sure, that he would stay at The Mill until they could find him a place at a parish. After ten days he stopped waiting and returned to the city and heroin. Less than a month later his mother found him dead.

Though tragic, Andrei's story is not unusual in Russia today. Like most HIV-positive injecting drug users (IDUs) in Russia, Andrei was young, only twenty when he died, and had been using heroin nearly half his life. He started using when he was just thirteen, at a time when heroin could be found in St. Petersburg as easily and as cheap as a pack of cigarettes. Often a person did not need to leave his apartment complex (*dvor*) in order to buy it. There is no doubt that many young Russians began to use heroin in times of social desperation related to the various economic crises of the mid- and late 1990s, but there were other reasons as well. Andrei first used simply because he did not want to appear scared in front of friends who offered it to him. Certainly not rich, his family was also not in any way poor. His father had died when he was young, and his mother had raised him and his sister to be loving and respectful children, and she always made sure Andrei took his studies seriously. He was also, he told me with a bit of nostalgia and still out of breath from his workout, becoming a fine young athlete. Then, in a social context where heroin was quickly becoming as common as marijuana and alcohol, young Andrei succumbed to peer pressure.

Years later, after having lost most of his non-heroin-using friends, dropping out of school, selling what he could from his mother's apartment, introducing his sister to heroin, selling heroin in his *dvor*, living in the streets, contracting HIV and hepatitis C, being arrested several times, and attempting to quit on his own on numerous occasions, Andrei entered the Church-run rehabilitation program. Like most who come to The Mill, Andrei understood that in order to quit heroin he would have to change himself, but he did not know what that meant. He was completely unprepared for the intensity not only of the daily schedule that attempted to regulate his every moment, but particularly for the intensity of the work he would have to do on himself. On several occasions I observed Andrei trying to find ways, including using me, to avoid therapeutic activities. This is not at all uncommon at The Mill, not because rehabilitants desire to resist the therapeutic process of the Church-run program, but because remaking oneself into a new, moral person is inherently difficult.[1] The overwhelming nature of the transformation can easily lead one to a state of hopeless resignation.

Like so many others, Andrei eventually returned to the city and soon thereafter to heroin. For a short period he tried to hide his use from his mother. But when all the signs of his use and his selling heroin from the apartment returned, Andrei's mother could no longer believe his lies. Her love never ended, but trust had disappeared. After she buried him she told the priest that at least now she didn't have to worry about him anymore; he was in God's hands, and she hoped that what he learned at The Mill would help him where he was now. With Andrei gone his mother only had to worry about his sister, whose whereabouts she did not know. She continued to pray for both of them.

In the view of many, Andrei is an example of a failed case of rehabilitation. If one's view of rehabilitation is that it is successful only if a person never again uses heroin, then I suppose they are right. But if rehabilitation can be seen in another light, as the possibility of living, even if for a very short period, some semblance of what might be called a normal life, then perhaps Andrei is not just another sad example of failed rehabilitation. I do not want to be misunderstood. No one would claim that Andrei had successfully experienced the rehabilitation process because for three short months he may have had moments of joy, comfort, and supportive social relations that he hadn't had in a long time. His fate was tragic and sad, and nothing can change that. But one of the things I hope to show throughout this book is that the rehabilitation process is not simply about overcoming addiction. If this were the case, nearly all rehabilitation programs would be considered failures, since studies show that up to 60 percent of clients treated for alcohol or other drug dependence begin to actively use again within a year.[2] There must be something more to this process.

This book is about that something more. One of the main goals of the Russian Orthodox Church's drug rehabilitation and HIV prevention and care program in the St. Petersburg area is providing the opportunity for injecting drug users to live what many Russians call a normal life (*normal'naya zhizn'*). But what constitutes this normal life? The normal life offered by the Church-run program is not necessarily the life it produces. To see how this is the case, the rehabilitation program will be considered as a process of ethically remaking one's moral way of being in the social world—one's moral personhood. This book discloses some of the possibilities for such an ethical project as they are lived out and experienced by rehabilitants within the assemblage of the Church-run program.

HIV IS GOD'S BLESSING

"HIV is God's blessing," I was told by Natalia Aleksandrovna. As the head of the Russian Orthodox Church's drug rehabilitation and HIV prevention and care programs in the St. Petersburg diocese, she was explaining their approach to combating Russia's HIV and injecting drug use epidemics. The phrase may sound crass, if not offensive, but her point was that from the Church's perspective the diagnosis of HIV, or even the fear that one may become infected, can be an important motivation for overcoming addiction. In a country where 80 percent of those who are HIV positive became so as a consequence of injecting drug use, in the Church's view only behavior change is the ultimate guarantee of prevention.

In the Church-run program this behavior change necessitates a complete remaking of one's moral personhood. Thus the rehabilitation process was often described by both the staff and rehabilitants like Andrei as a process of "stepping over oneself" (*sebya pridetsya perestupat*) by "working on oneself" (*rabota nad soboi*) and becoming a "normal person" (*normal'niy chelovek*) who can live a "normal life" (*normal'naya zhizn'*). It should be acknowledged from the outset that rehabilitation programs the world over are often considered by those who participate in them and by those who study them as programs of self-transformation.[3] Unfortunately, unlike the numerous anthropological studies of drug users, their lives and networks, there have been very few anthropological or ethnographic studies of drug treatment and rehabilitation programs.[4] There is thus no intellectual tradition addressing treatment and rehabilitation with which I can engage in terms of approaches, questions, and paradigms. What work has been done in this field has provided inspiration primarily by means of the lacunae in this literature, in particular the lack of studies from the perspective of those actually struggling through rehabilitation. As Hunt and Barker put it in their review of this "sadly sparse" literature, the client's experience "is probably the area of drug treatment research about which least is known," and what little has been shown of this experience tends to portray clients as "passive."[5] Such a portrayal seems particularly odd since most of the researchers writing on drug treatment and rehabilitation claim that these programs are primarily concerned with what they call identity transformation. What, then, happened to the people? One of the primary goals of my own research and the analysis of it in this book is to reveal the drug rehabilitation process from the perspective of rehabilitants like Andrei and their experience of the therapeutic process as an ethical process of making a new moral personhood.

To this end my analytic perspective is that of an anthropology of moralities that is concerned with the uses of the various discourses, practices, and processes that assemble in a particular context and come to constitute what *counts* as morality and ethics. In this sense the theory of moralities I outline in part I, and which is central to my analysis, allows us to recognize that particular social and ethnographic contexts are more appropriately described in terms of moral and ethical assemblages rather than defined by a totalizing morality. Morality can be considered as three different aspects—the institutional, the public discourse, and nonconscious embodied dispositions—each of which consists of a range of possibilities for what is recognizable as morality within particular social locations. Ethics, on the other hand, is those intentional and reflective tactics and practices utilized in moments of ethical demand when a person needs to work on herself in order to be with herself and others morally. Ethics is a process of working on oneself in order to remake oneself, even if ever so slightly, into a new moral person. This distinction is vital for understanding the rehabilitation process in the Church-run program as a process of making new moral persons. For it is my claim that the therapeutic process in this program, if not all therapeutic programs, is primarily a process of cultivating a particular kind of moral personhood.

As already mentioned, rehabilitation programs the world over are often considered programs of self-transformation. In this sense the Church-run program is not unique. What is unique is the peculiar assemblage of global and historical influences that constitute this program. From Soviet, Orthodox, and neoliberal discourses and practices of shaping, training, and making personhood, to Orthodox conceptions of sin and illness, to secular notions of therapeutics, to Orthodox and neoliberal ways of being in the social world, the Church-run program is not simply a rehabilitation and care program that combines both religious and secular therapeutics. Rather it is a context that brings together a unique genealogy of the mutual constitution of the sacred and the secular.[6] That is to say, neither of these concepts can be said to be strictly defined outside the context of their use. Rather they come to be so defined by means of the various discourses and practices that are used in certain ways within particular contexts, and as such come to be recognized as either sacred or secular. My primary intention in this book is to analyze this unique assemblage of what counts as sacred and secular in the Church-run program, the ways it shapes a particular kind of person, and to call into question the very distinction between a so-called sacred and secular therapeutics.

A significant aspect of the Church-run program is the way Orthodox moral theology in combination with the Church's recent notion of human rights frames the therapeutic process. Orthodox moral theology claims that all persons are born with the inherent duality of the image and likeness of God. The image of God is given by grace, but the likeness of God is merely a potentiality, the realization of which one must ethically work to attain. Recently the Russian Orthodox Church has made public its official document on human rights, which states that human rights are meant to structure a society so as to allow persons to more easily become moral, and in so doing ethically work to attain the likeness of God. The result of this process, in the Church's view, is the cultivation not only of moral persons, but of citizen-subjects responsible for morally

resurrecting the Russian nation.[7] The document names addiction rehabilitation as one area in which the Church can work to implement this
view of human rights. It is my contention that the Church-run program
can be viewed in just this way.

Ultimately the dispositional capacities the Church-run program
attempts to cultivate within rehabilitants provide them with the ability
to live very different life trajectories than the Church intends. Ever since
Foucault's insights into the intimate relation between techniques of subjectivization and political techniques,[8] anthropologists have attended to
the ways the production of certain kinds of subjectivities must be understood as at the same time the production of a particular kind of object on
which power is exercised. If the human rights discourse of the Russian
Orthodox Church links rights with good citizenship,[9] then what kind of
political subject or object is being produced by means of the practices
of this discursive regime?

Giorgio Agamben's philosophy of sovereign power and bare life is an
important theoretical lens through which to view the Russian Orthodox
Church's human rights intervention in the HIV crisis in Russia today.
According to Agamben, "Sacredness is a line of flight still present in contemporary politics, a line that is as such moving into spaces increasingly
vast and dark, to the point of ultimately coinciding with the biological
life itself of citizens."[10] Such is how he describes the modern political
relation, which at its very foundation links sovereignty with both the
sacred and bare life, that is, the biological life that can be killed, or at
least left to die. In his historical-philosophical analysis of the Roman legal
category of the *homo sacer*, the sacred man "who may be killed and yet
not sacrificed,"[11] in other words, the person who can be killed without
having the charge of homicide brought against the killer, Agamben
argues that the establishment of this category of exclusion was the originary sovereign decision that founded what has now become a global
hegemonic political order—a biopolitical order that is founded on bare
life as both subject and object and that now exercises the power of life
or death over all individuals as sacred men.

Whereas originally it may have been the sovereign's decision that
demarcated the sacred man as the exclusion that secured the political,
Agamben argues that over time and with the development of modern

democracies the sovereign and the *homo sacer* converged into one within individuals as modern subjects, who by this very convergence come to be endowed with certain inalienable human rights. But such a notion is a fiction, according to Agamben, who, following Arendt, points out that in the person of the refugee we see the erasure of rights, sovereignty, and indeed anything inalienable. The refugee is simply bare life. This is so because the refugee lacks citizenship status in any nation-state, and as such discloses the fact that it is citizenship and not humanness that provides the possibility for what is called human rights. It is this disclosure that reveals the tenuousness of the modern claim that rights are founded on the inherent dignity or sacredness of humans and once again exposes the fact that power lies in the power over bare life. As Agamben might put it, because in the modern world all individuals have become *homines sacri,* they must either become good citizens who contribute in appropriate ways to the sociopolitical order as nation-state, and as such enjoy their supposed inalienable rights, or expose themselves as those "who may be killed and yet not sacrificed." For Agamben the line between this either/or of the referent of sacredness is fuzzy and ever shifting in the modern world. A good citizen today may become one "who may be killed and yet not sacrificed" tomorrow.

This is clearly seen in the increasing decentralization of the power to decide over bare life in the modern world.

> If there is a line in every modern state marking the point at which the decision on life becomes a decision on death, and biopolitics can turn into thanatopolitics, this line no longer appears today as a stable border dividing two clearly distinct zones. This line is now in motion and gradually moving into areas other than that of political life, areas in which the sovereign is entering into an ever more intimate symbiosis not only with the jurist but also with the doctor, the scientist, the expert, and the priest.[12]

In the modern world of neoliberalism the power over bare life has moved from the hands of the absolute sovereign to those of bureaucratic functionaries and the instrumental intelligentsia. In today's world one's sacredness, that is, one's essential nature as one who can be killed or left to die, can be disclosed with untold consequences by the simple legislation of a new law, the discovery of a new disorder, or a diagnosis in a clinic.

If only those who are good citizens are entitled to human rights, then the attempt to provide human rights to individuals is the attempt to transform them into persons of good citizenship. It is little wonder that in a world in which biopolitics is increasingly focused on the bare life of all individuals that human rights have increasingly focused on the health of populations.[13] For what could be more vulnerable to the workings of a power that at one and the same time subjectivizes and objectifies than the fragile body of the sick, ill, and diseased, the fragile body that so openly reveals the bare life of all humans? As Agamben puts it, if humanitarian organizations, many of which claim to be working for the implementation of human rights, "can only grasp human life in the figure of bare or sacred life, [then], despite themselves, [they] maintain a secret solidarity with the very powers they ought to fight."[14] In this sense, rather than protecting individuals from the abuses of power that human rights–oriented organizations often claim to be doing, they are further subjecting individuals to the gaze of a power that makes them both subject and object. That is, by relying on, espousing, and enacting a discursive regime of human rights founded on the notion of the sacredness and dignity of all human persons, they are helping to create a world of sacred men, or *homines sacri,* "who may be killed and yet not sacrificed."

Agamben's arguments have been taken up by several anthropologists addressing the HIV/AIDS pandemic. I would suggest, however, that their use of Agamben focuses too much on his arguments regarding the exclusion of bare life in the constitution of the political. Thus, for example, Kistner argues that the so-called South African "AIDS war" is best understood in the stark terms of a sovereign-political rationale of the exclusion of the undesirable bare life of people living with HIV/AIDS.[15] Similarly Biehl describes zones of abandonment in Brazil where infected persons are mostly forgotten as they wait to die.[16] Responding to these anthropologists Jean Comaroff has argued for a politics that focuses on the "not-so-bare life" for the practice of a "more robust" citizenship.[17]

It is my contention that all of these examples miss Agamben's main point. Sovereignty does not simply exclude bare life in the process of constituting the political; rather, as Steven DeCaroli argues, it is bare life that is the very material on which sovereignty works to secure its power and "manage obedience" by means of various subjectivization disciplinary processes.[18] In other words, bare life is the border space located in and on the human body on which power works a double movement of inclusion-exclusion in order to discipline good citizen-subjects, and in the process solidify sovereign power.

It is this double movement worked upon the bare life of individuals that I find compelling about Agamben's work and that I see as going beyond the political-ethical techniques of power disclosed by Foucault. This is so because to speak about work on bare life goes beyond disciplinary work on the body. Whereas for Foucault the body may be docile, for Agamben the body is not only docile but expendable: the body as bare life can ultimately be killed or left to die. Thus in my reading of Agamben I see a twofold process of this double movement of inclusion-exclusion working upon bare life in the attempt to produce the political, and in doing so simultaneously produce subjects and objects of power.[19] First, while it may be the docile body that is ethically worked upon to cultivate morally good citizen-subjects, the failure of these subjects to properly embody these necessary dispositions often leaves them exposed as bare life in societies increasingly unwilling to accept or support such "untrainable" subjects. I have in mind here persons such as the homeless, refugees, the poor, drug users, convicted criminals, and the mentally and physically ill. Second, increasingly in what has come to be called the neoliberal world these "untrainable" subjects are placed in spaces of inclusion-exclusion where they receive "one more chance" to work on themselves to become acceptable citizen-subjects. I have in mind here spaces such as shelters, rehabilitation centers, camps, and various health and law-enforcement institutions. The failure to successfully work on oneself in these spaces of "last chance" is followed in many cases by the total abandonment of the state or private institutions in the care of the life of these persons. For this reason I consider Agamben's concepts of bare life and inclusion-exclusion to be vital for understanding the therapeutic process under way in the Church-run heroin rehabilitation and HIV treatment program. Both of these processes of the double movement of inclusion-exclusion are central to what occurs in this program. Therefore the analytical approach I use goes beyond a Foucauldian analysis of disciplinary regimes in that by utilizing this twofold character of the ethical and political work of inclusion-exclusion on bare life, I emphasize the always looming fatal consequence of the failure to embody the program's disciplinary ways of being.

Michelle Rivkin-Fish has argued that "sexuality has become a key site for moral struggles over the future of the [Russian] nation."[20] I will go further and say that the body as bare life as I have just described it has become this site of moral struggle. For in contemporary Russia it is the body as the locus of the distinction between health and disease, normality and abnormality, and productivity and unproductivity in terms of labor and reproduction that has become the material on which morality is to be molded, the failure of which has significantly contributed to the death of many marginalized citizens. As a space of inclusion-exclusion, the Russian Orthodox Church drug rehabilitation and HIV prevention and care program in St. Petersburg utilizes a human rights discourse founded in Orthodox moral theology in order to work upon the body as bare life and transform persons into good and responsible citizens, or what they call normal persons. It is my contention that because the Church-run program emphasizes the inherent worth and sacredness of all persons as the foundation for moral transformation, which manifests itself in this program as a moral transformation into good and responsible citizens, this program provides a clear and explicit example of the founding relationship between the sacred and political power that is less manifest in a more general and secularized human rights discourse.

NEOLIBERALISM AND POST-SOVIET RUSSIA

Others have pointed out the link between HIV/AIDS discrimination or methadone treatment and neoliberal governance and citizenship.[21] I want to take this a step further and argue that the tragic irony of the

Church-run program is that it is ultimately a space of inclusion-exclusion where responsibilized subjects are cultivated who are *better* prepared to live in the very neoliberal, Western-oriented world the Church discursively claims to be combating. Therefore, as Natalia Aleksandrovna's claim that "HIV is God's blessing" reveals, by working on the bare life of addicted and infected individuals, and utilizing a discourse of Orthodox morality and human rights to do so, the Church-run program unintentionally supports a regime of biopower that it claims is the root cause of the very social and moral problems the program was established to overcome. That this support is unintended is important, for as unintended it does not simply continue a long tradition of the Church's support of the ruling regime in Russia. Rather it indicates the unwitting participation in a form of power that transcends the Russian government and that the Church considers a foreign form of governance, morality, and lifestyle that is destructive of the Russian nation.[22]

This form of power is neoliberalism. Borrowing from recent explications of neoliberalism, in this book I consider it a paradoxical form of governance in which government actively creates the conditions within which appropriate kinds of behavior and activity are more easily enacted, and at the same time encourages a radical decentralization of responsibility requiring the institutional and personal cultivation of autonomy and discipline.[23] As a result of this radical decentralization, private institutions, organizations, and businesses have become increasingly responsible for providing the various services once offered by modernist states, and in doing so have increasingly become disciplinary spaces for cultivating self-responsible, disciplined, and autonomous subjects who bear the bulk of the responsibility for providing for their own well-being. This radical decentralization of services and responsibility has been accompanied by the shift Agamben described, of the increasing decentralization of the decision over life and death. It is my contention that within this new regime of biopower responsibility has become the hegemonic moral virtue that any good neoliberal subject must come to embody. By responsibility I mean an obligation to and for oneself as well as an Other, which is enacted by means of disciplined self-vigilance. Responsibility, then, is a dispositional attitude that enacts social relations by means of a hyper-self-aware individual who is able to stand outside of and be within those very relations at the same time. Thus through responsibility individuals at one and the same time constitute sociality and stand outside it as the very support that allows for its constitution. Responsibility is the moral disposition par excellence of the biopolitics of neoliberalism. Perhaps because of this, responsibility is also a central moral disposition for successfully living within a multidiscursive society.

Just as this new biopolitical regime was gaining dominance in the late capitalist world, the Soviet Union collapsed. Because of this and for much of the 1990s post-Soviet Russia became a space of experiment for the implementation of neoliberal forms of political, financial, institutional, and personal governance, so that by the turn of the millennium neoliberalism had become the dominant discourse in Russia.[24] In the post-Soviet years this discourse has been central for shaping new forms of business and administrative relations, consumer practices, and medical and welfare services, as well as the subjects who participate in, rely on, and live these ways of being in the social world.[25] One of the main arguments of this book is that the Church-run program is just one of the disciplinary spaces of inclusion-exclusion for cultivating the kinds of subjects who can successfully live what some have described as a sane life in contemporary neoliberal Russia.[26]

This idea of a sane life is central to my argument, for I consider it more or less the theoretical equivalent to what Russians call a normal life (*normal'naya zhizn'*), which is what many described to me as the goal of rehabilitation. The philosopher Susan Wolf defines a sane life as "a desire that one's self be connected to the world in a certain way—we could even say it is a desire that one's self be *controlled by* the world in certain ways and not in others."[27] Talal Asad has borrowed this concept and further argues that to live sanely in the world "presupposes knowing the world practically and being known practically by it, a world of accumulating probabilities rather than constant certainties."[28] To live a normal or sane life, I argue, is to cultivate a certain sensibility for living within a particular range of possibilities that *counts* as a normal or sane life. In this sense just as normalcy is defined by adherence to a certain statistical tendency,[29] so too a normal life is *not* the embodiment of a narrowly defined disciplinary and discursive regime, but rather the dispositional capacity to negotiate the range of discursive possibilities within a social world. Because every society is constituted by a number of competing discursive traditions this capacity is necessary for living a sane life. I suggest that in the contemporary world that is increasingly characterized by more and more competing discursive traditions, of which neoliberalism has become dominant, responsibility is a foundational moral disposition that allows for a normal and sane life.

It must be recognized, however, that although neoliberalism has become the dominant discourse in post-Soviet Russia, it has not necessarily brought with it an entirely new set of institutional and personal values and relations. In fact, as Stephen Collier has argued, more than anything the new neoliberal regime of living has reinscribed and reworked already existing values and practices into more efficient, rational, and reflexive forms.[30] Similarly Tatyana Teplova has shown that the radical decentralization of welfare and health services that are characteristic of neoliberal regimes was relatively easily done in Russia since the Soviet system of such services were already "highly decentralized"; they were not managed by the centralized government, but rather by each employment enterprise that worked as a "microwelfare state in itself."[31] These preexisting institutional structures and values have made the post-Soviet transformation to a neoliberal discursive regime that much easier, even if, as Teplova contends, in its current state it remains a unique mix of Soviet and neoliberal forms. Similar to these works I argue throughout this book that two of the most important values and practices that are central to neoliberalism—responsibility and ethical practices of work on the self—were also central not only to Soviet biopolitics, but to contemporary Russian Orthodox moral theology and practice as well. The sharing of values and practices by multiple discursive formations in contemporary Russia is just one of the reasons successful rehabilitants from the Church-run program can be considered well prepared to live sane lives in this neoliberal-dominated social world.

To understand how this happens I adopt the analytic perspective on the performative relation between discourse and subjectivity theorized by Judith Butler and utilized by Alexei Yurchak in his work on this relationship in the late Soviet and post-Soviet periods and Saba Mahmood in her analysis of women's Islamic piety movements in Egypt.[32] A performative approach to discourse argues that by means of various institutions and public media outlets a particular discursive formation is established that comes to define the range of possibilities for iterable speech and disciplined acting—and by extension thinking and emoting—within a particular social world.[33] While every society can be characterized as dominated by a particular discursive tradition, societies are also always constituted by competing discourses. Therefore this performative establishment can be understood to take place not only for the dominant discourse, which in post-Soviet Russia is neoliberalism, but also its multiple competing discourses, for example, Russian Orthodoxy. Living a normal or sane life entails the capacity to successfully negotiate between these competing discourses.

To live this kind of life a person must cultivate a disposition that allows him to live not only the dominant discursive form of life, but also one or more of its competing discursive forms. If the discursive range of possibilities is performatively established, then it is also performatively enacted, cultivated, and embodied by individuals through a process of what Butler calls iterability, or "a regularized and constrained repetition" within particular disciplinary spaces of inclusion-exclusion.[34] The result of this disciplinary process is the eventual remaking of individuals into new moral persons capable of sanely living in a multidiscursive society.[35] The Church-run program is just one of these disciplinary spaces in contemporary Russia for cultivating persons with this dispositional capacity. To show how this is true I follow Yurchak's lead in posing Foucauldian *how* questions of the relationship between discourse and subjectivization by means of ethnographically analyzing the disciplinary practices performed by rehabilitants in this program.[36] What becomes clear through this analysis is that the subjects cultivated by means of these practices are not necessarily those intended by the staff of the program.

To understand why this is so it is important to recognize that although the Church-run program self-identifies and promotes itself as defined by, organized according to, and propagating Orthodox discourse and practices, much of what is actually said and done in this program is very similar to some discourses and practices of neoliberal, Soviet, and secular therapeutic regimes of living. In other words, the Church-run program and Russian Orthodoxy in general do not recognize that some of the fundamental moral dispositions and ethical skills it considers essential to Orthodox moral theology are transferable and allow for successful living within competing discursive formations such as neoliberalism. There need not be a direct equality in terms of the particular value concepts or discursive foundational assumptions between these formations in order for subjects who have embodied their dispositional capacities to live sanely within competing discursive formations. Thus, for example, the moral virtue and ethical disciplining of responsibility is central to both neoliberal and Orthodox discursive regimes. But if the particular ethical and disciplinary practices utilized in the Church-run program and the underlying theological-discursive foundation for valuing responsibility as a virtue are not the exact same as those of neoliberal regimes, the disciplined and responsibilized subject that is cultivated within the Church-run program is still *better prepared* to live in the dominant neoliberal world of Russia than he was prior to entering these programs. Therefore the Orthodox discourse does not need to share the neoliberal assumption of autonomous individualism to share the moral virtue of responsibility. My argument throughout this book is not that the Church-run program unwittingly supports neoliberal regimes of living because they share the same foundational moral assumptions and standards. Far from it. Rather the support is unintended because of the very fact of the different foundational discursive assumptions, which despite this difference produce very similar disciplined subjects with very similar embodied dispositions, such as responsibility.

This book, then, is an intimate analytical description of what Deleuze and Guattari have called an assemblage,[37] a concept that Collier and Ong have expanded on with what they call global assemblage. That is, the Church-run program is a territorialized manifestation of global "abstractable, mobile, and dynamic" phenomena—heroin, therapeutic practices, human rights, Orthodox Christianity, Soviet discourses and practices, neoliberalism, and biomedicine, to name only a few—in which "the forms and values of individual and collective existence are prob-

lematized or at stake."[38] In part I I establish the background for understanding this assemblage as an Agambian space of inclusion-exclusion.
This includes a discussion of the current HIV and injecting drug use
epidemic in Russia, an explication of Russian Orthodox moral theology
and human rights, a description of the research sites, and a delineation of
the anthropological theory of moralities utilized in the second part. I end
the first part with a brief genealogical discussion of the Soviet emphasis
on working on the self as a means of cultivating moral personhood and
its influential traces on post-Soviet conceptions of personhood, as well
as its similarities to secular therapeutic practices of self-transformation.
This is the background necessary to understanding the ethical techniques
of work on the self done in the Church-run program. In part II I turn to
an ethnographic description and analysis of the Church-run program
and the ethical techniques and disciplinary practices used in the various
parts of the program. I focus my analysis on the ethical work of prayer,
confession, and various therapeutic processes as disciplinary practices
by means of which new responsibilized subjects, or normal persons, are
cultivated. In the end I argue that the Church-run program as a place of
ethical training is a paradigm for the kind of society the Russian Orthodox
Church would like to establish. In espousing a notion of human rights
as a means of cultivating a particular kind of moral person the Church
participates in reproducing much of the neoliberal order it attempts to
overcome, despite claims to offer an alternative human rights, moral,
and ultimately social vision. In a very real way, then, it is upon the bare
life of rehabilitants' bodies that various regimes of power unwittingly
battle for the future of Russia.

PART ONE Backgrounds

ONE HIV, Drug Use, and the Politics of Indifference

As a student in the late 1980s in a Leningrad (now St. Petersburg) medical university, Natalia Aleksandrovna was taken, along with her fellow students, to a hospital to see what they were told was the first person in the city diagnosed with AIDS. Whether or not this was in fact the first known person with AIDS in Leningrad is difficult to discern, as such information was tightly controlled by the Soviet government.[1] What is clear, however, is that this experience had a lasting effect on Natalia Aleksandrovna, for within a few short years she would be one of the cofounders of the Russian Orthodox Church's drug rehabilitation program, which in time eventually became one of the central features of the Church's HIV prevention and treatment program. The two programs have now essentially become one.

This is so because Russia's current HIV epidemic is primarily driven by injecting drug use. Unlike in many other parts of the world, where sexual contact is the primary means of transmission, about 80 percent of the estimated 940,000 people living with HIV in Russia today were infected through injecting drug use. Although there has been some recent evidence suggesting that the virus is increasingly spread through heterosexual sex, it is thought that so far this is primarily so with the sexual partners of infected injecting drug users (IDUs). Therefore despite this apparent shift toward heterosexual unprotected sex as a path of infection, Russia's HIV crisis remains today inextricably linked to injecting drug use.

There is little doubt that Russia today is in the midst of an HIV epidemic. While the official count of registered people living with HIV/AIDS (PLWHA) is more than 400,000, which most agree does not accurately reflect the scope of the crisis, it is generally thought that the number could be as high as 1.6 million, over 1 percent of the population. Most, however, tend to cite the UNAIDS estimate of 940,000 as of the end of 2005.[2] Most troubling is the fact that UNAIDS reported that at the end of 2002 the "unfortunate distinction of having the world's fasting-growing HIV/AIDS epidemic still belongs to Eastern Europe and Central Asia."[3] In this region Russia by far has the highest number of PLWHA and the fastest growing number of infections.

Yet very little is being done about it. Despite a proposed thirtyfold increase in budget allocation for HIV-related programs in 2006, the Russian government continues to underfund any programs or medical facilities related to HIV or drug use. In fact while the Russian government has pledged $20 million to the Global Fund, it generally allocates only $4 million to $5 million annually to HIV programs in the country.[4] In the 2008 budget this number was increased to $16 million for HIV vaccine research and monitoring programs. Therefore, the vast majority of funding for prevention and treatment programs is still provided by international funding agencies and Western charitable organizations, for example, the very Global Fund that Russia donates to. Indeed even the Russian Orthodox Church program is almost exclusively funded by these non-Russian sources; at the time of my research it received only a small amount of funding from the St. Petersburg City Committee on Youth Affairs and nothing from the Church itself. This lack of funding from the Church and government institutions is true for all locally run

Church programs in the country. Despite the lip service paid to the epidemic by President Putin prior to the G8 festivities in St. Petersburg in the spring of 2006, the situation has changed little in terms of how the government approaches the crisis.

In fact it has been argued that the drug policies of the Russian government are actually helping to fuel the HIV/AIDS epidemic. This is primarily due to the fact that the policies are characterized by a focus on the criminalization of drug use.[5] Because of this focus the majority of state funding goes toward anti-drug law enforcement rather than treatment and prevention programs. Additionally these punitive policies tend to focus on drug users and not the dealers, and have been widely criticized by human rights organizations for levying long prison terms for the possession of very small amounts of drugs. A recent change in the law should cut back on the number of arrests for these small possessions; the question remains, however, whether police will actually implement this law.

This remains a question because there is deep and widespread corruption within the Russian police forces and legal institutions. It is widely believed that the police work hand in hand with the so-called drug mafia, yet they also take advantage of drug users by routinely rounding them up to fulfill monthly arrest quotas. One example of this kind of police corruption takes place in Irkutsk.[6] An outlying section of Irkutsk called the Third Village is well-known as an open drug scene. In fact the police work together with the dealers in the Third Village, and when the police confiscate the heroin from users it ends up back in the hands of the dealers. But users need not always give up their heroin; a bribe can often get them off the hook. It is reported that the police take in up to 30,000 rubles (approximately $1,155) per month per precinct in this way.[7] In sum, by overly criminalizing and taking advantage of drug users, Russian drug policies and the corruption endemic to the Russian legal system help create a situation in which IDUs do all they can to avoid the world of official institutions, including the medical facilities that may be able to offer help.

Some have argued that these harsh drug policies are in part the unintended consequences of the Russian government's trying to follow the mandated drug policies of the UN.[8] It has been claimed that because countries like Russia feel international pressure to live up to the UN policies they have signed onto they are left with little flexibility to adapt their domestic policies to unique or newly arising drug situations and public health crises. Because two of the three UN treaties on drugs were implemented prior to the identification of HIV/AIDS, Malinowska-Sempruch and her coauthors claim that not only are they outdated but they continue to force nation-states to treat drug use solely as a legal problem and neglect its public health aspect. Indeed when it became undeniably clear in 1999 that Russia was experiencing a wave of HIV infections related to injecting drug use, their domestic policy was restricted by their UN obligations. This is not to say that Russia's drug policies would be any less punitive and harsh if it were not for the UN policies, but nation-states such as Russia do not work in an international vacuum when it comes to how they react to a social and health crisis, particularly when that crisis is driven by injecting drug use.

Despite the role played by the UN in shaping the Russian government's response to the country's HIV epidemic and drug use crisis, the government still bears the bulk of responsibility for their general inattention to the problem, manifest in the medical infrastructure available to PLWHA and IDUs. In terms of medical care, the ghosts of the Soviet medical system are still haunting the Russian people. The reforms necessary not only to ensure better medical attention but also to reduce blood-borne infections still have not been fully implemented.[9] Those who cannot afford private medical care are left to get the best they can from the underfunded, undersupplied, and technologically antiquated state medical system. Despite the promise of free care, many still must pay doctors or specialists to receive proper medical attention. If it is true that many Russians today fear falling ill because of the poor quality of medical care,[10] then this is even more the case for PLWHA and IDUs because of the institutionally entrenched stigma against HIV and drug use. Added to this is the looming possibility that medical personnel might involve the police.

One of the remnants of the Soviet system that remains in place today is that PLWHA can receive medical treatment only at specific hospitals or medical facilities designated for them. In the city of St. Petersburg there are three such locations, two hospitals and one ambulatory center. Care is denied at any other state medical facility to anyone who is known to be infected with HIV or to have contracted AIDS. It is also often denied at the private, for-pay facilities. This system not only perpetuates the already deeply embedded stigma against PLWHA, but also leads to a general lack of knowledge, skill, and perhaps even sympathy on the part of medical personnel who do not work at the AIDS centers. In addition, in order to receive treatment at one of these centers a person must first be registered as a PLWHA, further stigmatizing those with HIV or AIDS. It seems that the Russian medical system reflects not only the government's but also society's indifference to the HIV epidemic in their midst.

THE POLITICS OF PARANOIA AND INDIFFERENCE

This indifference also seems to be a remnant of the Soviet past, for in addition to the typical kind of indifference and lack of sympathy found around the world for people who suffer from HIV/AIDS and those most at risk of infection, many Russians, and especially the government and medical institutions, remain influenced by the anti-AIDS propaganda first perpetuated during Soviet times. When Western countries in the early and mid-1980s first recognized AIDS as an epidemic the Soviet media and the Communist Party relentlessly portrayed it as a disease of the decadent, immoral capitalist West. Soviet citizens were told that AIDS could not spread to the Soviet Union because the kinds of hedonistic behaviors, such as homosexuality, sexual promiscuity, and drug use, that are responsible for spreading the disease did not exist in the socialist homeland.[11] The portrayal of AIDS as entirely Other to the Soviet Union was further buttressed by the Soviet claim that AIDS was developed as part of the U.S. military's and CIA's biological warfare program, and that these institutions were using the marginalized and exploited populations of their own countries, as well as black Africans, to test this new weapon.[12]

The early years of Soviet discourse on AIDS took on what Susan Sontag described as the "dual metaphoric genealogy" of AIDS.[13] First it was metaphorically depicted as pollution, the result of participating in "dirty" and "immoral" behavior. Second it was depicted as an invasion, or in the Soviet case as a potential invasion. Sontag discusses the metaphor of invasion primarily in terms of the microprocess of the disease within the body, whereas Soviet propaganda politicized the metaphor so that AIDS came to stand as a potential invading weapon from the foreign and alien West. The fear of this invasion became manifest in Soviet laws that required all foreigners staying in the country longer than three months to be tested for HIV (a law that remains in place today), as well as all Soviet citizens who spent more than a month abroad.[14] There were also strong warnings against having sexual relations with any foreigners. These laws, as well as the metaphorical depictions of AIDS in Soviet propaganda, reveal what Sontag calls "the language of political paranoia, with its characteristic distrust of a pluralistic world."[15]

To a great extent these metaphorical descriptions, paranoia, and distrust remain in much of the public discourse on HIV/AIDS in Russia today. While during the Soviet period the Other of AIDS was represented as the West itself, today the Other of HIV/AIDS are those perceived immoral persons, such as IDUs and homosexuals, who have been infiltrated by and have taken on the lifestyle of the West that became possible after 1991. In other words, the Other has shifted from a political to a moral alien. In post-Soviet Russia the battle against HIV/AIDS is no longer primarily fought by securing national borders against the epidemic. Instead it is fought on the battlefront of lifestyles, values, and morals. It is widely seen as a battle fought within human persons, as an internal battle for morally disciplining persons in the post-Soviet world. This is the perspective not only of the Russian Orthodox Church, but of many Russian politicians, medical personnel, and media depictions.[16]

This distrust and paranoia extend to the very NGOs and foreign agencies that do the bulk of the work and funding of HIV prevention in Russia. In January 2006 a new law was signed that required all NGOs to reregister with the state. This was widely viewed as an attempt by the government to control the influence of foreign monies and ideas on Russian civil society, as well as to stem any revolution taking place in Russia as it did in Georgia and Ukraine, which the Russian government blames on foreign influence on civil society in these countries. As of this writing, I know of no NGOs working in the field of HIV prevention or with IDUs who have been shut down, but there has been clear harassment against some of these organizations, not to mention the time lost and effort put into the reregistration effort. It is widely believed among both Russians and non-Russians working within these NGOs that this kind of harassment is not the result of their legal status, but because of their work with the marginalized populations of IDUs and others most at risk for HIV. This paranoia toward NGOs also resulted in the Russian government's creating its own governmental nongovernmental organization, which is the recipient of a large grant from the Global Fund.[17] In its fear of the very organizations that have led the way not only in Russia but around the world in the fight against the spread of HIV, the Russian government is creating on the fly its own organizational mechanism for fighting the epidemic. This is indeed a dangerous path to take, especially when so many experienced and knowledgeable persons and organizations are practically begging the Russian government to let them help.

A similar distrust was conveyed to me by Father Maxim, the priest who runs The Mill.[18] Once while talking about the fact that the vast majority of the funding for the Church-run rehabilitation center comes from foreign agencies, Father Maxim told me that he is sometimes skeptical about these agencies. He said, "You know, we have many bigger problems in Russia than HIV, but these Western organizations make it seem like HIV is the only thing we need to worry about." He wonders if non-Russian organizations and agencies create and perpetuate the scope of the HIV problem in order to further their own interests. Just one of these interests, he told me, was the spread of Western political and moral ideas. Father Maxim works tirelessly with IDUs and PLWHA in St. Petersburg and the region, and therefore this skepticism does not prevent him from doing this work. Still this is even more reason to take note of his distrust of the Other of HIV/AIDS. Russia is in fact suffering numerous health problems that are larger in scope than HIV, for example, cardiovascular disease and alcoholism. Yet this is no reason to deny the significance of the HIV problem. In fact much of the infrastructural reforms that are needed to help in the fight against HIV could play an important role in combating these other health crises.

HIV, DRUG USE, AND THE DEMOGRAPHIC CRISIS

All of this—government neglect, stigmatization at nearly every institutional level, and a deep-seated distrust of the West and its ideas and lifestyles (including many of its HIV prevention strategies, such as harm reduction)—combined with what can only be described as widespread denial of the HIV/AIDS crisis will further the already obvious demographic crisis of Russia, a crisis that some have hyperbolically claimed could lead to the disappearance of the Russian people. This denial is even further supported by the relatively long period of time between initial HIV infection and the manifestation of clinical AIDS, which has potentially misled many Russians, politicians and nonpoliticians alike, into believing the crisis is not as severe as it is.[19]

The demographic crisis is what many observers call the fact that Russia is the first industrialized country in non-wartime or non-disaster conditions to experience such a sharp decline in its population.[20] Since 1992 there have been more annual deaths than births in the country. Perhaps most shocking is the dramatic decrease in average male life expectancy, which now stands at about fifty-nine years. Most have associated this demographic crisis with the societal shock of the collapse of the Soviet Union, but Mark Field argues that there were already signs of the crisis as far back as the end of the 1960s.[21] Whenever it may have begun, it is clear that the post-Soviet years have seen a marked increase in population decline and the kinds of socioeconomic factors that have contributed to it, such as increased poverty and the collapse of the social safety net, increased alcohol consumption, and an increase in violence and accidents. It is clear that we should now add increased injecting drug use and HIV/AIDS to this list.

According to one estimate, in the next decade as many as eight million Russians could be infected with HIV, which would amount to about 10 percent of the population.[22] Even if such a high figure is never realized, HIV/AIDS will have a particularly egregious effect on the Russian economy and national security because it is overwhelmingly found in the younger population who are already of or about to become of working age. Projections suggest that even a "mild" HIV epidemic could prevent the Russian economy from growing through 2025, and an "intermediate" epidemic could lead to a 40 percent decline in economic growth over the same period.[23] The Russian military would have difficulty maintaining its current strength, as the number of available young conscripts would also decline.[24] It should be noted that the military is where many young men begin injecting heroin and other drugs. Several of the young men I got to know through the Church rehabilitation program began using while serving in the military. In a sense the Russian military has itself become a public health danger.

Russia's HIV epidemic and its contribution to the demographic crisis can be traced back to the fact that Russia today has an estimated four million active drug users, one of the highest percentages of drug users in the world.[25] The Russian Ministry of Health estimates that drug use rose by 400 percent between 1992 and 2002 and that there are seventy thousand drug-related deaths each year. Perhaps most worrying is that the Russian Federation AIDS Center says that 56 percent of IDUs are HIV positive and make up over 80 percent of those registered as HIV positive. This public health crisis became very clear to most observers around 1999, and unfortunately little has changed since.

To this day very few long-term abstinence programs exist in Russia.[26] To the best of my knowledge, other than one other private, for-pay, evangelical-affiliated rehabilitation center in the St. Petersburg area, the Church-run program where I did my research is the only long-term (three to twelve months) and free rehabilitation program offered in the region. The only other option seems to be palliative detoxification programs, with a week to ten days of inpatient care.[27] This shortage of effective help in a city where there are an estimated 73,400 IDUs not only deters many drug users from seeking help in overcoming their addiction, but also contributes to a sense of hopelessness among medical personnel, who realize they can offer very little to help those who do seek it from them.[28] This shortage has also led to quite a long waiting list of those hoping to enter the Church-run program.

It has been said that drug use in Russia, especially heroin use, has become normal.[29] This is so partly because drugs are slowly beginning to replace alcohol as the intoxicant of choice, as alcohol consumption has slowly dropped in the same years that drug use has increased, primarily in the younger generation. Although marijuana remains the drug of choice in Russia, heroin has become the second most popular. This shift in preference began in the second half of the 1990s and boomed at the turn of the century, when registered heroin users in drug clinics rose from 33,721 in 1999 to 117,435 in 2000.[30] Indeed according to Pilkington, heroin is now commonly viewed by many of Russia's youth as a recreational drug to be used in one's free time.[31] While this may be so, in my experience I came across very few people who used heroin recreationally on a long-term basis. Although many of the rehabilitants in the Church-run program may have started using heroin in this way, in time their recreational use spiraled into addiction. Heroin use may have become common in today's Russia, but for many it is far from a leisure activity.

There are several reasons for this increase in and normality of drug use. One significant factor is that with the opening of the borders of the Soviet Union, the Russian Federation has become one of the primary transit countries on the global drug market. In terms of the exploding global heroin market, Russia has become particularly central not only because of its relatively low border controls, illegal migration, and rampant corruption, but also because of its location between the Central Asian heroin exporters and Western European consumer markets.[32] Another significant factor is the socioeconomic situation of post-Soviet Russia. Increased personal freedom, the upheavals of the transformation to a capitalist-like market economy, increased exposure to Western lifestyles, including the glamorization of drug use, increased spending money for some persons and a lack of hope in the future for others have all contributed to the booming heroin market.[33]

While these social and political factors are certainly important, personal motives also play a significant role in why persons begin using heroin. Vadim, who is now a factory worker in his early thirties and who used heroin for ten years, first started using because he came home from work earlier than the rest of his friends in the neighborhood. One day, out of boredom and curiosity, he bought some heroin, which he said was as readily available as a pack of cigarettes, shot up, and stopped using only a little over a year ago. Roma, also in his early thirties but from an upper-class family, said he started using because he wanted to be cool, and using heroin had become the newest cool thing to do. Eight years later he has been able to remain clean for nearly two years. And Zhenia, a young woman in her mid-twenties, first shot up when she was eighteen because her boyfriend, a heroin user, began to ignore her more and more and to break dates with her. Finally, out of jealousy, as she put it, she had to try it herself to find out what could be more important to him than she. When she told me this she had just returned from nearly one year of rehabilitation in the Church-run program.

As these and Andrei's stories suggest, in addition to the social and political reasons for drug use in Russia today, there are also personal motives, such as boredom, curiosity, peer pressure, and jealousy. Government policies, institutional structures, economic realities, and sociocultural assumptions certainly play a role in these epidemics, but it is actual persons with their own lives, hopes, families, and friends who begin to use and eventually become addicted. Some of these people, by this point often abandoned by the state, most institutions, and their family and friends, go through the rehabilitation process.

TWO The Church's Rehabilitation Program

It's seven o'clock on a Tuesday morning in late September and I'm waiting near a bus stop along a large city highway at one of the northern-most metro stations in St. Petersburg. It is early fall in northern Russia, but the weather this morning seems unusually warm. Still the people bustling around me on their way to work, or to wherever they may be heading, are wearing light jackets, some carrying umbrellas in prepara-tion for any change in the skies. As I stand there along the highway cars pass by at speeds that seem too high for city streets; buses inch along the edges of the road, stopping every so often to let people in and out of their confines. Groups of men stand near kiosks smoking cigarettes and drinking beer; those in suits are clearly on their way to work, others seem to have nowhere else to be anytime soon. Young women in skirts quickly move past them, ignoring their leering eyes, and old babushkas are already searching the nearby market for bargains. I begin to wonder how the priest will find me among all this bustle.

Just then a black Lada makes its way at a particularly sharp angle across two lanes, cutting off one of the buses that had just left the stop, and comes to a stop right in front of me. Through its dark tinted windows I can make out the figure of Father Maxim leaning across to open the door for me. "Get in!" he says to me with a smile that reveals a line of bright white teeth buried beneath his well-trimmed, hefty dark beard. Quickly I get in and barely close the door behind me before Father Maxim pulls back out into the steady stream of fast traffic. Before saying a word he reaches over and turns up the stereo, I assume back to the volume before I got in the car. I hear Miles Davis blaring away to the green and red lights flashing on the new removable face of the stereo. Father Maxim's large hands return to the steering wheel and begin to tap to the rhythm, while the icons attached to the dashboard also seem to be bouncing and dancing to Miles's trumpet.

This is not the Father Maxim I had expected. I had met him twice before this, once in May at a regional HIV/AIDS conference in Moscow and a second time at the church where he serves, located just off Nevsky Prospect in the heart of St. Petersburg. Both times he was wearing the black robes typically worn by Orthodox priests, with a large cross hanging from his neck. Today, however, he is dressed in jeans, a sweater, a black leather coat, and black leather boots. In this outfit one would never know he is an Orthodox priest. Only his demeanor—steadfast and reserved, with only a hint of joy—that along with his nearly two-meter-tall frame commands so much respect from those around him, suggests his calling.

As the cars around us begin to slow and we approach one of the many traffic jams that take place throughout the city every day, Father Maxim begins to tell me about the Church-run drug rehabilitation center that he leads and where we are now going. "The center is located outside the city because it is important to get the addicts away from this environment," he tells me, which not only suggests his recognition of the social nature of drug addiction but also highlights one of the Church's main tenets in their fight with drug addiction and the spread of HIV/AIDS: that it is a moral problem of both the individual and society. Because the Church and Father Maxim take the position that morality, or the lack thereof, is closely related to one's social surroundings, they believe that in order to change one's morality one must change one's social context. In other words, one must enter what Agamben would call a space of inclusion-exclusion in order to be ethically worked upon.

After finally making it out of the traffic jam and then outside the city onto a newly constructed highway, so new in fact that Father Maxim misses our exit because he is still not familiar with driving this route, we are on our way again. This new highway is just one example of the wave of construction hitting the cities of Russia today. It is of course a coincidence that this highway and the other roads that lead to The Mill follow the old *Doroga Zhizni* (Road of Life), yet its metaphorical significance does not elude anyone who knows this fact. Just as during the nine-hundred-day siege of Leningrad during the Great Patriotic War (World War II) this lone road between the city and Lake Ladoga remained open and allowed much needed supplies to enter the city, so today it is the path that many follow in their attempt to begin constructing a new life for themselves.

Once off the highway we make our way on old pothole-riddled roads barely wide enough for two cars to pass one another, through various villages, with dogs barking and people walking on the sides, near a fairy tale mixture of one-room dilapidated shacks and newly built walled-off mini-mansions. Finally the road disappears entirely, and we are on a dirt road that leads out of the village and into a small forest and then opens up again into large fields that spread as far as the eye can see. "Soon this road will be nearly impossible to drive on," Father Maxim tells me as we slowly maneuver around large ditches and mud puddles that engulf most of the single-lane path. I peer out the side window and notice the beauty of the early morning sun shining on the dew-covered high grass and can't help but think that this seems much farther than only twenty kilometers outside of the second largest city in Russia. It is indeed not simply a metaphorical, but also a physical space of inclusion-exclusion.

After we drive through another small batch of trees sprouting from the midst of the giant field, once again there are fields for as far as we can see, and just over the horizon I can make out a few small buildings slowly growing larger as we make our way toward them. This is The Mill, the Church-run rehabilitation center named after the last village we passed before entering the fields. "You can see," Father Maxim tells me, "that we have a position of natural surveillance. From the center we can see everyone who tries to come here or leave." As I would come to learn, surveillance is something that the staff of The Mill tries very hard to maintain over the twenty-five or so rehabilitants that are there at any given time. From the point of view of the staff this surveillance is vital for maintaining a well-run and disciplined community that will allow for the best chance of success for the rehabilitants. So too is the kind of mutual and self-surveillance and discipline the staff attempt to inculcate within the rehabilitants. Surveillance and discipline, however, are not something with which the rehabilitants always agree. Nor are they goals the staff can always accomplish.

Finally we arrive at The Mill. As we pull into the compound I see for the first time that this rehabilitation center in the middle of the field is essentially a small farm. There is one main building that houses most of the basics of the center: the sleeping quarters, the staff office, a meeting room, a recreation room with a Ping-Pong table and some exercise equipment, and a kitchen and dining room. A small plaque attached to one side states that the building was built with funding from the German Lutheran Church. A short walk away is the guesthouse, for visitors and, at that time, volunteers who are ex-rehabilitants themselves. By the end of my research the following summer the volunteers had been moved into the main building because of problems that had arisen between male and female volunteers living unsupervised in the guesthouse. The mixing of male and female rehabilitants, and volunteers for that matter, is one of the most frequent and difficult disciplinary problems the staff must try to manage at The Mill. Between these two buildings and set back about thirty meters is the small church where every day a morning and evening prayer service is held, as well as liturgy at least once a month. All three of these buildings are connected by rock-covered dirt paths.

On the other side of the dirt parking space outside the main building is the small sports rink, where in the winter the rehabilitants play ice hockey and in the summer soccer. The words "Orthodoxy or death" (*Pravoslavie ili smert'*) are painted on the wooden fence surrounding it. Painted in such a way that a rehabilitant will see them every time he or she leaves the main building, these words embody the focus on bare life as the ethical material between moral life and death that is central to this program. Behind the rink are the mechanic's garage, a wood shop, and a barn for farm animals. Here is where the majority of the male rehabilitants do their daily labor, maintaining the center's several vehicles and one tractor, building furniture for both the center and for sale, and tending the few cows, sheep, chickens, and geese from which the farm gets its milk and eggs. The wood shop is run by an ex-rehabilitant who mastered the trade while living in a monastery about a thousand kilometers away, the one option available to those rehabilitants who want to extend the rehabilitation process beyond the three months allowed at The Mill. The farm is supervised by a local man from a nearby village who comes two or three times a week to look in on the animals and to teach the ever rotating group of rehabilitants, all of whom are from the city, how to work a farm.

About a hundred meters' walk down a usually mud-covered road, past the fields in which they grow potatoes, carrots, cabbage, beets, and onions, and along which grow various kinds of wild berries, is the *banya* (sauna). This is where every Thursday evening, except for on the hottest of summer nights, the rehabilitants take turns in groups of five relaxing, talking, and laughing with one another as they sweat profusely in the healthfully stifling steam heat. For the *banya* to be properly ready for the evening the fires must be started in the early morning and maintained all day. Every Thursday morning two of the male rehabilitants light the fires in the *banya*'s furnace and spend the day chopping wood that has been taken from the nearby forest and stacked next to the building, keeping the flames going. This is a time and place of much activity and socializing, as other rehabilitants stop by to chat, smoke, and help chop wood.

A few hundred yards behind the *banya* another small forest begins, in which, after about three kilometers, a small village sits. Through this village and small forest runs the only road that makes The Mill accessible in the winter and most of the spring. It is also along this road

that in the spring of 2007 new houses were built for the Russian upper
middle class looking to get out of the city. In fact one of these houses
can be seen from the center's compound. The staff of The Mill is not
pleased with this increasing encroachment of the new Russia into their
sanctuary of moral training, as it is this very Russia that they see as the
cause of the drug and HIV problems they are trying to fight. As Oleg, a
thirty-three-year-old staff member, jokingly expressed his concern: "I'm
thinking about spreading a rumor in the local village that water used by
HIV-infected people contaminates the local water supply." He laughed
and added, "Then they definitely won't come." By making such a joke
Oleg uses the same stigma that PLWHA are exposed to every day as a
way, at least rhetorically, to suggest they have some power to stave off
the slow encroachment of a world they are trying to renounce. The joke,
however, also reveals Oleg's knowledge that it is a world that cannot be
renounced and at best he must learn to live with.

WHO IS AT THE MILL?

At any one time there are no more than about twenty-five rehabilitants
at The Mill. This number is generally split more or less evenly between
genders, and their ages range from eighteen to early thirties. Because
The Mill has recently received some of its funding from the St. Petersburg City Committee on Youth Affairs there is a rule that they can't
take anyone older than thirty. Nevertheless there are usually one or two
rehabilitants over the age of thirty, for whom the center's staff marks
a younger age on the official registration papers in case the Committee
asks. Because of this requirement the staff never admits a new rehabilitant over the age of thirty until one of the older ones has already left.

In the course of this book we will meet many rehabilitants and ex-
rehabilitants of the Church-run program. I will briefly introduce a few of
those who were particularly central to the research, which will provide
insight into the diversity of persons rehabilitating with the program.
Ivan is thirty-two and had been using heroin since he was twenty. He
lives in the center of St. Petersburg with his family, who owns a small

chain of pet supply stores in the city. He worked in the family business off and on over the years but was finally told by his sister, who now runs the business, that if he didn't get off drugs they would no longer support him. Ivan is an example of the many young persons in Russia who grew up in middle-class or well-to-do families who, counter to the common sociological discourse that focuses on the relationship between poverty and drug addiction, began using heroin and eventually became addicted. After staying at The Mill for nearly four months Ivan returned to the city and began working once again at the family business. Three months later he was using heroin again and has been in and out of the hospital since.

Zhanna is twenty-three; she began using drugs when she was ten and heroin when she was twelve. This is Zhanna's second time at The Mill. Her first was about a year ago, when she stayed for three months. After returning to the city following her first stint at the rehab center she went on vacation with some friends to the Crimea, where she began shooting up again. Zhanna was at The Mill for only two months her second time, most of which was spent in a deep depression, feeling as if her mother had abandoned her. This was something she was never able to get over. Eventually Zhanna was kicked out of The Mill for breaking too many of the rules, such as drinking coffee and wearing makeup. These rules are part of the disciplinary regime at The Mill and a central strategy for staff to monitor the disciplinary and moral development of rehabilitants. After Zhanna was forced to leave The Mill no one knew what became of her.

Anna, twenty-two, began using heroin when she was fourteen. Anna comes from a well-to-do family in one of the suburbs of St. Petersburg. She says that despite her drug use she has always had good relations with her parents, especially her mother, and they have done everything they could to try to help her stop using. When Anna first arrived at The Mill she told me she hated it because she wasn't used to all the work and the isolation, complaints that are extremely common among rehabilitants. Eventually, however, she came to like it at the center and felt as though she was making real progress. Indeed the work and isolation, she came to realize, was the best thing for her. As she put it, "Here nothing is allowed [*Zdes' nichevo nel'zya*]." Unfortunately there were temptations, and Anna gave in to drinking coffee. It was the fourth time she had broken the rules, and she was kicked out.

Dima is a young man of twenty-two with whom I several times helped maintain the fires in the *banya*. He had been using heroin since he was sixteen and had finally, as he put it, gotten tired of it. Unlike many others at The Mill this was Dima's first attempt at rehabilitation, and by all accounts he had done quite well. All rehabilitants are allowed to go to a parish, monastery, or nunnery, but only those whom Father Maxim deems ready are actually invited to go. Dima was invited and left before the end of his three months. For him, unlike for so many others, this was an easy decision. He told me he knew that three months at The Mill would not be long enough and if he had simply returned to the city he would be using again in a matter of weeks. He had decided at the beginning that he would work hard so that he would be allowed to go to a parish.

Officially rehabilitants are able to stay at The Mill for three months. After that they can choose to return to the city, where there are very few support networks, or go to a parish, monastery, or nunnery. This is often an agonizing decision, as many of them know that if they return to the city they will likely begin using again. But they also do not want to go to the monastery or parish because they're not certain that they can or want to live such a lifestyle. I have known several rehabilitants who have spent up to two extra months at The Mill trying to make this decision. Those who choose to go to the monastery or parish have a much better chance of not returning to heroin, but I know of several people who, after returning from this prolonged rehabilitation process, began using again.

There is also the possibility of remaining at The Mill as a volunteer. Father Maxim offers this choice only to those he believes have made the most progress while at the center, which in this case means not only progress in fighting their addiction but in beginning to live a life with the Church. These volunteers are entrusted with such jobs as driving the center's vehicle, which is used to run errands, pick up supplies in the local village, and drive to the train station and into the city. They also help supervise work done around The Mill, help the staff maintain discipline, and act as councilors to rehabilitants. The volunteers are extremely important to the running of The Mill, for they help make up for a lack in staff, but there have been instances when volunteers have breached the center's most serious rules on sex, alcohol use, and even heroin use.

One such transgression was committed by a volunteer with whom I had become particularly close. When I first met Misha he had been at The Mill for two weeks and had already struck me as one who was taking the rehabilitation experience very seriously. Misha and I were able to have many close conversations over games of chess, often during smoking breaks from group activities since we were the only two people at the center who did not smoke. During these conversations Misha was always very open about his past and his hopes for the future and how what he was now doing at The Mill was necessary for realizing these hopes.

The staff also quickly recognized that Misha was different from the other rehabilitants. In fact I was told by one of the staff members that he was "the most serious" about working on himself that she could remember. Eventually Father Maxim asked Misha to stay on as a volunteer. One of his duties was to drive to the city every Tuesday to pick up packages for the rehabilitants from their parents and to get medicine and antiretroviral therapy, the pharmaceuticals that suppress the HIV virus, from one of the hospitals. Tuesdays are also the day that Oleg, one of the staff members, holds a reception at this hospital for those IDUs interested in going to The Mill. During this reception Misha was often allowed to go for walks or to visit his mother in the city.

Unfortunately Misha was doing more than this. He was also buying heroin. The details are slim and no one seems to know how or when it began, but most think that Misha was meeting Andrei, who had recently returned to the city and started using again. It is from Andrei, who died a few weeks later, that Misha may have bought the heroin. Not only did Misha begin using again, but he would take the heroin back to The Mill and shoot up at the center. It is thought that he never sold it to anyone at The Mill, but this is something about which no one can be certain. Eventually Misha was caught and kicked out of The Mill. This turn of events was a shock to the entire staff, the volunteers, and anyone who knew Misha, myself included. The fact that this man, who so many thought of as a shining example of how a person can work to change himself at The Mill, could fall back into using again, and do so while a volunteer there, cast a shadow of doubt over the entire Church-run drug rehab and HIV prevention program throughout the city. Since this incident volunteers have lost a good deal of the freedom they were granted before, and a bit of distrust has tainted the relationship many of the volunteers have with the staff.

THE STAFF

In total there are four staff members who spend one or two twenty-four-hour periods at The Mill per week, as well as a psychologist who comes once a week, usually on Saturday afternoons, for a few hours. Other than the psychologist, the staff has very little professional train-ing for working with drug addicts, although one is currently studying psychology at a St. Petersburg university and Father Maxim wrote his dissertation on the history of drug use and HIV/AIDS in Russia and the Church's relationship to these problems. Despite this general lack of training the staff provides a unique combination of Church teachings and practical personal experience.

Father Maxim is the leader of the center. He comes to The Mill twice a week, on Tuesdays and also on Sundays for the church service. Still in his early forties he commands the respect of those around him in a way that it seems only a priest can. Nearly two meters tall he hovers above most around him, and I often noted how the behavior of both the other staff members and the rehabilitants changed when in his presence. In fact the atmosphere at The Mill is completely different when Father Maxim is there. For one, it is quieter. People are busy doing their assigned jobs and there is much less talking and certainly less laughter. All is done according to the daily timetable. On the days that Father Maxim is not at the center the rehabilitants are more likely to take cigarette breaks from work and have a chat; there is much more laughter; the staff may play music, which is against the rules; and the daily timetable is much more flexible and negotiable.

When Father Maxim is at The Mill he offers to hear confession. It seems, however, that few are interested or eager to give confession, though he is constantly reminding them that they *should* do so. Every one of the rehabilitants I spoke with has given confession at least once. Most of them said they were glad they did, for it helped to relieve them of many burdens, but many also expressed hesitancy about doing it again. It is, after all, quite difficult to express some of the things they have done and been through as drug users. But as Father Maxim reminded me several times, it is not only through confession, but also through therapeutic sessions that rehabilitants are able to talk to others about their experiences, as well as accept for themselves what they have done. This verbal and self-reflective acceptance is one of the first steps toward moving beyond addiction and, at least according to the hopes of Father Maxim, into a life of faith.

Each evening after dinner everyone at The Mill gets together for several hours of group activity. On Tuesday evenings Father Maxim commonly gives lectures or leads group discussions on the Church, the life of faith, and how to live a Christian life. As he and several others told me, The Mill can be thought of as a kind of kindergarten for Russian Orthodoxy. It is a place where people are often exposed to the life of the Church for the first time and where they can begin to learn, little by little, what it means to be Orthodox. Many rehabilitants are baptized for the first time. Many of these newly baptized told me that for them baptism was the most memorable moment of their rehabilitation because it symbolized the start of a new life. Unfortunately many cannot maintain this new life. Only about 25 percent of those who attend The Mill never return to drug use.

Aleksandr, a deacon from a local church, is another staff member at The Mill. When on duty he generally leads group activities about the Church and its teachings similar to those of Father Maxim. Although Aleksandr is a deacon, the rehabilitants do not treat him with the respect they show Father Maxim. When Father Maxim leads discussions few question what he says, all appear to be paying attention, and most respond to his questions in appropriate ways.

This is not always the case with Aleksandr. For example, one evening Aleksandr held a film therapy session. This is quite common at The Mill; rehabilitants watch films at least once a week and hold discussions afterward. The films shown are considered by the staff to have a good message and represent in some way Orthodox Christian values. Among films shown while I was there were Fellini's *Nights of Cabiria, Saving Private Ryan,* and *War and Peace.* On this particular evening they watched *Piter,* a recently popular Russian movie about young love. Afterward the discussion turned to premarital sex. Aleksandr was trying to emphasize the immorality of what the Church and the staff at The Mill call fornication. The rehabilitants, however, were having none of it. For over an hour they went back and forth about the question of the immorality of sex before marriage, questioning and debating Aleksandr's explanations at every turn. In the end the conversation just died out on its own, both sides seeing that no progress was being made. Such an interaction would never happen if Father Maxim led the discussion. One wonders how much of his religious message gets through and how much is a matter of respectfully listening to the priest.

Lena is an ex-heroin addict in her late twenties who rehabilitated at The Mill and at a parish and now studies psychology at the Orthodox university in St. Petersburg. Often smiling, laughing, and joking around, there is always a hint of sadness just below the surface. She attributes this sadness to her upbringing, which she says was mired in meaninglessness. She is originally from Nizhni Novgorad, where her father and mother, now divorced, own several businesses. Her mother, who is the more successful of the two, also has a business in St. Petersburg. While Lena was still a child living in late perestroika Nizhni Novgorad, her family's apartment was bombed by business competitors. From a very early age, she told me, she knew she didn't want anything to do with that life. For her it was completely useless and meaningless. It was this realization, she says, that turned her to using drugs, and it is the same motivation that now drives her to work to help others fight their addiction.

Despite Lena's good intentions and her practical and increasing professional experience, she sometimes has a difficult time controlling the rehabilitants. Several times I witnessed rehabilitants challenging her decisions and forcing her to change her mind, for example, about when the night's group activities should begin or about what time they should go to bed. According to the center's daily schedule the first call for lights out is at eleven and eleven-thirty is the final call. Every night I was there when Lena was on duty people were still up and about well after midnight. In fact Lena once apologized to me in embarrassment, saying that I should come only when others were working so I could see how things were supposed to be done.

Still Lena does her best, and for the most part she is well liked and appreciated by the rehabilitants. This is especially clear in the group activities she leads in the evenings, where she can get them to talk more openly than any of the other staff members can. Usually she leads either an art therapy session or a group discussion. The art therapy sessions generally consist of silent meditation while listening to classical music and then drawing what one saw or thought of while meditating. Afterward each person is asked to talk about what he or she drew. Lena is good at engaging them in these conversations, often leading them to say more about themselves than they were willing to at first.

She uses the same question-and-answer tactics in group discussions, which are generally started by one of the rehabilitants reading aloud a short essay on a topic about which they had been earlier assigned to write. Such topics include envy, prayer, faith, will, and responsibility. She uses these topics and the short essay as a way to begin a group discussion, which she is able to maintain very well by means of what can only be described as a kind of psychologically founded Socratic method of probing, questioning, and at times antagonizing. The discussions, which can become quite heated, have a naturalness that is missing in those led by Father Maxim and Aleksandr, perhaps because the rehabilitants recognize Lena as one of their own who was able to make it to where they want to be.

The same can be said for Oleg, a thirty-three-year-old ex-heroin user who rehabilitated at The Mill and a monastery before getting a job on the editorial staff of a St. Petersburg Orthodox magazine and becoming a staff member at The Mill. Like Lena, Oleg often smiles, laughs, and jokes around, and at times has a very thoughtful, insular manner about him. But the rehabilitants do not take advantage of him the same way they sometimes do Lena. One must wonder if this has something to do with gender difference, as Lena is in fact the only woman on the permanent staff. Be that as it may, it is clear from what I observed that most of the rehabilitants have a good relationship with Oleg and get along with him quite well, despite the fact that he is also known as the strictest disciplinarian at The Mill. His laughing and joking make it difficult for the rehabilitants to hold his discipline against him.

Perhaps Oleg is particularly popular because he always works on *banya* night. Other staff members lead some kind of group discussion or activity, which is almost always a trying and difficult time for everyone involved because it often uncovers some of the most personal and troubling experiences of the rehabilitants. In contrast, Oleg oversees a night of fun. Small groups are always rotating in and out of the *banya*, and those who are not in are free to play ice hockey in the winter and soccer in the other seasons, play chess or Ping-Pong in the recreation room, or just generally hang out and chat, laugh, and look at photos, which is something the rehabilitants often do with each other, recalling to each other not only their lives outside of The Mill but also the lives they have had here together. This time of *obshchenie*, or communing talk, was often described as one of the most significant aspects of the rehabilitation process.

GETTING INTO THE MILL

Those who hope to attend The Mill must first go through a screening process led by Oleg. Back in the city and about a ten-minute walk from the Aleksandr Nevsky Lavra is Botkin Hospital. Botkin is one of three hospitals or clinics in St. Petersburg that provides treatment for PLWHA. Every Tuesday afternoon, in a small room not far from the main gate, there is a reception for those who want to gain admittance to The Mill.

Every week about twenty IDUs and relatives line up to meet with Oleg. One at a time, or with a relative, usually their mother, they come into the small room, where Oleg sits in an armchair behind a small table. There is another armchair and a folding chair in front of him, where the IDU and the relative sit. On the other end of the room is a small couch, next to which is a table with a water boiler, tea cups, tea, coffee, and sugar. Next to the door is an old compact refrigerator that no longer works, on top of which usually sits fruit and candies. Seated on the couch and all around the room in folding chairs are ex-rehabilitants from The Mill who come here nearly every week to meet each other and catch up on news and gossip. Usually around five to seven come each week. The driver from The Mill is also there; he comes each week to get medicine from the hospital and to bring back bags of food, cigarettes, and candy left by the parents of current rehabilitants.

Persons who want to attend The Mill are expected to come to this reception every Tuesday until they are admitted. Depending on the available space at the center, the gender balance, and when Oleg judges the person is ready, this process of weekly visits can last up to two months. And Oleg is indeed judging. He takes meticulous notes as they talk so that he remembers each person well the next time they come. He often makes comments to them based on these notes, such as "You look better than you did last time" or "Last time you told me it was your aunt who died and now you say it is your grandmother. Why are you lying to me?" or "You said you were starting a job. Have you started?" Because Oleg spends more time meeting with them than does Father Maxim, it is ultimately his responsibility to decide who is ready and when, and Father Maxim relies on Oleg's experience and knowledge to make the right decision for The Mill and for the applicant.

It is not unfair to say that during this process of weekly visits to the reception Oleg is judging how much applicants are willing to and in fact whether they have already begun to work on themselves. He makes this very clear to those who come with parents or relatives or friends: the first thing Oleg tells them is that it is better for them to come alone. If they don't come alone, he tells them, he is not able to properly "analyze" (ana-lizirovat') their motives and intentions. He cannot determine how much the applicant actually wants to be there if he or she is with a parent; he does not believe the applicant is free to speak if a parent or relative is there; therefore he is unable to "judge" (*sudit'*) if the person is ready to go through the rehabilitation process. From the beginning Oleg makes it clear to everyone involved that the rehabilitation process will be successful only if the IDU is willing to do the work that is necessary. As he puts it over and over again every Tuesday, "Make no mistake, this is a very difficult process [*tyazhyolyi protsess*]."

The first time applicants meet Oleg he gives them a checklist of things they must do before they are admitted to The Mill. This list includes blood tests for HIV and hepatitis, an exam for tuberculosis, a checkup by a dentist (this is a special concern of the staff because of the many problems heroin users have with teeth and, as I was told, the potential interruption in therapy if the person needs to return to the city for dentistry work), identification to show Russian citizenship and residence registration, and a drug test. The applicant must collect several signatures, including from a psychologist and from Father Maxim. There is also a list of things they must bring with them to The Mill once admitted, including work clothes, for the women traditional women's clothing (*devushkam traditsionnaya odezhda*) such as skirts and dresses, and material for art therapy, all of which point to the kind of therapy and moral training that will take place during rehabilitation.

Oleg then explains what applicants can expect at The Mill and what is expected of them. He asks applicants their age, how long they have been using, if they have had any remission, the date of the last time they used, whether they are HIV positive and have hepatitis, if they have tried to rehabilitate before, and so on. He notes all the answers to these questions, including his general observation of their demeanor, in his notebook. He then explains the process of admittance, including going over what is on the checklist, where to get the tests done, where they can meet with the psychologist, and that they should visit Father Maxim at his church in the city on Saturday afternoons, when he has a small service for drug users and HIV-positive persons. Oleg then finishes by emphasizing the importance of coming to see him every week until a space opens up and he deems them ready to go, and that it is very important that they begin now to work on themselves so he sees that they are serious about going to rehabilitation.

When applicants come for subsequent visits the meeting usually focuses on the progress made on completing the checklist and getting signatures, as well as Oleg's continuing to assess the kind of work they have been doing on themselves. His questions are based primarily on his earlier notes, but also on what the applicants say during the meeting, how they look, and their demeanor. For example, I have seen him become very strict with persons who seem to not take the conversation seriously, or who are making too many jokes, or even those who don't answer his questions quickly enough. This is indeed odd since Oleg himself is often cracking jokes during the interview. Applicants must demonstrate their serious intent for rehabilitation and that they are taking responsibility for their life, while at the same time maintaining a friendly personality. This is often made even more difficult by the fact that ex-rehabilitants meet here each week to socialize with one another. During the interview applicants are surrounded by ex-rehabilitants and volunteers talking loudly, laughing, joking, and often listening to the interview and making comments about what the applicant says and how Oleg responds. It is not uncommon for them to address the applicant directly, as they are also judging the applicants. Although the others in the room ultimately have no say in the final decision, it certainly cannot make it any easier for applicants to act the way they think they ought to act knowing that everyone in the room is watching. This is just the first introduction to the kind of surveillance and disciplinary atmosphere that is awaiting them at The Mill.

For those who can maintain their composure the meeting may last only thirty seconds or so. Oleg simply checks to see what progress has been made on the checklist, asks one or two questions about how the person is and what he or she has done in the past week, and then lets the applicant go. It is those who seem to Oleg to be making little progress on the checklist or, more important, on the process of working on themselves—for example, not openly communicating or clearly lying or not spending their day in ways that Oleg deems productive—to whom he gives the most attention. This is especially so for those who come to the interview high on heroin; each week there are usually two or three. Oleg tries to engage them in normal conversation about the progress of the checklist, slipping in direct or indirect comments about their current state. He tells them that it is all right if they come to the interview high; in fact he says it is better to come high than not at all. But he also makes it clear that this only prolongs the process, for it is expected that applicants have not used for about a week before they go to The Mill. As with nearly all the rules at The Mill and at the reception, however, enforcement is left to the discretion of the staff; I know of several people whom Oleg has admitted who had used only one or two days previously.

It is always a big moment when Oleg tells an applicant that he or she can go to The Mill. Usually the applicants are not expecting it. They will come in, sit down, and give Oleg the checklist. He will acknowledge that all has been completed and then he will simply say that they can go on Thursday morning. The response is almost always one of utter relief and joy. There are also some who in the moment of realization of what they are about to go through will hesitate, although I have never seen anyone decline the offer. He then tells them to bring their things and meet him on the platform at eight in the morning at the Finland train station, where they will begin their journey to a hoped-for new life.

THE SUNDAY CLUB AND HOSPITAL PRAYER SERVICES

After rehabilitating at The Mill for three months rehabilitants have the opportunity to live in a parish, a monastery, or a nunnery. These are all located about a thousand kilometers to the northeast of St. Petersburg and offer rehabilitants the chance to do the kind of long-term ethical work most consider necessary for overcoming addiction. In these locations they can stay up to a year, although I have heard of some who stay longer, and they live a much more disciplined and rigorous life than at The Mill. Only about 25 percent of those who attend The Mill eventually choose to go on to live in a parish, monastery, or nunnery. Those who are the most successful at remaining heroin-free also tend to be the ones who choose to go on. However, this is not always the case.

Most rehabilitants choose to return to the city after their three months are over, despite knowing that this significantly reduces their chances of kicking heroin. As so many put it to me, they simply did not think they could live the kind of life expected of them if they continued rehabilitation at parish, monastery, or nunnery. Still there is another opportunity for them back in St. Petersburg. At the Aleksandr Nevsky Lavra, in a small room located directly below the Metropolitan's residence, a group of rehabilitants who have returned to the city meet on Sunday afternoons. For two to four hours each week from six to twenty persons use this opportunity to meet with and make friends, talk about things that are troubling them, help others with their problems, feel as though they are not alone in this process or in this world, and participate in some group therapeutic activities.

Reflecting the gender divide of injecting drug users and HIV-positive persons living in St. Petersburg, the participants of the Sunday Club are overwhelmingly males in their twenties. Of the core group of regular participants there are no women. This gender divide, however, seems to be more than simply a reflection of statistical difference. Based on the many conversations I had with women participants of the Club and rehabilitants at The Mill, it became clear that they tended to have a higher level of social support and networking available to them than do the men. Thus many of the women tend to report having better relations with their family than do the men with whom I spoke. The women tend to have friends or friendly relations who are not drug users, whereas many of the men told me they have absolutely no friends at all. Similarly several of the women are married, whereas most of the men are not, and several more women also have children. It seems quite possible that while many of the male participants of the Sunday Club told me they attend because it is an opportunity to socialize and perhaps make new friends, an opportunity it seems they do not have in other aspects of their life, the female participants do not need the Club for this reason and therefore attend in smaller numbers and quite a bit less often.

Each meeting begins with a prayer led by the Club's leader, Aleksei, a psychologist from Vladivostok who used to be the head of The Mill before Father Maxim took over and now works with a secular NGO that works with PLWHA. After the prayer Aleksei introduces himself and says a few words about the purpose of the group so that newcomers have a general idea of what happens during the meeting. He then turns to the person next to him and asks him to tell the group about himself. As is common in, for example, 12-step programs, the person begins by telling his or her name and then says something such as "I am a drug addict." Participants often tell their HIV status—most of them are positive—and how long it has been since they last used. Some stop with this basic information; others go on to tell something about themselves or bring up a recent problem, such as a work-related issue, a family problem, or a health concern. Aleksei always attempts, to varying degrees of success, to get participants to say more about themselves. He has the most success with the regulars. This give-and-take occurs as each person takes his turn around the circle created in the middle of the room.

Depending on the number of people attending the meeting this introduction can take up to an hour, sometimes longer if short discussions break out among the group when someone says something of particular interest or if Aleksei asks others to respond to what someone has just said. Usually after this introduction there is a smoking and tea break, which lasts about twenty minutes. During this time most of the participants go outside to smoke, while others remain inside and boil water and arrange plastic cups with tea bags for the group. Often someone has brought cookies and other treats. This time of smoking and tea drinking is perhaps one of the most fruitful periods of the meeting, for it is during this time that most of the participants do the kinds of socializing and communicating (*obshchenie*) that many report as the most helpful and useful aspect of rehabilitation. It is during this time, and after the meeting when many of them walk to the metro station together, that they talk about the more personal concerns and experiences they have, exchange music and DVDs, make plans to meet during the week, and generally chat with friends. These free moments help them construct among themselves what many of them refer to as a normal life.

After the smoking and tea break the group meets again, this time for a group activity, often art therapy. Similar to some of the therapeutic techniques at The Mill, Aleksei gives the participants a task, such as to draw a nonfigurative representation of themselves or their favorite letter of the alphabet. Afterward the group again sits in the circle of chairs and each person shows what he has drawn and tells about it and answers questions, most often asked by Aleksei. There are other therapeutic activities as well, such as one person leading a blindfolded other through a maze of upturned chairs and various exercises for learning how to better communicate with others. No matter the task, Aleksei once told me, these therapeutic sessions are meant to help the participants to explore and express their inner lives and to teach them to begin to trust others. Ultimately, Aleksei went on to say, they are meant to help them to continue to work on themselves once they have returned to the city.

The hospital prayer service is simply an extension of the therapeutic process offered by the Church. Every Wednesday at the Infectious Disease Hospital Number 10, Father Sergei arrives between three and four o'clock to give a short prayer service in the small church located on the second floor. In his mid-thirties Father Sergei is an energetic priest who, as the smile that often appears in the midst of his thick black beard and the steady stream of jokes suggests, has the kind of personality that is attractive to many young people. It is for this reason that so many of the young HIV-infected patients, the majority of whom are still using heroin, even while in the hospital, find it easy to talk with him. Perhaps it does not hurt that Father Sergei also wears a pair of black Converse All-Star sneakers along with his vestments.

Just over a year ago the church, which sits nearly exactly in the middle of the long second-floor hallway, was a large storage closet. In a complete reversal of what was done during Soviet times, when many churches were turned into storage halls, this closet was renovated by Church-rehabilitated drug users and made into a church. Because it has an altar it is truly a church and not simply a prayer chapel. Here Father Sergei gives weekly prayer services, hears confession, gives communion, has private talks and consultations with patients, and will soon perform a wedding.

On occasion Father Sergei brings an altar boy with him from his parish to assist him with the service, but usually he is assisted by Max, a thirty-three-year-old former heroin addict and mafioso who rehabilitated at The Mill and lived at a parish afterward for eleven months. Max now works at the hospital as a handyman; he helped build the church, acts as Father Sergei's assistant, and will marry his fiancée, herself a former injecting drug user and now rehabilitating at a nunnery, in the hospital church at the end of the summer. Max considers Father Sergei his spiritual father and several times expressed to me the central role Father Sergei had in helping him stay away from heroin and in advising him in various parts of his life—including the decision to put off his wedding in order to have more time to work on himself before he takes on the responsibilities of married life.

Father Sergei performs two prayer services at the church each Wednesday, one for the living and one for the dead. Following the second service he gives a short sermon, which is not given by all Orthodox priests after prayer services, during which he talks about such things as the importance of realizing that one is a sinner (and he constantly refers to himself as a sinner), the necessity of always working for salvation, and the importance of thinking about God at all times. It is, Father Sergei told me, during these short sermons that he tries to say things that will stick in the minds of the patients so that even those who do not meet with him privately are able to take something away that they can think over during the week while they pass the monotonous time in the hospital.

After the service, which ends with each person present receiving holy unction, or the marking of the cross on the forehead with oil, Father Sergei takes the oil and the cross to some of the rooms on the floor where he has been told a patient is too ill to attend the service but would like to see the priest. On several occasions I joined him on these visits and was able to see that besides giving holy unction and letting patients kiss the cross, he takes a few moments to speak to patients on a more personal basis, after which he encourages them to continue to fight to get healthy and to always pray to God. Occasionally a patient asks him to hear confession, which he will do after everyone else leaves the room. Obviously I was never able to sit in on these occasions, but according to Father Sergei he uses the opportunity to help patients find meaning in their life. As he told me, "I try to get them to think about what they have done and how it can be different in the future." He went on to say that the point of confession as he sees it is not punishment, or even redemption, but to help the person understand his or her life: "If they do one hundred bows and then go shoot up again, what good is that? We need to have conversation and get him to find some meaning in his life, to help him see that God needs to be a part of his life."

Reflecting the more therapeutic aspects of The Mill and the Sunday Club, the weekly prayer service at the hospital also emphasizes the need to keep working on oneself in order to overcome the sin of drug use and learn how to live a normal and moral life. For the priests and staff members who work at these various program sites there is no secret to how this is done. As Father Sergei put it during one of his short sermons, "There is no mysterious way to God, there is only the way shown by Christ and the saints." He went on to say in this sermon during the Easter fast period, "It is good to keep the fast, but it is more important to pray more, think about God more, and to watch your language." In other words, overcoming the sinful life of drug use does not necessarily come about by following institutional Church rituals (the fast), but instead by a constant working on the self, much of which is internal work (praying and thinking), but also social (speaking and acting), that will eventually bring one closer to God. It is this work that is the focus of the Church program on drug rehabilitation and HIV prevention and treatment. To understand why this is so, it is important to consider the Russian Orthodox Church's institutional perspective on HIV and drug addiction.

THREE

The Russian Orthodox Church, HIV, and Injecting Drug Use

When I first began research on HIV prevention and treatment programs in Russia I told several people who work for NGOs that focus on the epidemic that I was interested in the work the Russian Orthodox Church is doing with HIV. None of them knew of any work the Church was doing concerning HIV. They knew that the Church had some drug rehabilitation programs, but they did not consider this HIV prevention work per se. The fact is, however, that the Church has had various programs since 2001 that address the HIV epidemic. These programs include preventive programs aimed at educating children and youth about Orthodox morality and the harms of drug use, as well as programs for counseling HIV-infected persons and their loved ones. The Church also runs a telephone hotline for people to receive information about HIV/AIDS and has been holding educational seminars for priests and seminarians on how to offer spiritual support to PLWHA. Considering the correlation between injecting drug use and HIV in Russia, I suggest that the Church's drug rehabilitation programs should also be considered part of their HIV prevention and treatment program. Although secular organizations may not define some of these programs as HIV prevention or care, from the perspective of the Russian Orthodox Church that is precisely what they are.

It is not surprising that the NGO workers did not know about these Church programs, for there is almost no communication or working relationship between the Church programs and the secular NGOs who work in this field. This is so primarily because of the difference in how each views the epidemic, its cause, and its prevention and treatment. As a whole the NGO programs in Russia support harm reduction programs consisting of needle exchange and condom distribution and are lobbying for the legalization of substitution therapy in Russia; the Russian Orthodox Church is, as an institution, opposed to such programs. This fundamental difference has created a relational gap that appears to be very difficult to bridge.

Although the Russian Orthodox Church began its efforts in HIV prevention and treatment in 2001, it was not until October 2004 that it finally published *The Concept of the Russian Orthodox Church's Participation in Overcoming the Spread of HIV/AIDS and Work with People Living with HIV/AIDS*.[1] Approved by the Holy Synod it represents the official position of the Church on the topic of HIV/AIDS. Nearly a year later, on September 6, 2005, Church officials, with government and UNAIDS officials standing by their side, released *The Concept* to the media in Moscow's House of Scientists. The reaction by those present was mixed. Alexander Goliusov, an AIDS expert with the watchdog group Federal Consumer Rights and Public Well-Being, commented, "Federal authorities, those that deal with this problem, view the Orthodox Church as an extremely valuable and necessary partner in combating the epidemic."[2] Interestingly, however, Mikhail Narkevich, deputy head of the AIDS Coordinating Council with Russia's Health Ministry, rebuked the Church for their late response: "Unfortunately, this concept appeared [only] today—better late than never. . . . Other confessions have been more efficient in reacting to this problem."[3] In an attempt to lay the ground for future collaboration, Bertil Linblad, the UNAIDS country coordinator for Russia, expressed the hope that *The Concept* would provide for the "principles of tolerance and pragmatism" that he claimed are the basis of the Western approach to the epidemic.[4]

Although *The Concept* states that the Church is prepared to work in partnership with the state and society (meaning civil society), it also specifies that the "Church does not consider it possible to collaborate with those public forces, which by exploiting the theme of HIV/AIDS defend the way of life, behavior and ethical views that are unacceptable to Christian morals."[5] In particular it points out that it will speak against the "simplified" idea that sexual education is a "panacea for all misfortunes." This seems to be a direct reference to the same secular NGOs, such as UNAIDS, with which *The Concept* just one paragraph earlier claims to hope to work. As I already mentioned, there is no obvious working relationship between the Church programs and any secular NGOs, despite the fact that the vast majority of the funding for the · Church programs come from the very same international funding agencies *The Concept* seems to be referencing.

The Church's criticism of previous approaches to the HIV problem goes beyond secular organizations and includes churches of other denominations. Thus at the public presentation of *The Concept* one Church official chastised Western churches for their approach to the epidemic, claiming that in caving in to the "pressure of the liberal community," they took a position of "social pragmatism" that is "tolerant of sin."[6] He went on to promise that the Russian Orthodox Church will not make moral compromises in their efforts to fight the epidemic. Father Maxim echoed this position when he told me that harm reduction programs are "the legalization and legitimation of sin."

In fact the Russian Orthodox Church sees the struggle to respond to HIV as primarily a battle for the moral rectification of the Russian nation. According to *The Concept*, the social and medical factors that others see as the basis of the epidemic are secondary to the root cause of HIV/AIDS, which the Church defines as the "unprecedented growth of sin and lawlessness, loss of fundamental spiritual values, moral traditions and guidelines in society."[7] Thus the Church's primary strategy for fighting the "spreading epidemic of HIV/AIDS is the reinforcement of spiritual and moral norms in society."[8] This is to be accomplished through "religious education." *The Concept* emphasizes that this training is particularly important for children, but it says little about how this training will take place with PLWHA or those, such as sex workers and drug users, who remain most vulnerable to infection. To be fair, however, it is clear that *The Concept* is meant to be a declaration of intent and a motivational piece for Church members and priests who still hold a prejudice against PLWHA. A good deal of this effort is aimed at showing that it is not only safe, but also the duty of Orthodox people, to allow PLWHA to participate in the Church community and the sacraments. Other than stating, for example, that a person living with HIV/AIDS can be safely baptized and should be allowed to kiss an icon, *The Concept* is not meant to be a guideline for action; rather it simply states that the Church intends to work as an institution to fight the epidemic.

It is not surprising that the Russian Orthodox Church sees sin and immorality as the basis of the propagation of HIV/AIDS. As one of the Church officials who presented *The Concept* stated, "Society must not hide from the realization that there is a connection between sin and the disease."[9] Yet it is not entirely clear to which sin he is referring or what the connection should be understood to mean. *The Basis of the Social Concept of the Russian Orthodox Church*, the Church's public position on various social questions, states that disease and illness are the result of sin, in particular the sin of previous generations. Thus disease and illness are inherited immoral consequences.

It is important to remember that a genetic disturbance is quite often a consequence of the neglect of moral foundations, the result of a depraved way of life, as a result of which their descendants suffer. The sinful damage of man's nature overcomes spiritual efforts; if from generation to generation vice rules in the life of the progeny with increasing strength, then the words of the Saints Writings will be realized: "a terrible end awaits the unjust family." And conversely: "The blessed man is he who fears the Lord and deeply loves His commandments. There will be great strength on the land of his family; the family will be rightly blessed" (Psalms 111, 1–2). In this way, research in the field of genetics only confirms the spiritual law which was revealed to humanity many centuries ago by the word of God.[10]

Given this reasoning it is quite likely that the Church considers the cause of HIV infection to be not only the so-called immoral behavior of PLWHA (e.g., injecting drug use, extramarital and homosexual relations, and sex work) but also the genetic past of these individuals. On the other hand, *The Concept* on HIV/AIDS explicitly states that infection should not be thought of as a kind of "payback" for individual sins; rather it is the result of the sinful nature of humans. This inconsistency regarding the relation between sin and illness can be found within *The Concept* itself, such that "illnesses and the suffering they involve . . . are consequences of sin and neglect of God-commanded moral norms," but goes on to say that the "Church Fathers do not believe it possible to establish an unequivocal link between illness and a particular personal sin."[11] The matter is never settled within *The Concept*; Father Maxim told me that in his opinion this is one of the document's shortcomings.

Nevertheless it is clear from papers written by priests on the topic, as well as many comments I heard during my research, that there remains a widespread belief among the Church hierarchy, priesthood, and staff that HIV/AIDS is in fact a punishment from God for the immoral acts that led to infection. According to one priest who is very active in the Church's response to HIV/AIDS, "God allowed this new illness to appear to teach sinners and to stop the spread of several extremely destructive kinds of sin."[12] In this view, it is God's will that the sins of injecting drug use, prostitution, sexual promiscuity, and homosexuality be punished by death. The same priest draws an analogy between cutting off a limb to save a person's life, and individuals dying of AIDS to save society as a whole. We mourn the loss of the dead person but are joyful that by means of this death the community has become more healthy (spiritual, moral). Thus although the Church's official position is ambiguous on the question of whether or not HIV/AIDS is a punishment for particular personal sins, many of those who work within the Church on the epidemic are very clear about where they stand.

The Concept does make it clear that it is the duty of all Orthodox believers to "hate sin but love the sinner."[13] In the Orthodox tradition all persons are endowed with a natural and God-given dignity that entitles them to this love and the opportunity to repent. A significant aspect of this repentance is the chance to change oneself. The Church sees illness and the suffering it brings one as an opportunity to be motivated to change oneself.[14] This is what Natalia Aleksandrovna meant when she explained that HIV is a blessing because "it can lead a person to begin to change his life." Similarly a priest who is the head of a rehabilitation center said in an online interview that HIV is "not simply a disease, it is a call from God to realize oneself and endeavor to change."[15] The same priest quoted a young HIV-positive woman who turned to the Church after learning of her positive status: "I thank God that I have HIV. It helped me completely reinterpret and change my life. If it were not for HIV, I don't know where I would be now. I think our illness is not a punishment but a test." In a sense the Church's HIV prevention and treatment programs are not very different from each other, in that the main goal of both is to teach the person Orthodox morality and how to live a spiritual and moral life. As Natalia Aleksandrovna explained, "The Church's primary concern is helping a person secure a place in the afterlife." This is best done through the kind of spiritual and moral teaching the Church offers, and if HIV is motivation for learning these teachings, then so be it.

This does not mean, however, that the Church is prepared to do nothing to stop the spread of HIV. The Church sees the epidemic as a calling to perform its duty to educate Russian society about Orthodox spirituality and morality. This is clearly seen throughout *The Concept*, where it is repeatedly emphasized that the main task of the Church is to provide "religious education," a significant aspect of which is proper moral training. Such education should be directed not only to the youth, to prevent the spread of the "immoral" activities that may lead to infection, but also to those who are already infected, so they may learn to live with HIV/AIDS. Father Mefodii, the priest who made the analogy between cutting off a limb and an individual dying of AIDS, has argued that because HIV/AIDS is a disease that weakens the immune system, it is a sign of the loss of God's grace within a person. As God's grace protects one's spiritual health from sin, so the immune system protects the body's health.[16] It is the Church's task to train these persons so that they can regain God's grace and His protection of their spiritual health.

HIV IS GOD'S BLESSING

One afternoon in early September 2006 it became apparent to me that the Russian Orthodox Church programs of drug rehabilitation and HIV prevention and care focus their moral and human rights projects directly on the bare life of rehabilitants. Natalia Aleksandrovna, the St. Petersburg Diocesan program head, and I were speaking about the Church's stance on needle exchange and harm reduction programs, which the Church is officially against, when she said that from the Church's point of view HIV can be considered a blessing from God. I was a bit taken aback by such a claim and asked her what she meant. She continued:

> When a person receives some grief he gets a reason to think about his life and because of that it could change for the better. Many of our patients say exactly that: "When I found out I have HIV, I realized I need to change something in my life." And in spite of the fact that this is a grieving experience it helps the person change. And if it was not for that he could soon die because he was leading a criminal life, was using drugs and could die from overdose. Thanks to what happened he realized how strictly his life is limited and started to change something.

The Church views HIV as a blessing because the infection throws individuals into conscious awareness of their own bare life and mortality, making them more open to changing their way of being in the world. This is not simply the official view of the Russian Orthodox Church, but is also part of the public discourse on the ethics of HIV. I was told numerous times by persons attempting to enter the Church-run program that it was the diagnosis of HIV that led them to want to change their lives. Similarly Didier Fassin writes that in South Africa persons who discover they are HIV positive often desire a "reconstruction of the self" and work on themselves with "practices of moral regeneration." As Fassin puts it, this ethical work is instigated by the "modest ambition [of] wanting to live."[17]

From the Church's perspective this change is twofold. First an HIV diagnosis, or potential diagnosis, motivates one to ethically work on oneself in order to overcome addiction and start living a normal life as a responsible person. Second the primary goal of the Church and its program is to help secure eternal salvation for rehabilitants. The this-worldly consequence of such an aim is the attempt to cultivate responsible subjects.

Because the primary goal is eternal salvation, which can occur only after the death of the material body, the addicted and infected body of bare life is the border space between the life of a responsible citizen and the death of salvation upon which power works. From the point of view of the Church, ultimately it does not matter which side of this border space a rehabilitant ends up on as long as his body has been properly subjected to the power of the Church as the moral savior of the Russian nation. For while the Church recognizes the necessity of morally training individuals, ultimately their goal is the moral resurrection of the Russian nation. Thus one of the primary goals of their HIV programs is to contribute to "strengthening the moral and physical health of the nation."[18] These two metaphors of the strength of a nation—its morality and its physical health—disclose the Church's work on the bare life of IDUs and PLWHA.

FOUR Moral and Ethical Assemblages

Learning to live in this world in a particular way is the primary goal of The Mill and the Church-run program. As is clear from the sparse literature on drug rehabilitation programs, a vital part of this therapeutic process is the attempt to remake personhood.[1] Although this is true for drug rehabilitation programs in general, it is especially so for the Church-run program, which emphasizes the moral training aspect of rehabilitation. Indeed rehabilitation in the Church-run program is described in their public documents, and was often described to me, as a process of *rabota nad soboi*, or "working on the self," to make oneself into a new moral person. For this reason I approached my research from the beginning as an inquiry into rehabilitation and HIV prevention and care as a process of cultivating new moral persons.

To do this I paid close attention to the therapeutic *process* of rehabilitation at the Church-run program. In contrast to what they call the therapeutic procedure and outcome, Csordas and Kleinman argue that the therapeutic process is not only understudied by medical anthropologists, but in fact should be the focus of our studies.[2] They define therapeutic process as "all the meaningful activity that mediates procedures and outcome" and argue that it can be understood in several distinct senses: (1) as the unfolding of a specific treatment event; (2) in terms of an experiential process; (3) as the progression or course of an illness episode and the sequence of decisions leading to diagnosis and treatment; and (4) in the sense that therapy and healing articulate broader social issues and concerns.[3] Each of these ways of understanding the therapeutic process has informed the analysis of what follows.

What is particularly important for the way I approached the therapeutic process of drug rehabilitation in the Church-run program is that I see this process as one of making new moral persons. From this perspective the various therapies, ways of speaking, and practices performed are not so much aimed at overcoming addiction, although this certainly can be a consequence of the therapeutic process; rather they are aimed at transforming the moral personhood of the rehabilitants into what the Church would call spiritually moral persons. If one can make oneself into a spiritually moral person, then by definition one will no longer be a drug user. This is the therapeutic goal of the Russian Orthodox Church drug rehabilitation and HIV prevention and care program. It is my task to anthropologically describe and interpret the therapeutic processes that are meant to lead to this goal.

By personhood I intend a particular relationship to morality, as morality, and its various discourses and techniques, sets the range of possibilities within which persons are produced. Therefore I make an analytic distinction between self and person so as to be clearer about how this process works. Csordas defines the self as "neither substance nor entity, but an indeterminate capacity to engage or become oriented in the world, characterized by effort and reflexivity."[4] This capacity is an embodied capacity, which is to say that self is a way to describe the process by which human bodies are engaged, oriented, and actively attuned to their social world. The result of this process is what I call personhood. As Csordas puts it, the "person already objectified is a culturally constituted *representation* of self."[5] I take Csordas to mean that the person is the socially recognized disclosure of these embodied self processes. Throughout the rest of this book, then, when I speak of *self*, for example, *working on the self*, I mean that embodied capacity to dialogically and intentionally engage the social world. When I speak of *person*, I mean the socially recognized outcome of this engagement. The embodied self is the foundational process that allows for social and moral persons.

THE DISTINCTION BETWEEN MORALITY AND ETHICS

To understand how this process of remaking moral personhood occurs within the Church-run program I propose an anthropological theory of moralities that recognizes the multi-aspectual nature of what I call both morality and ethics. Elsewhere I have provided a framework for such a theory by taking a phenomenological approach to the study of the social uses of morality and ethics.[6] I find the phenomenological approach useful because a central analytical tool of this approach is the focus on the various aspects of a phenomenon that come to *count* as the whole.[7] From a phenomenological point of view, neither morality nor ethics can be considered as a total and unified concept, but can be found only in the social world in the various aspects I delineate below.

Because of this I argue that what comes to be called morality or ethics is constructed as a total and unified concept only after the fact of articulation in speech or thought. In the social world, that is to say, in the everyday interrelationships between institutions, discourses, and persons, one encounters only the *various aspects* of what might come to *count* as morality or ethics in a particular situation. Although the Church-run program claims to propagate and teach Orthodox morality and ethical practices, close analysis discloses the multi-aspectual nature of the local morality and ethical practices within the program. That is to say, the theory I outline in this chapter allows us to see that the Church-run program, like all particular social contexts, is not defined by one morality and its ethics, such as Orthodox morality, but rather by a unique local moral and ethical assemblage constituted by the various aspects I describe below.

Thus if there can be said to be any morality and ethical practices that characterize the Church-run program, they are a unique aspectual combination of not only Orthodox, but also Soviet, neoliberal, and secular therapeutic moral discourses and ethical practices.

The first analytical distinction between aspects of a local moral and ethical assemblage is between morality and ethics. Although this distinction is similar to ones made by other social and philosophical theorists, such as Ricoeur and Foucault, it differs in significant ways. For example, whereas Ricoeur makes a distinction between ethics as action aimed at the good life and morality as obligatory norms,[8] I speak of morality, on the one hand, as discourses articulated by various institutions and public outlets within a society, each of which have varying degrees of power to enforce these discourses. On the other hand, I speak of morality as the embodied dispositions that allow for nonconsciously acceptable ways of living in the world. As I have argued elsewhere,[9] I do not intend *acceptable* to be equivalent to *obligatory*. My interpretation of embodied morality is much more about being existentially comfortable in one's world, which is another way of saying living sanely in one's world. Because these institutions and public outlets do not usually have the power to implement their respective moral discourses in a totalizing manner, and embodied morality is about acceptable existential comfort, it is impossible to speak of morality as either obligatory or normative in a strict sense. Similarly ethics in my terms is the process that is aimed not at the good, but at cultivating this existential comfort in and between the ranges of influence of these various moral aspects.

Foucault, on the other hand, regards ethics as the kind of relationship one ought to have with oneself in order to be a moral subject, and morality as the institutionally imposed codes one is obliged to cultivate.[10] He is clear that moral systems tend to emphasize either moral codes or ethical practices of the self, yet ultimately all moralities are composed of both.[11] I agree with Foucault on this to a point. There is no doubt that at the level of what I call the institutional and public discourses of moralities there is almost always some interrelationship between what he calls codes and ethical practices. Yet my theory goes beyond this discursive level and allows for the kind of analysis of very particular social and global assemblages, such as the Church-run program. At the level of the assemblage there are clearly present not only any number of the three aspects of morality I discuss below, but also a unique set of ethical practices that emerge out of this localized assemblage of various moralities. In this sense ethics as I describe it is not tied to any one particular moral discourse, as Foucault would have it, but is tied to the particular assemblage that is partially constituted by multiple moralities. Thus whereas Foucault might talk about ethical practices within a discursive formation, I am concerned with the ethical practices unique to a particular assemblage. How this moral and ethical assemblage is constituted will become clearer as we move forward.

Once this initial distinction between morality and ethics is made, then further distinctions become necessary. In terms of ethics, these distinctions become clear in the various practices utilized. In terms of morality, further aspectual distinctions are made in the different kinds of discourses and the nonconscious embodiment of ethical practices.

Morality can be considered as three different but interrelated aspects: (1) the institutional; (2) that of public discourse; and (3) as embodied dispositions. Institutions, for our purposes, can be loosely defined as those formal and informal social organizations and groups that are a part of all societies and wield varying amounts of power over individual persons. All humans have at least some nominal contact with or participate in some of the institutions that make up their respective societies. Most humans are intimately entwined within the overlapping spheres of influence of several different institutions within and beyond their own society. Some examples of such institutions are governments, organized religions, village elder councils, the workplace, and international organizations such as the United Nations and International Monetary Fund.

An institution claims to be the bearer and securer of the truth or rightness of a particular kind of morality. Institutions have varying levels of power available to them to propagate and enforce their version of morality; however, it is generally a formal prerequisite of interacting with the institution that one adheres to this morality, at least publicly. For example, the Russian Orthodox Church has a particular moral view on sexuality, which is part of the Church's larger moral system, and it is expected that all Orthodox should believe and live according to this moral doctrine.

However, it is obvious that not all Orthodox, or all the participants in any institution for that matter, always follow to the letter the claimed morality of the institution. It is also obvious that those who do not follow the institutional morality are not always punished or reprimanded for not doing so. In fact their behavior may go unnoticed. It is also clear that all societies, including small-scale societies, are made up of a plurality of institutional moralities. Despite the fact of the plurality of institutional moralities within all societies and that persons do not always precisely adhere to one or any of these institutional moralities, the influence that institutional moralities have on individual persons is clearly real and substantial. For this reason it is not uncommon that when asked what morality is, a person will give some version of, for example, the Ten Commandments, the law, societal tradition, or something of the kind. Institutional morality, then, is a significantly influential moral discourse that is often supported by very real expressions of power, but that nevertheless is not totalizing and is more akin to a very persuasive rhetoric than it is to a truth.

Closely related to institutional morality, but yet not quite the same, is the public discourse of morality. This distinction is very similar to the distinction Voloshinov made between official ideology and behavioral ideology,[12] where the former is that which is upheld by official and state institutions and the latter is the result of the everyday dialogical interactions between persons. Although these two kinds of ideologies, like the institutional and public discourse of morality, are separate and distinct from one another, they are in constant dialogue with one another. Thus both of the ideologies about which Voloshinov speaks and the two moralities I am discussing (as well as the third aspect I will discuss next) not only support and authorize one another, but at times also undermine and subvert one another.[13] The public discourse of morality, then, is all those public articulations of moral beliefs, conceptions, and hopes that are not *directly* articulated by an institution. Some examples of the public discourse of morality are the moral position of media outlets, protest, philosophical discourse, everyday articulated beliefs and opinions, the arts, literature and stories, and parental teachings.

The public discourse of morality can be very closely related to institutional morality, but need not be. In any case, the two aspects of morality are always in a dialogical relationship with one another. Thus, for example, certain television news networks may articulate a moral discourse that is very similar to that of the institutional morality of the government, yet when the network is not itself run by the government it cannot be said that it is itself a part of that institutional moral voice. This is so because given even relative independence from the institution of the government, there is always the possibility of dissent and debate within the network and by speakers on its broadcasts. Indeed it has become a trademark of most modern media outlets to provide some diversity of moral voices on their broadcasts or in their pages.

Because in the contemporary world the media have become so entwined with many institutions, perhaps it is better to consider some other examples of the public discourse of morality to see how it is a distinct but dialogically interacting aspect of morality from institutional morality. Take, for example, the arts and literature. In the Western world these have provided an alternative moral vision to institutional morality since at least the time of ancient Greece; Sophocles, Shakespeare, Dostoevsky, Stravinsky, Picasso, among many others have all provided, in their own ways, distinct moral views of the world. The same can be said of the arts and literature of the non-Western world, and I have no reason to think the same cannot be said for the oral narratives and arts of small-scale societies around the world. Likewise the arts and literature also often support institutional moralities.

Similarly it is very clear that people in their everyday articulations of their moral beliefs and concepts also offer an alternative moral voice to that of institutional morality. Earlier I said that it is not uncommon that one would reference, for example, the Ten Commandments or the law when asked what morality is. This shows the pervasive influence of institutional morality, but that is not the end of the story. Once one begins to press a person a bit more, for example, in the kinds of moral debates that arise in everyday life or in the context of anthropological interviews and conversation, one often finds moral articulations that differ, sometimes radically, from the dominant institutional moralities of a society. Such moral articulations are a part of the public discourse of morality.

They are also, I suggest, an articulation, or a reflexive verbalization of the third aspect of morality, that is, morality as embodied dispositions. This third aspect of morality is similar to what Mauss called habitus, or unreflective and unreflexive dispositions of everyday social life attained over a lifetime of socially performed techniques.[14] Morality as habitus is, as Mahmood puts it, a product "of human endeavor, rather than revelatory experience or natural temperament [and is] acquired through the repeated performance of actions that entail a particular virtue or vice."[15] Especially important about this notion of habitus is that it emphasizes the conscious and intentional work necessary to acquire a particular kind of habitus, and thus avoids the largely unconsciously acquired and socioeconomically determined view of habitus offered by Bourdieu.[16] What I call ethics is just this conscious and intentional work that cultivates moral habitus.

Unlike morality as codes or obligatory rule-following or conscious reflection on a problem or dilemma, morality as habitus is not thought out beforehand, nor is it noticed when it is performed. It is simply done. Morality as embodied dispositions is one's already cultivated everyday way of being in the world. It is because all persons are able to embody their morality in this unreflective and unreflexive way that most persons most of the time are able to act in ways that are, for the most part, acceptable to others in their social world seemingly naturally.

Ethics, on the other hand, is a conscious reflection on, or the turning of one's attention toward, this third aspect of morality as embodied dispositions. In this ethical moment a person becomes reflective and reflexive about her moral way of being in the world and what she must do, say, or think in order to appropriately return to her nonconscious moral mode of being. What must be done is a process of working on the self, where the person must perform certain practices on herself or with other persons in order to consciously be and act moral in the social world. In this way, ethics is a conscious acting on oneself either in isolation or with others so as to make oneself into a more morally appropriate and acceptable person not only in the eyes of others but also for oneself.

This working on oneself in what I call the ethical moment is brought about by a moral breakdown. This occurs when some event or person intrudes into the everyday life of a person and forces him to consciously reflect upon the appropriate ethical response (be it words, silence, action, or nonaction). Once he has experienced this moral breakdown, he works on himself by utilizing certain ethical tactics not only to return to the unreflective and unreflexive disposition of morality, but in so doing to create a new moral dispositional self. Thus this moment of ethics is a creative moment, for by performing ethics new moral persons and new moral worlds are created, even if ever so slightly.

This moral breakdown, or what might also be called an ethical dilemma, occurs in those moments traditionally associated with such dilemmas as when a good or right action must be decided upon. But perhaps more important the moral breakdown occurs in those moments when one is forced to reflect on the kind of person one wants to be in one's social world. As Jason Throop has convincingly argued, the experience of pain and suffering is just one such moment when this shift to an ethical mode of being occurs.[17] The Church-run program provides the context in which ethics can be performed by those IDUs who have already experienced the moral breakdown brought on by the various forms of social suffering related to their heroin use.

This ethical moment of the moral breakdown is a moment in which the three aspects of morality come together to *inform* the ways a person works on herself. I say *inform* because none of the aspects of the institutional moralities, the public discourses of morality, or the person's own embodied dispositional morality determines how this person will work on herself in this ethical moment. It may be true that one or several of these aspects will play a very significant role in the workings of the ethical moment (so significant that some might be tempted to say that it or they are determinant). Nevertheless, because this is a moment of conscious reflection and dialogue with one's own moral dispositions, as well as with the other two aspects of morality, it is also a moment of freedom, creativity, and emergence. It is because of this moment, and the way it feeds back into the social world, that one's own embodied moral dispositions change throughout a lifetime and the possibility arises for shifts, alterations, and changes in the aspects of institutional morality and the public discourse of morality. It is because of this creative aspect of ethics as a conscious work on the self that, though clearly influenced by the work of Foucault, I ultimately agree with Critchley in his rejection of Foucault's seeming emphasis on work on the self as an ethics of self-mastery.[18] I view ethics instead as a lifelong process of adjusting and readjusting to the breakdowns of social and moral life. Rather than conceiving of ethics as aimed at what Critchley calls Foucault's emphasis on "the autarchy of self-mastery," I view ethics as the lifelong struggle to remake oneself in the face of finding oneself over and over again in a state of inauthenticity.[19]

With all three aspects of morality, but also with the practice of ethics, there is always a range of possibilities that define the recognizable options for what counts as either morality or ethics. Similar to how MacIntyre has characterized tradition as consisting of a recognizable range of debate over its key concepts, ends, and practices,[20] so too with morality and ethics. As Douglas Rogers has put it, morality (and I would also say ethics) consists of those shades of similarities and differences that fall within the range of what is recognizable by both oneself and others as possible.[21] It is this range of possibilities that is altered, even if ever so slightly, by the creative and free process of ethics.

This analytical approach to the anthropological study of moralities is vital to the study of the Russian Orthodox Church's approach to injecting drug use and HIV, for central to the Church's view of this dual epidemic in Russia today is that they are both the result of what the Church considers to be the current immorality of Russian society. This immorality is often said to be the result of the negative influences of globalization and Westernization that took place in the post-Soviet period. In the Church's view this dual epidemic must be addressed by providing the context in which so-called traditional Russian and Orthodox morality can be taught to rehabilitants.

However, there are several moral discourses and sources of ethical practice that constitute the local moral and ethical assemblage of the

Church-run program. The program is uniquely constituted not only by an Orthodox institutional discourse of morality and its ethics, but by various aspects of Soviet, neoliberal, and secular therapeutic institutional and public moralities and their respective ethics. It is for this reason that a theory such is this is necessary to make distinctions between the various aspects of the local morality that characterizes a particular assemblage and the unique set of ethical practices that are the result of this assemblage.

FIVE *Synergeia* and *Simfoniia*

ORTHODOX MORALITY, HUMAN RIGHTS,
AND THE STATE

As should be clear from the discussion of the Church's institutional view of HIV/AIDS, the Russian Orthodox Church sees drug addiction as a sin and a problem of immorality. It is not uncommon for priests and laypersons writing on the topic of drug addiction to mirror this view in their public discourses. For example, in his paper titled "The Christian View of the Problems of Drug Dependence," Father Maxim calls drug addiction a "social evil" and writes that no "disease is so connected to sin as drug addiction."[1] Similarly an Orthodox psychiatrist writing about drug addiction claims that "using drugs is a deliberate [*coznatel'nyi*] sin, which in time 'becomes' many other sins"; he later reiterates, "I repeat, the sickness of drug addiction is a sickness of sin."[2] In the institutional view of the Church and in Orthodox public discourses drug addiction is a particularly dangerous sin because it can lead to the performance

73

of other sins, as well as the HIV infection of the user and the spread of the infection to others.

But the sin is not simply a matter of the immorality of the individual who uses drugs; it is also a reflection of the general lack of morality and spirituality in contemporary Russian society. This was emphasized by Aleksii II, who prior to his death near the end of my research was the patriarch of Moscow and All Russia. At a Church conference on Russia and drug use he said, "The Church of Christ proclaims that drug addiction is, first and foremost, a spiritual problem, and it cannot be solved without overcoming today's spiritual crisis of our people. The reason why this disease spreads so widely and quickly is the distortion of the traditional spiritual foundations of Russian society. We cannot seriously hope to get rid of drug addiction without curing human souls befouled by sin."[3] This comment discloses what the Church sees as the integral relationship between society and the individual. Individuals fall into the sin of drug use because society as a whole has lost its spiritual and moral foundations. To stop the spread of drug addiction the Church must begin the task of reestablishing these foundations in society. But this can be done only by "curing" individual souls, one at a time, person by person, of their sinful nature. The social body is morally and spiritually renewed by retraining and changing the individual body. This is precisely the method used in the Church's drug rehabilitation program.

What is sin in the Orthodox view, and why is drug addiction considered a sin? To answer this question I turn to a more detailed explication of Father Maxim's thesis on the Orthodox view of drug addiction, which is the most extensive analysis of this view available, where he attempts to give a theological and moral description of drug addiction. Using the definition of M. Olesnitsky, an important Orthodox moral theologian from the turn of the century, Father Maxim defines sin as a "conscious and free disobedience of human will to the morality and will of God." Referencing John Chrysostom, one of the Church Fathers, he argues that sin is not in nature, but rather is the result of the "disposition of the soul and in free will."[4] Sin, then, is an embodied capacity to deviate from the way of God and to go one's own way in this material earthly world.

As an embodied capacity sin can become habitual, and when this habit becomes nonconscious it becomes a passion.[5] It is important to emphasize the nonconscious nature of passion, for as Father Maxim argues, passion "is truly spiritual slavery: by its means people as slaves are conducted to evil, even against their will, against their wish."[6] A person with an embodied passion does not choose to sin. In fact he may wish to choose not to sin. But he must sin. It is who he has become: a sinner. Only by means of proper ethical training can an embodied capacity to sin, a passion, be gotten rid of.

There are also different stages of embodied passions. The first stage is ethical sloth and carelessness, when persons do not reflect on their "duties and the results of their activity . . . and forget the necessity to change and improve their lives." The next stage is self-delusion, when persons deny the necessity of trying to change and improve their lives. Ethical slavery is the embodied state of no longer desiring or having the strength to get rid of one's passion. Persons in this state can attempt to change themselves, but these are almost always fruitless attempts because "sin has already entered them and mingled with them." Sin has become who they are. When one has reached this state of passion, it often leads to bitterness, or the sinful state when the person has been cut off from any "ethical sense."[7]

According to Father Maxim, drug users have at best acquired the embodied state of ethical slavery and at worst that of bitterness. He describes the inner being of drug users as having received a nuclear strike, which leaves within them "a deep and ominous silence announcing the death of everything animate."[8] In this state of being all that was once moral and had the potential for a spiritual life with God has been destroyed. Now only communication with the demons that possess one is possible. From this state of extreme moral and spiritual withdrawal one might expect that there is little hope for a return. Indeed Father Maxim describes this hopelessness as a cold nuclear winter of ethical slavery and bitterness. But as the Church Fathers have shown, the passions are not incurable, and in their example drug users can find hope for their own spiritual and moral renewal. It is this renewal that the Church offers in its drug rehabilitation program.

In fact Father Maxim claims that only in the Church is true recovery from drug addiction possible. This "true recovery" is what he calls the "maximum goal" of The Mill: for the ex-drug user to become a "church-going" person and "to step on the path of salvation and to accept Christ." The maximum goal is contrasted with the "minimum goal" of the rehabilitation center, which recognizes that not everyone is able "to answer the call of God," and therefore sobriety and a return to a "normal life in society" is the goal of these people.[9] "True recovery," then, is not simply sobriety; it is not simply defined as no longer using drugs. This is the "minimum goal." "True recovery" is "spiritual rehabilitation." It is becoming what is often called enchurched (*votserkovlenie*).

From my own observations it became clear that very little pressure to fully convert was ever put on rehabilitants or other drug users who came into contact with the Church program. Nevertheless, based on the sources I've discussed so far and my own observations it is also clear that conversion is in fact considered "true recovery." Most never achieve this "true recovery"; in fact most are unable to reach the minimum goal. Still conversion is the primary goal of the program. As Father Maxim once told me, it is very rare that anyone is able to gain true sobriety without having become enchurched.

To become enchurched, which is the acquisition of an embodied disposition of an Orthodox way of living, a person must come to embody Orthodox morality and learn to live a spiritual life. This is done by a long process of laboriously working on the self. But to understand what the final goal of this working on the self is and why certain ethical practices are utilized, we must first understand what is meant by Orthodox morality and how it leads to a spiritual life. That is, we must understand why the embodiment of Orthodox morality results in enchurchment.

ORTHODOX MORALITY

The Russian Orthodox Church views drug use and HIV/AIDS as moral problems of both the individual and society. The drug rehabilitation program and the Church's motivation for establishing it cannot be understood separately from the Church's concept of morality, for morality is the raison d'être for the program. And Orthodox morality cannot be understood outside its theological basis. Although I am not qualified to fully delineate this theology, I will do so in a cursory manner, by focusing on the Orthodox view of the human person and her relationship with God. Orthodox Christianity shares many foundational theological and moral concepts and practices with both Catholicism and Protestantism, but there are some significant differences. Orthodoxy, true to its name as "right belief," finds its theological and moral foundations in the Patristic Church Fathers of the fourth century, whereas the Western Christianities, still recognizing the importance of the Church Fathers, have developed various interpretations of these foundations throughout the millennia.[10] Particularly significant to this difference is the much stronger influence of philosophy on the theology of the Western Churches.

Perhaps the best starting point for an understanding of Orthodox morality is the Fall. The Fall represents the separation of humans from God, a separation that was foreshadowed by the fall of Satan from the angelic realm. The Fall of humans was made possible by the freedom with which they were originally endowed. With this freedom the original persons, Adam and Eve, had the choice to follow God's will or to disobey. In their free choice to disobey God they also chose to separate themselves and all of humankind from God. According to Orthodoxy, humans have been carrying this burden of separation ever since.

This first sin, or we could also say this first immoral act, set the scene for human nature. Unlike the predominant Augustinian view in Western Christianities, in the Orthodox tradition the original sin is not conceived of as inherited guilt.[11] Rather the original sin is that which created the separation between God and humans that allows sin and immorality to exist in this world. Whereas prior to the Fall sin and immorality did not exist in the world, after the Fall they became, if you will, the norm against which humans must take on the burden to struggle. In other words, the struggle against sin and immorality is the struggle to reunite oneself with God, a struggle to undo the Fall. Thus there is an important distinction between the Western Christianities and Orthodoxy. Whereas in the Roman Catholic and Protestant traditions original sin is inherited by individuals, and thus each person bears the responsibility of living with this inherited guilt in the world, Orthodoxy primarily views original sin as that rupture which allowed for a world in which sin is the norm. Therefore in the Orthodox view it is not individuals as such that are guilty of original sin, but individuals as part of a fallen world that must struggle against the ease of sinning in such a world.[12]

What, though, is sin? Orthodox definitions of sin tend to mirror the separation from God that was caused by the first sin at the time of the Fall. That is, sin is an act against the will of God, and as such in performing a sin a person is recreating and reestablishing the separation of the Fall. For example, one of Orthodoxy's Holy Fathers, St. John Chrysostom, defined sin as "nothing but an action against God's will," and the moral theologian Olesnitsky defines sin as a "conscious and free disobedience of human will to the morality and the will of God."[13] Sin, then, is a deliberate and intentional act, thought, or emotion that is against the will of God and thus further separates one from Him.

Because sin is an act that further ruptures the relationship between the sinner and God, it can be seen as a disturbance of the sociality that Orthodoxy posits as the basis of the relationship between humans and God.[14] This sociality is disturbed by means of free acts of the will. In contrast, the Roman Catholic view of sin is conceived in legalistic and rationalist terms. According to the *Catechism of the Catholic Church*, sin is an "offense against reason, truth, and right conscience," and following Augustine and Aquinas is "an utterance, a deed, or a desire contrary to the eternal law."[15] Therefore it is possible to see sin in the Catholic tradition as the irrational transgression of an impersonal legal order.

However, sin as the willful disruption of the natural sociality between humans and God describes only what might be called the first level of sin. Because sin is described in terms of consciousness and intentionality, it references those sinful acts that are chosen. But as I showed earlier, sin can also reach a state within a person such that it is no longer chosen but is instead embodied. In other words, one can acquire a sinful habitus and perform sin in a nonconscious manner as one's way of being in the world. This state is called passion, and there are several stages of passion that demark the extent to which one has come to fully embody a sinful habitus. The final and most complete embodiment of sin as passion is at the level of ethical slavery and bitterness, when one no longer desires to be free of sin and has lost all moral sense. This, however, is a stage that very few ever reach; the vast majority of persons remain capable of working on themselves to rid themselves of sin. Indeed even those who have reached this highest level of passion are able with the help of God to slowly disentangle themselves from this state of embodied sin.

This is so because despite the separation from God created through the Fall, and recreated through sin and passions, all persons have the capacity within themselves to reunite with Him. This capacity exists because of the uniqueness of humanity in the order of things. In the Orthodox tradition this uniqueness is founded in the fact that humans are created in both the image and likeness of God, which separates humans from the rest of creation and allows for a special relationship with God. It is this special relationship that, among other things, allows humans to be free and moral beings.[16] This is, if you will, the static reading of the image/likeness nature of humanity. Similarly in the Catholic tradition as outlined in the *Catechism of the Catholic Church* humans are conceived in terms of being created in the image (but not the likeness) of God.[17] In both the Catholic and the Orthodox traditions this fundamental image within all persons is the basis for their dignity and what sets them apart from the rest of creation in a special relationship with God.

In the Orthodox tradition, and in distinction from the Catholic tradition, there is another, dynamic reading of the image/likeness nature of humanity, which is predominant in the Russian Orthodox Church's documents on moral issues and topics.[18] This reading makes a clear distinction between the image and the likeness and allows for a dynamic person to struggle against sin and work toward moral perfection. The image of God within each person signifies that humans are endowed with such capacities as intellect, emotion, ethical judgment, and self-determination.[19] These capacities have been diminished by the Fall, but they remain within all persons as the image of God. The likeness of God, on the other hand, is the "human potential to become like God."[20] That is to say, by means of spiritual and ethical work every person has within them the potential to become God-like, or to achieve divination or *theosis*. Jesus Christ and the various saints serve as examples of this potentiality.[21] In other words, the full potentiality of human nature is to become like God. The duality of the image and the likeness within each person provides the dynamic basis for the spiritual and moral work that is possible for all persons and by their very nature provides them with a moral imperative to develop themselves.[22] Therefore, while the image of God provides the foundations for moral personhood, such as ethical judgment and self-determination or freedom, true human nature can never fully be realized without having realized the likeness of God.

This dynamic view of human nature, which has its end point in the realization of the likeness of God or *theosis*, necessitates a kind of developmental view of the moral nature of human beings. Since all persons are born with the dual nature of the image and likeness of God and also separate from God and therefore in a natural state of sin, they must learn to develop themselves so as to realize their potential true human nature. This moral and spiritual development, which in the Orthodox view cannot be considered distinct, necessitates the conscious attempt to work on oneself ethically. As Metropolitan Philaret puts it in his work on moral theology, one "must observe oneself in all respects and . . . must also consider what must be done at any given moment."[23] This self-observation is not only of one's outward actions but also of one's inner life. As Philaret argues, to be a moral Orthodox Christian "one must not only do good for others, but work on oneself, struggling with one's insufficiencies and vices, developing in oneself a good, Christian-valued foundation . . . . [A] Christian strives, of course, not to *seem*, but to *be* good."[24] Moral development in the Orthodox tradition, then, is not only developing the ability to do good toward, with, and among others, but, just as important, developing within oneself morally good intentions, motives, thoughts, feelings, and emotions.

This moral development, this working on the self, is not something to be done on occasion or in certain moments, but should be done continuously. It is that which should define one's mode of being in the world. As Philaret writes, "Life is a moral struggle, a path of constant striving toward good and perfection. There can be no pause on this path, according to the law of the spiritual life. A man who stops working on himself will not remain the same as he was, but will inevitably become worse—like a stone which is thrown upwards and stops rising, it will not remain suspended in the air, but will fall downward."[25] Even those who have reached this moral perfection, for example the saints, never stop this working on the self. That is to say, even the morally perfect, acting according to the moral virtue of humility, continue to strive to better themselves. If they do not continue this work, there is always the possibility that the gravity of the Fall will pull them once again into sin.

Not only does the image and likeness of God within every person give them the natural ability and duty to morally develop and attempt to perfect themselves, but as I mentioned above, so too does it provide them with a natural and God-given dignity.[26] As Patriarch Aleksii II put it in his greeting to a Church-sponsored conference on biotechnologies and Christian ethics in 2006, human dignity is not given to a person by another or by human law, but is revealed by God. That is, dignity is endowed by God and helps persons recognize their moral commonality to all others.[27]

This God-given dignity has a double significance for Orthodox morality. First, as we just saw, the recognition within oneself of this dignity provides motivation to ethically work on oneself in the struggle to morally perfect oneself. Second, it provides an obligation for each person to recognize the community of persons united in this God-given dignity and, because of this, the duty to act toward all others in a morally proper way. In this sense Orthodox morality is a social morality that begins in the individual. This is vital for understanding why the Russian Orthodox Church sees their drug rehabilitation and HIV prevention and care programs, which focus on the cultivation of individuals' moral personhood, as contributing to the moral revitalization of Russian society. In a very real way, from the perspective of the Russian Orthodox Church the morality of the Russian nation can develop only as the morality of the individuals within it develops. In this sense the kind of ethical work on the self the Church espouses through its moral theology and advocates in its social programs tries to develop and cultivate a new moral personhood, and at the same time to create closer bonds between the individual and social groups. The bonds created go beyond the individual and the Church and nation; perhaps more important, they include the family, social networks, and the workplace.

The image and likeness of God found within every person, in addition to providing each person with dignity and the dynamic nature to act on this dignity, also endows every person with a free will. According to Metropolitan Philaret, freedom of the will is "freedom of choice between good and evil."[28] In the Orthodox view this freedom of will is a gift from God because God does not want humans to mechanically submit to His will, but to choose freely out of love to be morally good and follow His will. Ultimately it is a person's free will and how it is exercised that determines whether one achieves salvation or not, for moral responsibility cannot exist without freedom.[29] This is so because it is only through God-given freedom of will that a person can make any choice at all, and it is by means of making this choice that responsibility comes into question.

Indeed it is through freedom that morality and ethical decision making and working on the self become possible at all, for with freedom sin becomes possible. In the Orthodox perspective, if God did not endow all humans with freedom, they would automatically and mechanically submit themselves to God. But because God loves humans and wants them to love Him back, He gave them the gift of freedom, for love must be given freely. Therefore while freedom is that which makes sin possible, it is also that which makes love possible.[30] Because of this, freedom is the condition that allows for the only true basis for acting morally: love.[31]

Freedom of will and choice are essential for any person fully realizing his human potential of becoming God-like. Although no one can achieve this state, or salvation for that matter, without the grace of God, God's grace is not enough. For God cannot force anyone into the Kingdom of Heaven. Instead the Orthodox tradition sees an essential *synergeia* between God's grace and human freedom that is the only possible way for persons to achieve salvation or moral uprightness or even to do singular morally good acts.[32] Therefore, although it is impossible for a person to be moral or to work on himself without the grace of God, these are equally impossible without the freedom of the will and choice.

The relationship between grace and human freedom has been a central debate within Christianity since at least the time of Augustine and the

Pelagian controversy, and is the source of one of the essential distinctions between the various Christianities.[33] The *synergeia* between God's grace and human freedom that is essential to Orthodox moral theology is very similar to the Roman Catholic view on the debate. However, while the Orthodox position on grace is founded on the teachings of the early Church Fathers, such as St. John Chrysostom and St. Cyril of Jerusalem, the Roman Catholic position was not officially established until it was decreed at the Council of Trent in the sixteenth century. This decree was issued in condemnation of the Protestant position on grace, which in its most extreme form of Calvinism claims that grace is given by God only to the elect few predestined for salvation. This distinction within the various Christianities can be articulated as follows. Within the various Protestantisms it is grace bestowed by God and not the acts and ethical work of individuals that determines salvation. In contrast, the Orthodox and Roman Catholics share a similar notion of grace that works in synergy with human freedom, and thus while God's grace provides the necessary foundation for salvation, one's specific acts and ethical work ultimately determine if one is saved.

This freedom of will that is both necessary for salvation and a necessary aspect for morality and ethics is also that which allows for the uniqueness of each individual person. As Bishop Ware puts it, because every person is free in his will, "each human being realizes the divine image within himself in his own distinctive fashion."[34] This means that every person is unique and "unrepeatable," and therefore "infinitely precious." As such, each person is "irreplaceable." This irreplaceability sets Orthodox morality squarely against the kinds of utilitarian theories that attempt to calculate the moral worth of individual persons or groups of persons. As Ware puts it, using Kantian language, each person "is irreplaceable, and therefore each must be treated as an *end* in his or her self, and never as a means to some further end. Each is to be regarded not as object but as subject."[35] Freedom, then, is an indispensable concept for understanding Orthodox notions of morality, ethics, and personhood.

It is important to address the question of individualism versus collectivism in Orthodox morality. In the West Orthodoxy has, perhaps a bit stereotypically, come to be associated with collectivism. There is no doubt that Orthodoxy emphasizes the Church as community or *kollektiv*, and that the Church as a *kollektiv* considers itself to have a central role in revitalizing the morality of the Russian nation. Nevertheless Orthodox moral theology, as well as several recently adopted documents of the Moscow Patriarchate, for example those on society, human rights, and HIV, clearly articulate a morality that starts with the moral development of individuals, which in turn leads to the moral development of society. It is in this sense that the concept of *sobornost'* should be understood. *Sobornost'*, which is difficult to translate but is often described as unity in multiplicity,[36] articulates this emphasis on the moral responsibility of each person to morally develop herself. This responsibility is important not only for one's own salvation, but also for the salvation of the whole. In this sense it is true that Orthodox moral theology has a concern with the morality of society, but as I argued earlier, it is a concern that begins with the moral development of individual persons.

It is important to pause for a moment to reflect on the roots of this Orthodox notion of morality and personhood. It is tempting to read into this Orthodox moral tradition a continuity with various schools of ancient Greek philosophy, even more so, perhaps, due to the recent revival of Neo-Aristotelianism in the social sciences. There is no doubt that the Patristic Church Fathers who shaped the foundations of Orthodox moral theology were well aware of the various Greek philosophies and to some extent were influenced by several of them. For example, I have argued elsewhere that the Stoic notion of the divine spark of *logos* found within each person has striking similarities to the Orthodox notion of the image/likeness duality.[37] For the Stoics the spark of the divine reason that animates the universe and that is found within each person provides the capacity for developing moral personhood. For the Orthodox the image of God found within each person allows them to ethically work on themselves in order to strive toward God-likeness.

Despite such similarities, however, it would be a mistake to read the Orthodox tradition as a kind of Christianized ancient Greek or Roman philosophy. Indeed in contrast to developments in Western Christianity these ancient philosophies had much less influence on Orthodox theology. While Catholic and Protestant theology were primarily shaped by the philosophically influenced works of Augustine and Aquinas, the Orthodox tradition to this day continues to find its theological roots in the Church Fathers of the fourth century.[38] In fact the Church Fathers are perhaps best understood as working out their theological position as an alternative to the very philosophies that so influenced Western Christianity.[39] Thus, while much of Catholic theology as outlined, for example, in the *Catechism of the Catholic Church* continues to this day to be significantly shaped by Aquinas's adaptation of Aristotle to Christianity, no such systematic use of Aristotle or any other ancient philosopher has been taken up in the Orthodox tradition.[40] One significant result of this difference is that in Catholicism, as well as the various Protestantisms, the relationship between God and humans, on the one hand, and individual persons and their bodies, souls, and morality, on the other, are viewed in rational-juridical terms,[41] whereas in Orthodoxy these relationships are conceived in unitary and holistic relationships of mutuality.

Because of this Orthodox notions of morality and personhood are perhaps better understood as strongly influenced by what Ware calls the Hebraic-biblical tradition.[42] Ware argues that Orthodox morality and personhood are strongly reliant on a holistic understanding of the human person, which he claims is central to the Hebraic-biblical tradition. In contrast, the Hellenic-Platonist tradition holds a dualist notion of the person, in which the body and soul are to various degrees sharply separated. Ware points out that although the Stoics had a very similar notion of the holistic view of the person,[43] the Hellenic-Platonist tradition was primarily understood by the early Church Fathers as that against which their theological positions were being formed. This holistic view of personhood, in which no distinction is made between body and soul, as the basis for Orthodox morality is central for understanding how morality is disciplined in the Church-run rehabilitation program. That view is the basis for a notion of ethically working on oneself that does not make a distinction between the disciplining of one's body, one's emotions, and one's thoughts. Several of the disciplinary techniques utilized by the Church-run program are meant to work on all three of these as aspects of one unified and holistic embodied person.

ORTHODOX HUMAN RIGHTS

The Orthodox notion of human rights is a driving moral motivation behind the Church's efforts in drug rehabilitation and HIV prevention and care. Recently the Church released *Basic Teaching on Human Dignity, Freedom and Rights,* which delineates its official institutional view on human rights.[44] This document is rich with information for understanding the Church's moral perspective, particularly its view of the moral person, which are key for understanding how and why the Church is involved in drug rehabilitation and HIV prevention and care. In fact drug addiction is mentioned in *Basic Teaching* as one of the immoral activities that must be addressed to ensure people's human rights.

The Russian Orthodox Church's view of human rights calls into question the liberal assumption that a universal human rights already exists. Metropolitan Kirill, who became patriarch after the death of Aleksii II and is one of the main defenders and authors of *Basic Teaching,* has argued in several public speeches that the so-called universal notion of human rights now dominant in the world is, in fact, a reflection of a certain liberal ideology predominant in the West.[45] This characterization contrasts with the Catholic view of, for example, the *Universal Declaration of Human Rights,* which since the *Pacem in Terris* encyclical of 1963 has supported the basic tenets of the UN document.

Basic Teaching is an attempt to give a Russian Orthodox perspective on human rights, and in so doing provide an alternative view of what rights can do for the relationship between persons, society, and states. Ironically, in the Church's attempt to offer this perspective on human rights against the claimed universality of the dominant human rights discourse, it is also claiming a universality that overrides that of the dominant discourse because of its foundation in the Orthodox Christian moral theology outlined above, a theology that the Church sees as universally binding and true. Paradoxically this universality is meant to secure the moral and spiritual existence of the local over against the threats of the universalizing threat of the ideology of globalization and neoliberalism.[46]

The universal basis of the Russian Orthodox Church's notion of human rights is founded on the "singular unalienable worth" of each person. This worth is given by God because of the very fact that humans are created in the image of God. This singular worth of each person must be, so the Church argues, protected with human rights. At first glance this notion doesn't seem very different from the secular notion of human rights,[47] against which the Church is rhetorically arguing. In both human rights discourses that which is claimed to be the essential nature of human beings, their inherent worth and dignity, or what Agamben calls their sacredness, is what makes their inherent rights undeniable. But by explicitly tying this unalienable worth to the sacredness of every person, the Orthodox version reveals what Agamben would call the originary connection between rights, sacredness, and bare life. In other words, by explicitly returning to this originary connection, the Russian Orthodox human rights document reveals the centrality of bare life to all human rights discourse.

This is further seen in how the Church envisions human rights being enacted within society. A secular (neo)liberal discourse of human rights utilizes a rhetoric of empowerment as motivation for the subjectivization of individuals-cum-citizens, which is an implicit discourse of limitation.[48] In contrast, the Russian Orthodox Church explicitly states that human rights should put limits on a person in order to preserve her unalienable worth. Therefore the Church is against such secular rights as freedom of sexuality and abortion. From the Church's perspective these are not rights that protect the worth of human persons at all, but instead, through a misunderstanding of the true notion of worth, provide the opportunity for individuals to demean their own worth. In other words, they are "rights" that encourage and support sin.

The Russian Orthodox Church posits that human rights must be closely guided by universal standards of morality in order to protect the God-given worth of human persons. As a preliminary Church document on human rights puts it, "the religious tradition that has God as its Origin [that is, the Orthodox Church] is called to help discern between good and evil" in the guidance of establishing human rights.[49] Therefore it is the role of the Russian Orthodox Church to authorize and establish the moral structure of society that promotes those human rights meant to support the worth of persons. Human rights should provide a structure or context within which moral behavior becomes more easily acted upon.

This is clearly seen in the list of human rights included in *Basic Teaching*. Preserving the rights of nations and ethnic groups to their religion, language, and culture; protecting against ethnically and religiously motivated crime; supporting the traditional understanding of family; protecting the free confession of faith; opposing prostitution and drug addiction—these rights should be established to encourage one to act in morally appropriate ways to help foster one's dignity. For the Russian Orthodox Church human rights are not meant to allow what they consider immoral behavior, such as homosexuality, abortion, or the public demeaning of religion, since these kinds of activities do not promote human dignity but instead belittle it. Rather human rights provide a structure or context within which moral behavior becomes more easily acted upon and ultimately helps make society and the persons living in it more moral.[50] Therefore the Orthodox Church's notion of human rights is not about securing rights for individuals, but about providing the means by which a moral society can be cultivated and secured.[51] It is my contention that the Church's drug rehabilitation program is a paradigm for this societal moral structure.

The concept of dignity is central to the Church's view of human rights as providing the societal structure within which morality can be cultivated. In a speech on human rights and moral responsibility Metropolitan Kirill argues that there are two aspects of dignity: that a person has an inherent worth and "that the life of a subject corresponds to this worth."[52] Thus, although all persons are naturally endowed with dignity from God, this dignity can be darkened by not living an appropriately moral life. Nevertheless because this dignity can never be fully erased, it remains to be purified and grown. As *Basic Teaching* states, repentance provides "a powerful stimulus for seeking spiritual work on the self [*dukhovnoi raboty nad soboi*], making a creative change in [a person's] life, preserving the purity of the God-given dignity and growing in it."[53]

Related to this, the Church's view on human rights relies on the Orthodox notion of freedom. *Basic Teaching* makes a distinction between two kinds of freedom: inner freedom from evil and freedom of moral choice. The first is good on its own. The second has value only if it is used to choose good. Human rights are related to both. First, they provide the context in which a person can more easily choose to do the morally appropriate thing. This is so because the Church does not separate rights from moral obligations and responsibilities. Second, in providing this context in which persons are more likely to choose rightly, human rights, much as they help reveal the God-given worth of each person, help to bring about a personal state of freedom from evil.

Human rights also help bring about a society free from evil because rights are "inseparable from human obligations and responsibilities."[54] Rights and morality are inherently social, for they are meant to always be related to "the neighbor, family, community, nation and all humanity." Similarly Kirill stated in a speech at a human rights conference in Strasbourg that freedom and human rights "ought to be harmonized with morality and faith, and this harmonization, in turn, ought to be reflected in the structure of contemporary society."[55] *Basic Teaching* ends on this same harmonizing note that sees human rights as uniting individuals with both national and international communities: "Unity and interconnection between civil and political, economic and social, individual and collective human rights can promote a harmonious order of societal life both on the national and international level."[56] For the Russian Orthodox Church human rights help structure a society in which both individual persons and society as a whole can more easily harmonize and move toward moral perfection.[57]

The Church's moral theology is the foundation for its view of human rights. Based on the image/likeness duality, this moral theology claims that every person has a natural capacity to ethically work on themselves and strive for moral perfection, or God-likeness, and in so doing work at the same time for the moral betterment of society. As we have just seen, this view of human rights envisions the creation of a moral-political society by means of the creation of responsible and normal persons and lists the overcoming of drug addiction as one of the social areas in which Russian Orthodox human rights should be implemented. Thus, according to *Basic Teaching*, the "social value and effectiveness of the entire human rights system depend on the extent to which it helps to create conditions for personal growth in the God-given dignity and relates to the responsibility of a person for his actions before God and his neighbors."[58]

This moral theology is also the basis for the Russian Orthodox Church's programs on drug rehabilitation and HIV prevention and care. Although the Church sees drug users as having reached the highest level of embodied sin or passion, Orthodox moral theology argues that within these persons is the ability to change themselves, to overcome their embodied immorality, and to move toward God. The Church-run program hopes to set rehabilitants on this path. It is not expected that rehabilitants will attain the sainthood that defines having achieved God-likeness, but it is expected that each of them will ethically work on themselves so as to become moral persons who are able to be responsible citizen-subjects and live normal lives in contemporary Russia. It is for this reason that I am arguing that The Mill and its related programs can be viewed as a paradigm for the kind of society the Church would like to establish based on its view of human rights. By establishing the structures and standards of morality within which those who come to The Mill must live, the Church hopes that these persons can exercise their rights to realize their God-given worth and dignity and, if not reach the main goal of enchurchment, then at least become responsibilized and normal persons.

CHURCH-STATE RELATIONS

This approach to human rights as that which provides the moral structures and standards of society raises the question of the contemporary relationship between the Russian Orthodox Church and the Russian state. During the Soviet period the Church suffered much persecution, including the imprisonment of clergy and laypersons, state interference in internal Church decisions, and the closing of innumerable parishes, monasteries, nunneries, and seminaries. Then, after World War II, the Church as an institution was to a certain degree accepted by the state for propagandistic and pragmatic purposes. Thus even during those darkest hours the Church had a unique institutional relationship with the Russian state that, despite its periodic redefining, dates back a thousand years.

Because of these various uses and abuses of the Russian Orthodox Church by the Soviet regime, how to reorganize Church-state relations in the post-Soviet period has been a primary question in contemporary Russia. The position of the state seems to be pretty clear: the 1997 Federal Law on Freedom of Conscience and Religious Associations recognizes the Church's "special contribution [to the] development of Russia's spirituality and culture," and legalizes the Church's priority status within the contemporary plurality of religions in Russia. This priority status allows the Church access to particular public, political, and financial support from the state that other religions do not enjoy. Nevertheless Russian Orthodoxy does not enjoy the status of a state religion or hold any privileged position for *officially* influencing state policy. The 1997 law can thus be seen as the result of a political project for controlling the religious pluralism that came to characterize the post-Soviet religious field,[59] a project that was heavily lobbied for and supported by the Russian Orthodox Church. In turn the Russian government at least tacitly expects that it will receive both public and private support from the Church.[60]

In contrast, there appears to be a range of views within the Church hierarchy about how this relationship should be constituted.[61] Irina Papkova, a political scientist who writes on religion and the state in Russia, describes the various positions as ranging from the marginalized liberals, who support universal religious freedom and resist the legal institutionalization of the Church's privileged status, to the "monarchist apocalyptic" faction, who claim that an Orthodox tsar ruling according to Orthodox ideology and leaving no room for religious pluralism or social tolerance is the only acceptable form of government for the Russian state.[62] The moderates, and the currently ruling faction within the Church, are those Papkova calls the "conservative pragmatics." For this faction, to which both Patriarch Aleksii II and Patriarch Kirill clearly belong, Church-state relations should be defined according to the ancient

Orthodox Byzantium notion of *simfoniia,* which can be defined as "a model of governance in which the Church and state are engaged in an active partnership aimed at achieving the best possible material and spiritual conditions for human development."[63] Thus, just as the Orthodox see a relationship of *synergeia* between God and individual persons that allow for the development of moral personhood, the Orthodox political concept of *simfoniia* envisions good governance in the form of a mutual relationship between sacred and secular powers. Indeed this political concept of *simfoniia* underlines the Church's political vision of human rights.

In this political vision the form of government the state takes is of little concern to the Church (Soviet-style, atheistic communism is obviously excluded from this vision) as long as the state privileges the Russian Orthodox Church for defining, shaping, and propagating the moral values that define the Russian nation and her people.[64] A significant aspect of this is helping Russian society withstand the shocks of the post-Soviet transformation, in particular the influences of globalization and neoliberalism, which the Church believes seriously threaten the spiritual and moral foundations of Russian society and persons. According to Alexander Agadjanian and Kathy Rousselet, the main social and moral documents of the Church in the post-Soviet period, which have been either authored or coauthored by Patriarch Kirill and include *The Basis of the Social Concept of the Russian Orthodox Church* and *Basic Teaching on Human Dignity, Freedom and Rights,* are best understood as establishing a theological position that is both antiglobalization and anti-neoliberalism.[65] In the view of Agadjanian and Rousselet this position mirrors, supports, and works in tandem with the current predominant political position of the Putin-Medvedev regime, perhaps best encapsulated in the neologism of sovereign democracy, that seeks to reestablish Russia's political power and position over and against the universalizing nature of the ideology of globalization and neoliberalism.[66] I agree that this partnership between the Russian Orthodox Church and the government exists, but as I pointed out earlier, although the government often utilizes an anti-neoliberal discourse, the dominant political-economic discourse in contemporary Russia is in fact that of neoliberalism.

In a very real way the Church-run drug rehabilitation and HIV prevention and care program I studied can be seen as providing the spiritual and moral support thought to be needed for the Russian people to overcome the moral diseases of globalization and neoliberalism. Yet in Russia's neoliberal political environment, which is partially defined by the radical decentralization of services, it comes as little surprise that the government is more than pleased to allow the Church to take the reins of such programs. And if the content of several of the Church's recent public documents are any indication, the Church appears more and more eager to organize and offer such programs with at least the political, if not financial, support of the state.[67] In an environment where both the Church and the state are eager to utilize the other for the purposes of solidifying their respective institutional and moral foundations and have found antiglobalization discourse a convenient means of expressing this partnership, it is no surprise that the unintended consequences of the Church-run program are the cultivation of persons better prepared to live in just the kind of world this theological, political, and moral rhetoric seeks to overcome.

SIX Working on the Self

One afternoon in October I went to the Aleksandr Nevsky Lavra to attend an orientation and introduction meeting offered by a psychologist for the various Church-run rehabilitation centers. The small room next to the Lavra café where the meeting was held is only a short walk from the metro, but on this walk it is possible to see so much of recent and not so recent Russian history. Sushi restaurants and a McDonald's share a building with a Soviet-era hotel across the street from the Lavra; new BMWs, Fords, and Toyotas race past the giant statue of Aleksandr Nevsky, who defeated the invading Swedes in the Battle of the Neva in 1240; and legless veterans of Chechnya and Afghanistan compete with old *babushky* for handouts along the walkway between the two cemeteries where many of Russia's most famous artists, intellectuals, and politicians are buried.

Outside the small room waiting with me were fifteen or so drug users and parents and relatives of IDUs who came to hear the introduction and have a short one-on-one meeting with the psychologist. He finally arrived and opened the door. After helping everyone find chairs, Vladimir Alekseiovich began his talk. In addition to the general information he gave about the different centers from which they could choose, he spoke about the particularities of the Church-run rehabilitation process, while continually emphasizing the need for the rehabilitants to do work on themselves.

He told everyone, "Nobody is going to do it for you. At detox, yes, there they will load you up and you will rest. But that is not healing, that is erasing your problem, that's what detox is. And you are still going to have to solve your problems. One way or the other you are not going to find an easy solution anywhere. You are going to have to set yourself for serious work [*rabota*], for humbleness, for patience." Vladimir Alekseiovich was making the point that there is no quick fix for addiction: it is a time-consuming and difficult process of remaking oneself. In this view a person does not overcome addiction; instead a new, unaddicted person must be made.

Vladimir Alekseiovich described a process that can be accomplished only by means of the focused hard work of the rehabilitant himself or herself. This emphasis on the centrality of the individual was the most common way the rehabilitation process was described to me and others by staff members and rehabilitants. But although it is certainly true that a good deal of the success of rehabilitation depends on the work done by individuals on themselves, it still remains largely a social process. Examining this tension between the individual and the social is vital for a proper understanding of the moral approach of the Russian Orthodox Church in their fight against drug addiction and the spread of HIV.

One aspect of this tension can be seen in the way working on the self is articulated and conceived by those involved in the rehabilitation process as an actual process of labor. This is how Vladimir Alekseiovich described it to the group: "In order to break out of this circle of madness dictated by the drug addiction, you need to labor [*trudit'sya*], everyone needs to labor—both the family and the drug addict." Throughout his talk he repeated these two words, *rabota* and *trudit'sya,* so often that at one point one of the mothers became confused. He had just told them that "the most important thing is that a person starts to work and looks for and accepts help. This is the main thing which you need to start with." To this a mother replied that drug users are often not hired for jobs, which is certainly a true statement that reflects the widespread stigma of injecting drug users and HIV-positive persons in Russia today. However, this is not the kind of labor and work about which Vladimir Alekseiovich was talking, and after nearly forty minutes of speaking, most of which was on this very topic of the need to prepare oneself to work on oneself, for the very first time he explicitly stated what he meant: "To work on oneself [*rabotat' nad soboi*], this is the most important work that will help one get sober." This working on oneself, then, is conceived as actual labor or work.

Father Sergei, who leads the hospital prayer service, once described the process to me as one of *perestroika* or rebuilding, which connotes the necessity of laboring and working to rebuild who one is. And Oleg, the staff member at The Mill who runs the Tuesday reception at Botkin Hospital, told me that rehabilitation at The Mill is not effective unless the person is willing to work until he has bloody blisters (*rabotat' do krovavykh mozolei*). This phrase actually has various interpretive layers. On the one hand, it clearly indicates the labor therapy that is a central aspect of the rehabilitation process at The Mill. Everyone who goes there must be prepared to do manual labor and keep a schedule that they most likely are not used to keeping. But it also references the need to work on oneself, the main rehabilitation strategy of the Church-run program. Even the labor therapy is a central aspect of this more important labor on oneself. In fact I suggest that the phrase "work until they have bloody blisters" is more indicative of the metaphorical process of the difficult labor of rebuilding oneself than of the relatively nonintensive labor therapy, for to rebuild oneself, to work on oneself with such intensity, is in fact a labor-intensive process that leaves one with metaphorical bloody blisters.

The goal of rebuilding oneself is articulated by many in the Church-run program as the construction of an entirely different moral person.

For example, Max, Father Sergei's assistant at the church in the hospital, described his current relations with old friends from before he began rehabilitation: "The people I hung out with three years ago, they do not recognize me, they just say that I have become a different person." Zhenia, the young woman who first used heroin out of jealousy of her boyfriend's addiction, told me something similar about the difference between her former and current personhood: "I am now something completely new and even interesting for myself." Over and over again I heard statements such as these from ex-rehabilitants. They have become new persons, even if, as in Zhenia's case, they eventually begin to use again.

This process of creating a new person entails working to move beyond who one has become. As Vladimir Alekseiovich put it in his introduction, "You are going to have to step over yourself [*sebya pridetsya perestupat'*]." This same phrase was used by Dima, a twenty-one-year-old who told me this while he was preparing himself at the Botkin reception to go to The Mill: "Sometimes it is hard, sometimes you have to really step over yourself. . . . I do not have any other way out. I understand that if I do this I will have to limit myself a lot and step over myself, bite my lip and go forward. And if I am not going to do it I will soon die like Andrei. And I want to live. I have something to live for." Unfortunately Dima left The Mill and returned to the city three days after arriving. He was unable to begin the process of stepping over himself, which is, as Dima quite rightly put it, hard, as it means working on one's bare life—the life of the self that can die, and at least in Dima's view, will die if he doesn't do the work.

SECULAR THERAPEUTICS AND
THE CHURCH-RUN PROGRAM

I have been arguing that this therapeutic focus on working on the self is intimately connected to Orthodox notions of morality, human rights, and personhood. But as is clear from the fact that psychologists such as Vladimir Alekseiovich are a significant part of the therapeutic process, the

Church-run program has also been significantly influenced by secular therapeutic and rehabilitation programs that have their origin in Western Europe and North America. In fact when Natalia Aleksandrovna and her cofounder first sought to establish a rehabilitation program in the St. Petersburg area in the early 1990s they did not intend to associate the program with the Russian Orthodox Church. Their original idea was to establish a private rehabilitation program run along the lines of Narcotics Anonymous, but one that was affordable for all. Only after several unsuccessful attempts to find a suitable location and financial support did Natalia Aleksandrovna and her cofounder decide to associate their program with the Church. Natalia Aleksandrovna eventually converted to Orthodoxy and now runs the program out of the Aleksandr Nevsky Lavra; her cofounder continues to play a significant role in the financial and organizational support of the Church-run program, but also is one of Russia's most staunch activists and organizers of secular therapeutic and harm reduction programs.

These origins played a significant role in shaping the eventual therapeutic process in the Church-run program. Central to this was the hiring of Aleksei, who now runs the Sunday Club but who was originally hired in the mid-1990s to be the first director of The Mill. He was considered best qualified for this position because of his unique experience being an active Orthodox believer who had a degree in psychology and previously worked with IDUs in various secular rehabilitation and therapeutic programs. These programs were based on various rehabilitation philosophies from the West, primarily Narcotics Anonymous, and it was from these examples that Aleksei borrowed when he was given the job of organizing the first therapeutic plan for the Church-run program. In his study of Alcoholics Anonymous in St. Petersburg Eugene Raikhel has shown that the late 1980s and 1990s saw a great influx of 12-step programs, as these were viewed by many as offering not only a more successful, but also a more compassionate therapeutic model for treating addiction.[1] Therefore it is not surprising that a newly established drug rehabilitation program in St. Petersburg would be significantly influenced by these secular therapeutic models, even more so after Patriarch Aleksii II gave his blessing to 12-step programs in 1993. His blessing officially opened the possibility for the Church-run program to adopt certain aspects of this secular therapeutic model.

Rehabilitation and therapeutic programs around the world are programs of self-transformation.[2] Whether these are 12-step programs for alcoholics or drug users or psychologically focused therapeutic programs based on religious teachings, the goal is often to induce and follow through on a process of transforming the personhood of those undergoing treatment.[3] Because of this focus on self-transformation these programs match well the Orthodox position that drug rehabilitation is a process of remaking the moral personhood of drug users. Therefore it was not difficult for Aleksei to create the Church-run program by integrating secular therapeutic models with Orthodox notions of self-transformation. The result is the current Church-run program that cannot be categorized as either secular or sacred; it offers a unique mix of such secular therapeutic strategies as talk, art, and film therapy with Orthodox teachings on God, personhood, and society, as well as prayer and confession.

A significant aspect of the therapeutic process in the Church-run program is various forms of talk. That is, therapeutic activities such as art and film therapy, as well as much of the therapeutic work that takes place outside of official activities, are just as reliant on speaking for their efficacy as is the more aptly named talk therapy. The Church-program emphasizes a certain kind of dialogical talk, *obshchenie,* that is perhaps unique to the Russian context, but talk of various kinds is central to the therapeutic and rehabilitation goal of self-transformation around the world. For example, Kelly McKinney in her analysis of a rehabilitation program for survivors of torture and refugee trauma in New York, points out that one of the primary therapeutic assumptions of psychotherapy is that first-person narratives of traumatic experience are essential for the reconstructing of the personhood of these survivors.[4] These narratives are significant in part because they help survivors come to terms with their memories of trauma. So too participants in Alcoholics Anonymous meetings retell their experiences to remind themselves and each other who they are and what they need to change.[5] By talking the therapeutic participants in these programs are able to work with their past and present selves in order to begin to cultivate a new future personhood.

Talking is also central to the therapeutic process in the Church-run program. In fact to an outsider like myself it is not immediately obvious that the program is run by a Church. An entire two-hour art or talk therapy session can go by without any mention of God, Orthodoxy, prayer, or any other religious subject. Often an Orthodox topic is only tacked on at the very end as a reminder that the work done in the therapeutic session should always be related back to what the program claims is the foundation of the rehabilitation process. This is not to say that the Church-run program is a secular therapeutics in the guise of religion. Rather, and this is one of the central claims of this book in terms of both therapeutics and the cultivation of self-governing persons, it is impossible to make clear distinctions between secular and sacred techniques of therapeutics and self-transformation. In the Church-run program it is just as difficult to define the difference between a secular and a sacred therapeutic process as it is to define the difference between the self-governing characteristics of an enchurched and a secularized rehabilitated person.

SOVIET PRACTICES OF WORKING ON THE SELF

As is well-known from the works of Foucault and others, there is a history in the Christian tradition that goes back to its earliest years of the individual working on the self to become a new moral person. As I have shown, this tradition is significant for the Church-run program, as are the techniques of self-transformation in secular therapeutics. But there is another important supporting history of working on the self that came out of the Soviet tradition. And it is perhaps this history that is more important for the way many of the rehabilitants and staff understand and accept the Church's emphasis on working on the self, for more than the Church tradition or Western secular therapeutics, the Soviet tradition has almost certainly had an influence on rehabilitants' everyday ways of understanding themselves and being in their social worlds.

One of the proclaimed ends of the Soviet Union was to create a New Soviet Man who embodied the communist ideal of collective values, and the tactics utilized for this endeavor focused on individual persons working to change themselves into this new type of person. As the anthropologist Michele Rivkin-Fish puts it, and similar to the Orthodox moral theology I described earlier, this is a history of targeting social change at the level of personal consciousness.[6] Perhaps most interesting about this history is what appears to be an underlying assumption to the discourse of Soviet practices of working on the self: that although it is possible to change individuals to varying degrees, the goal of societal change by means of cultivating individuals can come about only over an extended period of time. In other words, just as Orthodox moral theology does not expect most humans to be able to reach God-likeness, so too there was little expectation that most Soviet citizens could become New Soviet Men or Women. Instead the goal of creating the New Soviet Man would be reached only after decades, if not generations, of individuals incrementally cultivating themselves into new moral persons, and by extension incrementally building a communist society. Thus the underlying assumption of Soviet practices of working on the self can be considered a kind of social Lysenkoism, which sees the minor alterations in personhood acquired by certain individuals within a lifetime transmitted through generations, eventually resulting not only in the full cultivation of the New Soviet Man but also the achievement of a fully communist society.

I suggest that a similar assumption is at the basis of the Church-run program, in that although full conversion is the main goal, the secondary goal of living a normal life is the more expected and common outcome. Therefore, if the ultimate aim of the program as part of the Church's larger human rights project is to rebuild a moral Russian nation, this can be done only over the longue durée of incrementally cultivating each generation, one individual at a time, into an Orthodox nation. That is to say, since it is unrealistic to expect the immediate and full conversion of all Russians, an Orthodox nation can be realized only by gradually coming to define a normal life in Orthodox terms.

Shelia Fitzpatrick claims that Soviet individuals had to begin working on themselves in order to remake their identities from nearly the moment of the revolution onward.[7] Although working on the self was

conceptually important to Soviet power from its inception, Oleg Kharkhordin convincingly argues that only in the postwar period did it come
to be associated with individuals working on themselves.[8] Prior to that,
when this shift to the individual slowly began, working on the self was
generally associated with working on the collective body as self. That is,
the group of which one was a member, for example, a reading group, a
work group at a factory, and even the nation as a whole, was the self-
referent for which work must be done. Of course individuals were recognized as making up these various groups, yet the work these persons did
was done not for their own self-perfection but for that of the collective.

A shift slowly began toward individuals working on themselves with
the purges of the late 1930s, when individuals had to learn to assess
themselves in light of what they could discern as the expectations they
were supposed to meet. But even this tragic period was not enough to
fully move the emphasis from the collective to the individual. In some
sense the purges were still about perfecting the collective at the cost of
the individual. It was not until Zhdanov's 1948 speech criticizing two
newspapers in Leningrad that a full shift of emphasis from the collective to the individual appeared.[9] Zhdanov claimed that Stalin had for
a long time been emphasizing the necessity of Soviet citizens "to work
ceaselessly at improving oneself," something Kharkhordin claims is not
supported by the archives of Stalin's speeches. According to Kharkhordin it was this speech that "opened a flood of literature on working
on oneself."[10]

Catriona Kelly concurs that it was this "flood of literature," much of
which focused on self-help, that marked a significant shift in the post-
Stalin period from a collective work on the self to individual work on
the self.[11] In addition to the self-help literature and brochures, as well
as journal and scholarly pieces on morality that came out during this
postwar period, perhaps the most well-known is the 1961 Communist
Party program "The Moral Code of the Builder of Communism." Rivkin-
Fish claims that the Code was a central strategy in the postwar push for
moral education, providing "a template of ethics with which each citizen
was to model his or her individual character . . . [with] the obligation for
each individual to internalize societal interests as his or her own, and

work to fulfill them in daily life."[12] With such principles as "honesty and truthfulness, moral purity, modesty, and unpretentiousness in social and private life," "a high sense of public duty [and] intolerance of actions harmful to the public interest," it is clear that a full shift had occurred in the public moral discourse toward the individual. Although the individual is still meant to work on himself in the interests of society and collectives, the emphasis now lands squarely on each individual necessarily making himself into a proper moral person so as to fulfill this obligation toward society and to contribute to the eventual realization of a communist nation. We may very well call this shift of emphasis the *responsibilization* of the Soviet person. If the postwar period saw the acceptance of Lysenko's theory of genetics in the Soviet biological sciences, then by extension a similar mechanism can be discerned in the assumption of how individuals work on themselves and in doing so contribute to the long-term project of building of a moral nation.

The Code was certainly important because of its status as the official moral code of the Communist Party, which meant that it was taught in schools and explained by Komsomol members going door-to-door. Rivkin-Fish, however, claims that the moral concept of *kul'turnost* (culturedness) came to be a much more useful concept for officials, teachers, and parents for morally disciplining and educating Soviet persons.[13] *Kul'turnost*, she argues, allowed for an everyday perceived separation between state power and moral values. In other words, by linking a morally good person with, on the one hand, modernity and civilization, and on the other, personal respect and dignity, the concept of *kul'turnost* allowed for the perception that one was learning to embody a natural morality. Because *kul'turnost* was viewed as distinct from Soviet power per se, it came to be associated with a morality that was natural, human, and transcendent of politics. To be sure *kul'turnost* was already an important ethical goal for some persons, particularly Party members, in the prewar Stalinist period.[14] In the late Soviet and post-Soviet period, when so many became alienated from politics, it clearly became significantly more important, for in this alienation *kul'turnost* became a central moral concept for judging and remaking oneself.

Despite the consistent discursive use of *kul'turnost,* as a moral concept its meaning shifted throughout the Soviet period. In the prewar period it referred primarily to public cultured behavior such as hygiene and modesty; in the postwar period *kul'turnost* campaigns and literature increasingly aimed to cultivate the private sphere, such as the proper decorating of the home or the propriety of paying alimony.[15] Thus if *kul'turnost* was perceived by Soviet citizens as a natural morality, as Rivkin-Fish argues, it was a natural morality that was increasingly aligned with what might be called middle-class and bourgeois regimes of everyday life. In other words, the Soviet discourses and practices of working on the self as a cultivation of *kul'turnost* increasingly contradicted the Soviet political discourse of building the New Soviet Man and a communist society. Kelly sees just such contradictions and discontinuities in the history of the Soviet moral concept of *kul'turnost* as contributing to the decline of social consensus and the eventual collapse of the Soviet system.[16]

Nevertheless individuals remaking themselves seemed to become a necessity in the perestroika and post-Soviet years, as persons sought to overcome their own Soviet past and once again begin to construct a new kind of society.[17] But today the discourses of working on the self seem to focus less on projects of *kul'turnost* and instead, reflecting the political discourse of the time, focus more on projects of perestroika or rebuilding oneself. No longer is the emphasis on acquiring a preconceived moral ideal such as culture or a Soviet self; instead the focus is on cultivating the particular characteristics of a moral individual such as responsibility and discipline. This shift of focus can be seen, for example, in Nancy Ries's report of informants talking about the necessity of transforming themselves in the context of overwhelming social change. Using words that echoed Father Sergei's claim that the rehabilitation process is one of perestroika, one informant said, "We must rebuild [*perestroit'*] our very selves."[18] Similarly Dale Pesmen claims that her informants considered self-analysis (*samoanaliz*) synonymous with work on the self and an important characteristic of a developing moral person in the post-Soviet context.[19] In her work on reproductive health in contemporary St. Petersburg Rivkin-Fish found that medical personnel emphasize the need for women to work on themselves and cultivate self-responsibility.[20] According to these public discourses of working on the self, if post-Soviet Russian society is going to morally develop it will be a rebuilding process done one person at a time.

The end of the Soviet Union did not bring about the end of various discourses and practices focused on the necessity of individuals working on themselves to change or rebuild not only their moral personhood but also Russian society as a whole. Thus the emphasis by the Church-run program on work on the self as a means of changing Russian society seems to be a continuation of this long-held tradition. Not only is this tradition part of the Soviet legacy, but so too is it part of the much longer Orthodox legacy. When secular therapeutic models were brought in to be adapted to and adopted by the Church-run program, their emphasis on self-transformation seamlessly fit in with these two local traditions.

CONTINUITIES OF PRACTICE IN CHURCH-RUN PROGRAMS

Oleg Kharkhordin has argued that there were three stages of working on the self that were prevalent in the late Soviet period. He further delineates the methods used to realize the fulfillment of each stage. In what follows I consider those methods most closely linked to what I observed in the Church-run program. What I hope to make clear is that there is some degree of continuity between these late Soviet techniques of working on the self and much of the ethical work done in the Church-run program. Because of this continuity, and as I have been arguing, it would be incorrect to think of this ethical work simply in terms of the Christian practices, morals, and goals that the Church and its programs discursively emphasize. Rather it is a unique combination of Orthodox, Soviet, and secular therapeutic models.

According to Kharkhordin, the first stage of Soviet techniques of working on the self is self-cognition, resulting in self-evaluation.[21] This self-evaluation leads persons to realize certain deficiencies and shortcomings they may have, which they can then begin to work to overcome. Three of the most significant methods of this stage are recognizing oneself by means of others, solitary self-reflection and observation, and self-accounting or reporting of oneself. Each of these is meant to set the individual on the process of working on himself by taking the first step of coming to understand just what it is that needs to be worked on. The assumption underlying this stage and its methods, as well as the others discussed below, is that the self is not simply an internal and private self discernable through a psychologically focused reflection, but is additionally constituted by its external and public behavior, as well as by means of verbalization. Therefore working on the self entails certain practices meant to alter and cultivate very specific aspects of the internal, external, and verbalized self.

This first stage makes up the bulk of the work on the self done at the Church-run program. A significant amount of time is spent doing activities, participating in therapy sessions, and engaging in talks, all meant to get drug users, rehabilitants, and ex-rehabilitants to begin to realize what they need to work on. This first stage is a process of coming to know the self not as a whole, but as that which is constituted by various aspects all of which can be worked upon in specific and differing ways. For example, one of the weekly evening activities at The Mill is to meet as a group and talk about each rehabilitant's personal qualities. When individuals first arrive at The Mill and first attend this meeting, they put two to three words or phrases naming what they think they should try to change about themselves next to their name on a chart on the wall. Examples of such qualities they hope to take on or get rid of are responsibility (*otvetstvenost'*), confidence (*uverennost'*), and laziness (*len'*). In meetings every week thereafter each person stands up and puts a number from 1 to 10 next to each quality indicating how she thinks she has done during the past week working on this particular focus. In the group discussion individuals often offer their own view of the matter and come up with their own number indicating what they think the person's progress has been that past week. In this way the person comes to recognize herself through the eyes of others, which she can then integrate into her own cognition of herself. This recognition allows for the person to better hone in on the aspects of the self that need to be worked on, how she has been doing thus far in her work, and what she will need to do next.

A second method of self-cognition and self-evaluation is what Kharkhordin calls solitary self-reflection and self-observation.[22] This method is meant to be a response to the first method of seeing oneself through others. By reflecting in solitary moments upon what others say, the person is meant to fix his energy on working on those particular qualities, feelings, and motives that need attention. This kind of self-reflection and observation is clearly seen at The Mill during the long working hours of labor therapy. While this labor is certainly a necessity in terms of keeping the rehab center running, it has a secondary role of providing long daily hours for rehabilitants to reflect upon themselves and the work they are doing on themselves. As Oleg once described the therapy process at The Mill, all the various therapies are supposed to work together and thus allow for a kind of temporal expansion of the therapeutic experience. With this temporal and therapeutic expansion work on the self can be done much more intensively, as differing therapies not only work together, but each therapy contains within it various therapeutic processes. For example, what is discussed in group and art therapy sessions in the evening, as well as lectures on religious topics, are meant to be the impetus for self-reflection during labor therapy. Many of the rehabilitants told me this is precisely what they do for much of the day. Whether folding clean clothes, weeding the garden, or tending the cows, rehabilitants think over such things as how they have treated their parents and loved ones, the illegal or immoral acts they have done in the past, or why they have a problem with anger or low self-esteem. In these moments of self-reflection they can begin to realize those aspects of themselves that most need to be addressed.

Self-reporting or self-accounting is the third method of self-cognition. This is a public accounting of oneself and the work being done on oneself. It is a very common practice at The Mill and in the Sunday Club. In a way this is what is happening when each rehabilitant at The Mill rates himself on the wall chart, although that activity tends to focus more on what the group says about each person. Other therapy sessions, and most particularly the art therapy at both The Mill and the Sunday

Club, are examples of this self-reporting. During art therapy sessions rehabilitants are asked to draw, for example, a representation of their dominant feeling or emotion, their hopes, or something about themselves that they like and dislike. Each person then takes a turn showing the drawing to the group and talking about it, explaining how they plan to achieve this hope, stop acting in a certain way, or learn to express more or less of a certain feeling or emotion. These public self-accountings are just one more way for persons to recognize certain aspects of themselves and realize what they need to do to start working on themselves in an appropriate way.

According to Kharkhordin the second stage of Soviet techniques of working on the self is self-transformation.[23] Having achieved certain realizations through the first stage of self-cognition, the person begins to work on herself in earnest. This is set in motion with what Kharkhordin calls self-injunction or self-stimulation, or the process of bringing "oneself to start acting." This also seems to be the case with many of the rehabilitants at The Mill, especially those who have successfully remained drug-free back in the city. Self-stimulation comes about because of the success of the first stage of self-cognition; having realized that they were a kind of person who hurt their parents, stole from the family, went to jail, or participated in prostitution, and that they need not be this way anymore, they find the motivation to begin working on themselves. Often this stimulation is a social motivation. Thus several rehabilitants and ex-rehabilitants told me that they will finally begin to make the changes necessary in their lives because they don't want to hurt their parents any longer, or because they realize they need to begin to be responsible for their child and wife, or simply because they want to have a family of their own some day. Whatever the case may be, it is clear that many of those with whom I spoke experienced a certain kind of realization about themselves, which then motivated them to begin to work on themselves.

Although the practices of working on the self as self-transformation that are performed at the Church-run program go well beyond the two that Kharkhordin discusses, these two Soviet practices have also been integrated into the Church-run program. The first is what Kharkhordin calls personal planning: adopting promises or obligations toward oneself and the necessary list of rules of conduct for meeting them.[24] Kharkhordin claims that this was the most common means of working on oneself in the late Soviet period, and it is the most common way that rehabilitants work on themselves in the Church-run program. For example, for both rehabilitants preparing to return to the city from The Mill and for those attending the Sunday Club, it is important to have a personal plan for how they will avoid the social contexts that may lead to using drugs again. Plans may consist of never having more than fifty rubles (about $2) on them at one time, getting a job to avoid too much free time, attending church services several times a week, and forming a new circle of friends. Personal planning is the enactment of self-responsibility and self-discipline.

Besides avoiding heroin, beer and marijuana also played a significant role in the plans of many of the rehabilitants I spoke with at The Mill. The staff and Father Maxim are clear about the need for drug users to avoid both of these; rehabilitants, however, are less certain. Each seems to have his own view on the matter. Most think that having a few beers at home with dinner or in front of the television is not dangerous, yet they are very hesitant to go out to a bar or club and have the same amount of beer. It is not so much the beer, then, but the social context that they consider dangerous. Others believe that any amount of beer in any context poses a risk to their future sobriety, and therefore they have made it a part of their personal planning to refrain from all alcohol drinking. Interestingly some of these very same people will smoke marijuana. As Nika, a former DJ who became quite open with me at The Mill, once explained as we weeded the potato field together, alcohol is dangerous because it loosens your inhibitions, but because marijuana just relaxes you it is not dangerous. However individuals define their goals, a significant part of the rehabilitation and postrehabilitation program is for each person to set goals and plans for themselves and to internalize the rules of conduct necessary to attain them.

The second technique of working on the self as self-transformation during the late Soviet period is what Kharkhordin calls hero identification. The aim of hero identification was not to replicate the actions and feats of one's hero, but to form an internal world similar to the hero's. This new internal world allowed one to persevere "in fulfilling whatever goals one set oneself in everyday life."[25] The point was to enact an internal transformation of the self so as to allow for the fulfillment of certain socially and morally expected behaviors.

The Church-run program uses this technique as well. The staff and Father Maxim push Jesus Christ and certain saints to serve as role models, or heroes, but I found that the most common role models identified by the rehabilitants themselves were the staff members who were former drug users. On occasion someone would reference a saint's act or the life of Christ to provide an example for how she should be, but rehabilitants most often spoke about the staff members as examples of what they could become. This difference between *should* and *could* is important: the ideal examples of the saints and Jesus were less helpful to rehabilitants than the real living example of someone who had once been just like them and had now become a "normal person." I was told several times that if only they listened to the staff members, took their advice, and tried to embody what the staff members had become the rehabilitants could become just like them.

The third and final stage of Soviet techniques of working on the self is what Kharkhordin calls self-control by means of self-restraint and self-renunciation.[26] Kharkhordin tells us that this stage was influenced by the Christian imperative to fight temptation. There is little doubt that this too is the ultimate goal of the Church-run rehabilitation program. Nevertheless persons who were able to successfully embody this final stage are unfortunately quite few, as only about 25 percent do not return to drug use.

For those who have been successful—and success is always conditional, for, as the saying goes, "heroin can wait"—the key was achieving self-control and the discipline to avoid the social contexts of temptation. Especially important is the need to control one's emotional world; for many of the rehabilitants and ex-rehabilitants I spoke with loneliness and feelings of worthlessness are major obstacles to overcome. The same persons also spoke about their inability to feel comfortable or to communicate (*obshchat'sya*) with other persons, which suggests that these obstacles are not psychological per se but rather social. Learning to overcome these obstacles, so they told me, contributed to their success in staying away from resuming drug use.

It is not my claim that the Soviet practices of working on the self were simply transferred in toto to the Church-run program I studied. Rather, I am suggesting that we can find the traces of specific techniques that have their origins in the Soviet past. Those who practice and endorse these techniques may not even be aware of their origins, yet the techniques have legitimacy because of those origins. That is, the very idea of individual persons working on themselves to change themselves into another moral person has a familiarity to it that allows it to go unquestioned.

Not only does this Soviet tradition support and complement the Orthodox discourse of rehabilitation as a process of remaking moral personhood, but it also greatly facilitated the adaptation and adoption of certain secular therapeutic models of self-transformation. In fact the three stages of Soviet techniques of working on the self are from a certain perspective so broad that they can describe the basic model of both Orthodox and secular therapeutic regimes of self-transformation. Thus these practices would be familiar to those working on themselves in Orthodox and Catholic monasteries as well as to participants in secular 12-step programs.[27] For example, self-accounting as autobiographical narration, hero identification of a sponsor, and self-restraint as the ultimate goal are all parts of Alcoholics and Narcotics Anonymous. I suggest that the familiarity of this Soviet legacy, along with the continued post-Soviet public discourse of the necessity of individuals to work on themselves, greatly facilitated both the mixing of Orthodox and secular therapeutic ethical tactics as well as the acceptance of both of these by rehabilitants and staff. Finally, because of this mixing it is clear that the Church-run program cannot be defined by a singular and totalizing morality, but is more productively considered a local moral and ethical assemblage of various aspects of diverse and conflicting moral discourses and ethical practices.

PART TWO Practices

SEVEN Enchurchment

In part I, I provided an overview of not only the general social context of the current drug use and HIV epidemics in Russia today, but also the various discourses addressing these epidemics. In part II, I will slow down a bit and closely analyze some of the specific ways persons ethically work on themselves in the Church-run program. In doing so rehabilitants try to make themselves into new moral persons, the even partial success of which constitutes them as responsible subjects and as such participants in the gradual remaking of a new moral Russia. Many of these techniques have much in common with secular therapeutics, and as such invite us to question any clear distinction between a so-called secular and sacred therapeutic regime. I will begin, however, with two techniques that are solidly in the Orthodox tradition: prayer and confession.

PRAYER

As usual on Wednesday afternoons Father Sergei was giving his weekly prayer service at the Infectious Disease Hospital. He had just finished with the prayer for the dead, and before proceeding to holy unction he paused for a moment, looked around at the four patients in the small church—three female and one male—and as he would tell me later decided in that very moment to say a few words on the importance of prayer. As I mentioned earlier, it is not unusual for Father Sergei to end his services with short sermons, or what might be better described as words of advice or wisdom, but his obvious spontaneity on this day made his words seem all the more important. Here is what he said to those four HIV-positive patients on that day: "We all need to realize that within each of us is an evil person and we need to struggle with it and we do this through prayer, and God provides us with the Church to help us with this process. And we should remember that all the saints were once just like us." Like most of Father Sergei's sermons, this one was short and to the point.

It is also ripe with Orthodox assumptions about personhood, drug users and PLWHA, and the process of ethically working on the self. To begin, Father Sergei does not make a distinction between any of the persons present at the service. Instead he is addressing a general "we." All of us—the HIV-positive patients, at least two of whom I know were still using heroin at the time; Max, Father Sergei's HIV-positive assistant and a former drug user and mafioso; myself and my assistant; and Father Sergei himself—are sinners and have evil within us. According to Orthodoxy there are different types and degrees of sin; nevertheless all of us on that day in that small church were united in our humanity as naturally born sinners. This is our very nature as human persons in the Orthodox view.

If one chooses to attempt to be good, this attempt is necessarily a struggle (*borot'sya*). The necessity of struggle to overcome the evil suggests that evil is the default state of our personhood, and indeed this seems to be confirmed by the Orthodox notion of fallen humanity, a humanity born with the trace of original sin. This being the case, one cannot do nothing and expect to be good and moral. One must work, struggle, and strive to be so. It is a process that one must consciously choose to undertake. It is, in my distinction between morality and ethics, clearly an ethical process.

Father Sergei's plea for us all to realize our evil nature reveals that this is an ethical process that must be undertaken by our own conscious and deliberate efforts. It is, however, not a solitary and individual process. The Church and its saints stand ready to help, providing an authoritative structure and tradition to guide one in the ethical process of working on the self and also providing authoritative examples of what one can become by means of this work within the tradition and through the grace of God. In his short sermon Father Sergei was communicating to us that although the necessary struggle to work on oneself is a process that must be consciously and deliberately undertaken by each individual person, this process can be done properly only within the very particular social context mediated and structured by the tradition of Orthodox Christianity. This necessary ethical relationship of the individual working within a shared tradition is revealed in the lives of the saints. It is also indicative of *sobornost'*, or the unity in multiplicity, that many nineteenth-century Slavophile writers saw as defining not only the Orthodox Christian community but Russian society in general.[1]

Most important to this process of ethically working on the self within the authoritative tradition of Orthodoxy, Father Sergei's words suggest, is the technique of prayer. Indeed prayer can be considered one of the two primary Orthodox techniques of ethically working on the self. For in its very performance prayer reveals the necessary ethical relationship between the individual and its empowering authoritative tradition. This is so because, on the one hand, it must always be articulated and performed by an individual who chooses in certain moments to act the prayer, and on the other hand, as Mauss pointed out, prayer is possible and effective only within its authorizing social context.[2] It is this dialogical aspect of prayer as an ethical technique of working on the self that Father Sergei articulated.

Saba Mahmood and Joel Robbins have each shown how ritualized prayer can be an important technique for ethically working on the self in two very different societies. In both cases the act of ritualized prayer, as Mauss argued, has both a social and a personal ethical effect. Mahmood provides an important example for understanding how ritualized prayer is understood as a vital part of ethically disciplining the self. Her vignette of a conversation between three older and more experienced members of an Egyptian women's piety movement and a young woman seeking advice on morning prayer shows that prayer is conceived by these women as more than a ritualized form of worship; it is a means for creating a "pious self."[3] The repeated effort of making oneself wake up early enough to perform the morning prayer eventually leads to the cultivation of the internal desire to pray; it also leads to an ethical sensibility that better equips one for living morally in the social world. Thus the young woman is told that in performing the morning prayer every day she will be better able to do her daily chores, refrain from anger with her sister, and speak more appropriately. Ritualized morning prayer as Mahmood describes it is an important ethical technique for these Muslim women for remaking themselves into moral persons.

Robbins shows that among Pentecostal Christian Urapmins living in Papua New Guinea ritualized forms of prayer serve as an ethical technique for working on the self.[4] One such ritualized form of prayer is the anger-removal ritual, a traditional Urapmin ritual that has been co-opted by Christian concepts of ritual and expiation as well as practices of prayer, so that, Robbins tells us, it may now better be called a sin-removal ritual. Prayer has now become a central aspect of this ritual, in which persons who have committed "socially consequential, legally actionable sins," such as violence, theft, or adultery, undergo the rite in order to temporarily remove the burden of sin until the person goes on trial *and* confesses his sin.[5] This prayer ritual is a process by which a person is at one and the same time relieved of his internal, personal burden of anger, regret, and guilt and made able to return to the social world during that period of time prior to the trial and confession. It is, if you will, the first step of ethically working on the self that culminates in confession.

Similarly I found that prayer becomes a central technique for ethically working on the self among those in the Church-run program. Whether starting and ending the day with a prayer service in the church at The Mill, beginning and ending a session of the Sunday Club with a prayer, praying to oneself while doing one's daily labors at The Mill, or praying with Father Sergei at the hospital's church, prayer is emphasized over and over in each of these settings. What is particularly interesting about the importance of prayer in the lives of rehabilitants and ex-rehabilitants is that in all my time doing research only once did I witness instruction from a priest or a staff member on how, when, or to whom to pray. This was during a talk given by Father Maxim at The Mill, and even then it constituted only a few minutes of his discussion on the sacraments and focused on the ritual processes of prayer during liturgy.

However, several interlocutors told me that they did in fact receive what might better be called words of advice on the power of prayer to help someone in difficult and emotionally stressful situations. In other words, this advice came as an authoritative suggestion that what one does in ritualized and public form can also be done in a nonritualized and private manner as a means of working through the moral break-downs in one's life. Prayer, then, is introduced to rehabilitants as a significant ethical technique by means of individualized and private conversations between them and priests or staff members, rather than through the formal and public teaching of how to pray. As such this individualized and private mode of authoritative transfer of ethical techniques further supports the notion that prayer as a technique for working on the self is that which must be undertaken and cultivated by the person who prays.

Following the lead of Mahmood and Robbins I argue that prayer was articulated in the narratives of many of my interlocutors as a central technique for ethically working on the self. But whereas both Mahmood and Robbins focus on the ritualized practice of prayer, the nonritualized practices of prayer are perhaps more important for understanding this ethical process among those with whom I worked. This, however, does not diminish the social impact of such prayer, for even the practice of internal private prayer has a social dimension that is manifest through the person who prays. Prayer as a technique for ethically working on the self encompasses two separate processes, one external and one internal. Yet although this internal/external distinction is helpful for analytic purposes and reflective of the way people spoke about prayer, it does not accurately depict the integral connection between these two aspects of prayer. That is, prayer is a technique for ethically working on the self that serves to create an integral link between the internal life and the social world of the person, and in doing so contributes to the cultivation of responsible subjects.

Prayer as Working on the Social World of the Person

Zhenia, the young woman whose jealousy led to her heroin addiction, began attending the Sunday Club meeting at the Aleksandr Nevsky Lavra about a month after I first attended. She had recently returned from spending the summer in Odessa, where her grandmother lives and where she had gone after returning to St. Petersburg after seven months of living in a nunnery. For a time she attended these meetings regularly and actively attempted to make friends through the Club. Eventually she joined a tight-knit group of young men, one of whom is Max, the assistant of Father Sergei, all of whom also worked as palliative care volunteers at the same hospital where Father Sergei gives prayer services. In just a few months Zhenia would marry one of these young men, Misha, and become pregnant; slowly the two of them disappeared from social circles. The consensus among those I asked, including Misha's closest friends, was that both had begun using heroin again.

Before all of this, however, Zhenia was actively trying to use what she learned at The Mill, in the nunnery, and at the Sunday Club to help her continue the process of making herself into a moral person. One of the methods she used was prayer. For Zhenia prayer had become a way to negotiate the dangers of once again living in the tempting world of St. Petersburg. Not long after Zhenia began attending the Club the group was discussing various ways of dealing with difficult situations that could arise in the city, such as finding oneself in the middle of a fight on public transportation. Zhenia did not think this situation pertained to her at all, but she listened attentively and learned that most agreed the best one could do in such a situation is pray.

While riding a minibus (*marshrutka*) home after the Club that evening Zhenia was suddenly in the middle of a fight that broke out between a young couple and three young men, all of whom were quite drunk. After getting over the initial shock that this was happening to her right after it was discussed in the Club, she realized that she had to do something since she was literally in the middle of fists flying all around. She told me her first instinct was to begin throwing fists as well and to try to fight her way out of the situation. But she quickly remembered what the others had said not more than an hour earlier, and so she sat quietly in her seat with five sets of fists violently swinging around her head and began to silently pray while holding her prayer beads in her pocket. As she told me, "I didn't even pray as I should with the beads, I just held on to them and prayed that everything would sort itself out [*vse raz-reshilos'*]." Eventually it did, as another man was able to calm everyone down. The couple eventually got off the minibus and the conflict was over. Zhenia told me that although it was clear that this man was the one who was able to stop the fight, she believed that her prayer was a significant factor in supporting his actions.

Zhenia's use of prayer had a dual effect. First, it was prayer that prevented her from following her initial instinct to fight her way to safety. Her prayer, which seems to have taken the general form of invoking the help of God in a plea for order and safety rather than a formal prayer, helped her to overcome her "natural" response to meet violence with her own use of violence. In other words, prayer helped her to overcome herself with a form of self-discipline in order to cultivate, in this very moment of moral breakdown, a nonviolent and peaceful response. In the words of Stanley Harakas, prayer helped Zhenia to stay "in the sphere of God and in proper orientation to God, [her] fellows, [herself], and to the rest of creation."[6] In other words, prayer helped Zhenia remain true to her chosen trajectory of Orthodoxy and sobriety.

Second, Zhenia's prayer played a vital role in reestablishing social order within the minibus. Zhenia told me she believed that her prayer was heard and responded to by God, who in turn provided the man with the strength and courage to stop the fight. It should be added that such strength and courage must certainly have also been given to Zhenia in order for her to remain nonviolent in the midst of the violence, and in doing so to ethically work on herself in this moment of breakdown. Her prayer in this moment, then, had both a personal and a social effect, which must be understood as intimately connected, for in being able to remain still and not react to the fight with her own violent act, Zhenia further contributed to the eventual halt to the violence by not adding to it.

Particularly interesting to note about this example is the way prayer contributes to what we might describe as both Orthodox and neoliberal moral ways of being. It is quite clear that from Zhenia's point of view her use of prayer was the enactment of an Orthodox ethical technique that contributed not only to her own nonviolence and calm, but also to the eventual social overcoming of this event. But this Orthodox technique of prayer also contributed to neoliberal notions of order and control in public space. If a significant aspect of neoliberal governance is the radical decentralization of control, discipline, and responsibility to the individual level, then Zhenia certainly provides an example of one way this can be enacted in public space. In a contemporary world constituted by a range of possible moral and ethical ways of being in the world, as well as the increasing disclosure of the intimate links between the so-called secular and sacred that partially comprise modernity, it should come as no surprise that an ethical technique originally taught to Zhenia as a way to control her temptations by intimately connecting her with God for the purpose of achieving salvation should have a secondary affect of allowing her to act as a responsibilized subject in public space.

The most common way I heard about prayer being used to ethically work on oneself in a particular moment of social disturbance or moral breakdown was in moments of temptation, and in particular temptations to once again use heroin or to fornicate. Prayer, I was told several times, is the primary means of fighting these kinds of temptation that are abundant in the social world. Prayer helps in such situations in two ways. First, and this was emphasized over and over, prayer provides a distraction from the temptation in that it helps the person who prays to refocus on what is important and good in his life. That is, prayer helps a person maintain fidelity to the path he has chosen toward God and a sober life. It is thus for many of my interlocutors a central technique of maintaining hope.[7] Second, and connected to the first, prayer helps the person who prays become stronger so as to avoid such situations or to better handle them in the future. By utilizing such techniques when these difficult situations arise, a person slowly cultivates self-discipline and control so that one day he will no longer be tempted.

When I met Misha at the Sunday Club he had been in the city for seven months, after having spent eleven months at The Mill and then in a parish. Like many of those returning to the city from a parish he was having a difficult time adjusting to a sober life in the same social context in which he had been using heroin for seven years. He was doing his best to make new friends and find new ways of spending his day so as to avoid the old life. This was mostly done through the network of friends Misha was able to find at the Club, which included Max, who helped Misha find work at the hospital.

Eventually, however, one of Misha's old friends with whom he used to shoot up called him and asked if he wanted to meet. Misha reluctantly agreed, but only after telling him that he no longer uses. When they met in the center of St. Petersburg Misha was eager to tell his old friend about how much he had changed, that he no longer uses and had become an active member of the Orthodox Church, and about his experiences in rehabilitation and at the parish. His friend was impressed, and when their time together was finished he offered to drive Misha to the church where he had planned to receive communion later that evening. Misha accepted the ride.

On their way to the church Misha's friend made a quick stop to pick up another of their old friends. As soon as the other guy got into the car they began preparations to shoot heroin. Misha was terrified. He was also very tempted. He did not know what to do and he didn't know how he could say no if they asked him to shoot up with them. He felt himself getting weaker and wanting the drug more and more. Thrown into a moment of moral breakdown and intense temptation Misha did the only thing he thought he could do: he began to pray. Silently he began to pray the Jesus Prayer: "Lord Jesus Christ, son of God, have mercy on me a sinner." He repeated this prayer over and over and over as he sat watching his two old friends shoot up. Not once did they offer him any, nor did Misha ask. Within a few minutes Misha was dropped off at the church and he hasn't seen them since.

When Misha recounted this experience to me he said that he had learned about the Jesus Prayer while living at the parish, and that the priest there had told him that it was a particularly powerful prayer for fighting temptation. Misha even went as far as to read a book about this prayer that the priest had given him. He was quite impressed by one thing he read in the book, "that a time will come when the Jesus Prayer will be more powerful then the strongest steel on Earth." I asked him how he interpreted this. He replied, "It will destroy any temptation, any passion. People will be saved with the help of this prayer." Indeed Misha's life may have been saved by this prayer in this situation. Having been told by a priest who he had come to trust that the Jesus Prayer is particularly powerful for fighting temptations, and having this confirmed in a book about the prayer, Misha uses this prayer whenever he needs to fight temptation of any kind. It has become a primary technique for him to utilize in moments of difficulty or breakdown to refocus his fidelity to his trajectory of a sober life and to help him continue to remain strong against any undesired temptations.

The Jesus Prayer holds a special place in Orthodox Christianity. This prayer originated in the mystical tradition of hesychasm, the followers of which sought inner stillness and silence (*hesychia* in Greek) through the internal and silent repetition of the prayer. Hesychasts often prayed while sitting in special poses and using various breathing techniques, with the eventual goal of embodying the prayer to such an extent that it spoke itself at all times within the person. Despite this mystical origin, the Jesus Prayer has today become a common prayer for laypersons to utilize in their everyday lives in moments of ethical challenges or moral breakdowns. This is clear from the narrative descriptions of such situations by my interlocutors at the Church program, as well as the narratives of those with whom I did research in Moscow on moral experience.[8] I suggest that the authoritative tradition of this mystical history of the prayer, along with its simplicity, makes it particularly powerful and useful for many in their everyday lives. As Misha said, many view the prayer as the most powerful of all prayers for providing calm, stillness, and the ability to refocus on what is truly important in even the most difficult situations.

In reciting the Jesus Prayer one is invoking the name of Christ and asking for his help. In the hesychast tradition the prayer is said to call God into one's presence, which provides one with the ability and strength to act in the way required in a particular situation. The continued use of the Jesus Prayer in such situations helps one cultivate an ethical sensibility of standing with God, and as such embody the moral strength to handle any difficulties and temptations the world may bring.

Another example of the use of the Jesus Prayer was told to me by Vadim, the factory worker in his early thirties who had started to use heroin out of boredom. Vadim is no longer very worried about returning to a life of drug use; he is, however, worried about living the kind of immoral life he lived when he was a user. Most particularly he is concerned about his desire to fornicate. For Vadim this desire becomes most pronounced and obvious when he rides the metro, where many people are forced together in very close quarters and he often has no other choice but to look directly at attractive women. It is a social context that he cannot avoid while living in the city, and for some time he has had difficulties controlling his thoughts and desires in this context. Recently, however, he was reading a book on prayer that he bought at his church and in it he learned how prayer, and especially the Jesus Prayer, is a powerful way to fight such temptations. Whereas in the past Vadim tried to recall passages from the Gospel or to memorize the liturgy as a way to avoid such temptations, now he simply closes his eyes and repeats the Jesus Prayer to himself whenever he rides the metro. In this way he does not fixate (*osmyslivat'*) on his desires for women, but instead can refocus himself or keep himself busy (*ya zanimayu sebe*) with the work he needs to do on himself so that these desires will not arise in the future. As both Vadim and Misha told me, if one continues to repeat this prayer in such situations eventually it will become a part of one and so prevent these situations from arising again. In other words, both Vadim and Misha have accepted the hesychastic notion that the Jesus Prayer in time becomes embodied in such a way that the prayer speaks itself with no intentional effort by the person. As such, the prayer is always with one, providing inner calm and silence and the power of God's presence, so that one has acquired an ethical sensibility that allows for the relatively easy handling of ethical challenges and moral breakdowns.

Vadim, Misha, and Zhenia all used prayer in particular moments of moral breakdown in order to avoid giving in to certain temptations brought on by particular social contexts. Max, on the other hand, used prayer to avoid temptations that were not imminent, but expected. Max was in his final weeks as a rehabilitant at The Mill and was desperately trying to decide what he should do next. He did not want to go to a parish, but he knew if he returned to the city after only three months at The Mill he would immediately begin using heroin again. He was stuck, scared, and already feeling the temptations of the city. One of the staff members at The Mill noticed that Max was very concerned about this and suggested that he pray in front of an icon of Amvrosy of Optina. Not knowing what else to do, he began praying in front of the icon. He continued to do this for the next two days whenever he had free time. On the third day Natalia Aleksandrovna, the head of the Church program in the diocese, called The Mill asking for Max and offered him the chance to live at the Optina Monastery for a few months in order to help rebuild some buildings. Recognizing this as a miracle, Max immediately accepted the offer and was at Optina within a week. After his stay at the monastery he decided to go live in a parish, where he stayed for eleven months. To this day Max has no doubt that it was because of his prayer that all of this occurred.

Max's case may appear at first glance as an inappropriate example of prayer as a technique for ethically working on the self. But in fact I think it very well illustrates how prayer is used by persons in a moment of ethical concern or indecision, when, for example, one does not know what one should do next and fears the many temptations that lie ahead. Prayer in this case not only helped Max refocus his attention on the trajectory of sobriety he had chosen, but it also prepared him to accept an offer to work in a monastery that he might not have otherwise accepted. That is, it helped him cultivate a certain sensibility that allowed him to take the risk of going to a monastery rather than back to the city. The fact that the offer was to work at the Optina Monastery, the very same monastery associated with the icon, provided him with even more evidence of the power of prayer to see him through such difficult moments. Indeed it was this miracle that firmly and resolutely set him on the trajectory that has kept him sober for nearly four years. As he told me, "This [miracle from the prayer] is what encouraged me. From my point of view it was a miracle that I just prayed and the Lord responded to my prayer. So I had to go [to the monastery and parish]."

As can be seen prayer has effects not only on one's moral way of being in the world, but also on one's social world and the context in which one lives. In this way, the ethical technique of prayer serves not only to cultivate an Orthodox person working toward eternal salvation by means of overcoming temptation in this world, but also helps cultivate a person of self-discipline and control who can act responsibly in public space. In other words, by means of prayer both a sacred and a secular subject are cultivated.

Prayer as Working on the Internal World of the Person

When I asked Max how he felt when he received the phone call from Natalia Aleksandrovna to go work at the monastery, he told me, "I felt calm [*spokoino*], I realized that the Lord is taking care of me. And later I have been convinced many times that every time I am in any sort of trouble or I start feeling desperate I pray and then something happens and you cannot just call it a coincidence." Max's response highlights the interconnectedness between God and the internal and social worlds of the person who prays . Situations arise in the social world that cause a person's inner world to become unsettled; just as likely, an unsettled inner world can lead to a disturbance in a person's social world. The two worlds are inextricably linked in a dialogue of reciprocity. Prayer serves to render the dialogue negotiable through the mediation of God.

Consider the advice given by Vladimir Alekseiovich, the psychologist who runs the orientation and introduction meetings for the Church program, to those rehabilitants who are experiencing inner turmoil, such as fear or anger: "All the time I suggest to them to try and pray because prayer is a universal means. I think that it allows one to get out of this submersion in the self [*uglublennosti v sebya*], in one's own negative feelings, and to see that in fact everything is not that bad in there. It gives support and hope." Prayer serves to pull one away from oneself—remember that it is Vladimir Alekseiovich who emphasized the need for IDUs to "step over" themselves—to ground oneself once again in the social world and realize that things are not as bad as they seem. Vladimir Alekseiovich asks rehabilitants to step back and reflect upon themselves through prayer and to do this from the point of view of their social world, where "there are never the extreme" situations that fear and anger imagine. Thus stepping away and reflection on oneself is at the very same time a reflection upon the reality of the social situation that may have influenced one's inner world in the first place. This stepping away, a vital part of ethically working on the self, is facilitated by prayer.

When Max prayed in order to relieve his internal suffering and to help resolve his indecision, he was in fact performing this very stepping away. The result of this process was the offer to work at the monastery and, perhaps more important, that he "felt calm." This combination of internal and social effects of prayer set Max on his current life trajectory and showed him that when he experiences troubles or desperation he should pray in order that such situations can once again be resolved through the combination of his own prayerful efforts and that of God. In other words, this was the founding event that set him on his current moral trajectory and has motivated him to continue working on himself through prayer and other means.

It would seem that prayer is the perfect technique for IDUs choosing to ethically work on the self, for many of them told me several times that one of the biggest hardships they suffer is controlling their inner world, specifically their emotions. Zhenia is one who often struggles with her emotions. When I asked her how she tries to control her emotions, she told me, "Only with prayer because nothing else works at all." Just as she prayed on the minibus when her first reaction was to fight, a reaction accompanied by strong emotions, Zhenia says she prays the Jesus Prayer using prayer beads to try to calm down: "Let's say when I redline and my feelings are on the edge and then it is only 'Lord have mercy, Lord have mercy.' And sometimes the feelings redline so bad that I cannot even say the whole prayer. But then you calm down and start saying the entire prayer again and your feelings go back to normal." She added, "[The] Jesus Prayer is very powerful, especially when you are struggling inside. It just saves you."

For Zhenia prayer is a vital technique for controlling her emotions in social contexts when she feels that they are out of control or in some way negatively affecting her ability to morally be in the social world. But prayer is also an important way for persons to overcome the emotional guilt and embarrassment they feel for what they have done in the past. This was a common use of prayer among people at The Mill. If those such as Zhenia, Misha, and Max, who have already returned to the city after rehabilitating at The Mill and a prolonged stay at a parish or monastery, have learned to use prayer in their daily lives to help negotiate the ethical difficulties and moral breakdowns of their inner and social worlds, then for many of those who are just beginning their new moral trajectory at The Mill prayer is a means by which they can begin to deal with the inner suffering they experience because of their past life.

Rehabilitants at The Mill described prayer as a significant technique for moving beyond the past, or for beginning to step over oneself. Some used prayer as a way to ask for forgiveness from God and eventually from their family. One young man in his early twenties told me, "In my life I have caused my parents a lot of suffering and so I pray to God to help them and so that they will forgive me." Guilt is another central theme in the narratives of many of the new rehabilitants, and another reason many choose to pray. One young woman at The Mill told me about how aggressive she had become after starting to use heroin. She said that it was only after she went to The Mill that she could understand all the things she had done: "You feel embarrassment for so many things and you just don't know where to run. There is some guilt still with me. I know I'll be forgiven at home, but I think it will take a long time to pray for forgiveness for all of the things I've done." This young woman is sure her family will forgive her, in fact she went on to tell me that she has always been able to count on them and she knows they already have forgiven her. So to whom is she praying for forgiveness? It seems likely that one answer is from God. But I also think it is clear that she is praying to find a way to forgive herself, to find a way to move beyond the guilt and embarrassment so that she no longer feels the need to run and hide from what she has done. For this young woman who is just beginning the long process of rehabilitation and trying to move onto that trajectory of sobriety and faith in God, prayer is a technique for beginning to control her emotional world so that it will be prepared and open to the kind of ethical work that will be necessary in her very near future.

In fact that is precisely how prayer was described to me by Aleksei, a young man in his mid-twenties who had spent over a year in a monastery after first attending The Mill. Here is how he described what he learned at the monastery: "You are always learning, how do I say, this is difficult, to keep an inner peace and to pray, to keep prayer inside at least to some small degree—some kind of order both inside and on the exterior." I asked him how prayer helps him keep this order. He replied with a very interesting analogy between the result of prayer and social life in the monastery: "When I was living at the monastery we were living in a separate house, the three of us [he and two other rehabilitants]. We had to keep the house clean and orderly so the rector would be able to come and see and so that his eyes would rejoice when seeing that his pupils are living properly and that peace and brotherly love rule the house. It is the same in my soul. When I pray and call on God I try, well at least I should try, so that the Lord comes and sees that he can enter my soul. It is some kind of inner order, a readiness to accept."

At the monastery Aleksei learned that prayer helps one establish and maintain an inner order. This notion of prayer, I suggest, is repeated in all the examples given in this section. Prayer helps align and realign the order of things in one's soul. But this order is not an end in itself; rather it is a means to something greater and more significant in the moral life of an Orthodox person or someone struggling to enter upon this trajectory. Prayer and the order it establishes allow for the possibility of or the readiness to accept (*gotovnost' prinyat'*) God within oneself. If the main goal of Orthodox morality is to become God-like, to embody God-likeness, then prayer is a means for preparing oneself and opening oneself up to this possibility. Just as the rector of the monastery is joyful upon seeing the order of the rehabilitants' living quarters and interprets this as a sign of their good living, so too God rejoices at the sight of a well-ordered soul as a sign of one who is trying to live a good life, and because of this, enters that soul.

While Aleksei clearly meant this analogy to be a straightforward way of explaining the workings of prayer on the inner person, I believe his narrative can also be read as a metaphor for the way prayer links the inner and exterior social worlds of a person. This reading is possible because he begins the analogy between the well-ordered living quarters and the well-ordered soul directly after telling me that by keeping prayer within oneself one is able to achieve both inner and exterior order. Prayer, then, is that which not only orders the soul, but also helps order the social world. In his analogy the living quarters could not become ordered, they could not become a sign of the rehabilitants living right (*normal'no*) and according to peace and brotherly love without prayer. That is, prayer is the prerequisite that allows for the exterior order in the social world that serves to explain the effects of prayer on the soul. Prayer is the unspoken condition of the first part of the analogy. As Aleksei put it, prayer is that which allows for both inner and exterior order.

Aleksei's analogy mirrors the words of one of the Orthodox Church Fathers, St. John Chrysostom: "It is totally impossible to live in virtue without prayer. . . . When prayer enters the soul, every virtue comes in with it. What the foundation is to a house, prayer is to the soul. It is necessary for prayer to be first, having been set as a sort of base and root in the soul, so that all can firmly build temperance and humility upon it, as well as justice and care for the poor and all of the laws of Christ, so that subsequently we can live in accordance with them and receive the good things of heaven."[9] Whether the Jesus Prayer or some other form, prayer is the foundation for, and the first and primary technique for creating, a virtuous and moral person in the Orthodox tradition. This technique is clearly passed on to and practiced by those who attend the various Church programs.

I have been arguing that through the dual efficacy of prayer—as that which helps establish and reestablish order both within the person and in his social world—rehabilitants and ex-rehabilitants are able to ethically work on themselves. Clearly each of the persons who spoke to me about prayer is at a different phase of utilizing this ethical technique. While it is safe to say that none has yet achieved the goal of embodying constant inner prayer, there is a clear distinction between those who are just beginning on the trajectory of sobriety and Orthodoxy and use prayer as a means to work through the emotive memories of their past life, and those who have persevered on this trajectory for several years and have learned that prayer is a powerful technique for helping them through both inner and social moral breakdowns. All of them, however, have learned during their time in the Church program that prayer is one of the central ethical techniques offered by Orthodox Christianity, and that the continuous attempt to practice this technique will help them cultivate an embodied sensibility that allows one to better face the ethical challenges of living in a world of temptation and desire. Prayer as an ethical technique, however, goes beyond the fighting of temptation and desire and has a secondary consequence in helping cultivate rehabilitants as responsible subjects who are able to enact self-discipline and control in public space. As such, prayer is not only an ethical technique with sacred consequences, but also supports neoliberal notions of decentralized and individuated responsibility.

CONFESSION

If prayer is one of the primary Orthodox techniques for ethically working on the self, then confession is the other. One afternoon in late winter I met Olga Viktorovna in the café inside the Aleksandr Nevsky Lavra for an interview. Olga Viktorovna heads the department that helps orient some of those who wish to attend the Church-run rehabilitation centers. Nearly an hour into our interview she told me that many of the rehabilitants at the centers eventually become quite ill. She attributed this to the body's reaction to no longer receiving drugs regularly, which, she told me, "activates" all the chronic illnesses within their bodies. She then went on to make a distinction between those who take medication for these illnesses and those who do not. She was quite surprised to discover that some of those who do not take medications return to health at the same pace as, or even faster than those who do take medications. She realized that these are the persons who put their trust in God. As Olga Viktorovna put it to me, "I realized that these are the guys who say that 'nobody can help me but God.' And [they pray] more and [trust] God more and there are miracles. And I looked into the matter more and found that these guys go to confession and receive communion more frequently. It is they who trust the Lord more and it is they who work on themselves with such intensity, and here are the results!"

Olga Viktorovna, as did Father Sergei, told me about the importance of ethically working on the self by means of Church sacraments and authoritative tradition. This time, however, the purpose is not to overcome the evil within, or at least not solely for this reason, but to return to health. In the Orthodox tradition, however, these two processes are interconnected: to overcome evil and sin is to return to a state of health, for illness is a sign of sin. In fact Olga Viktorovna pointed out that it was the body's reaction against not receiving drugs, and not the low immune level of most of the rehabilitants, that causes activation of these illnesses. Is this activation, then, a sign of the desire for drugs? That is, a sign of sin?

Perhaps, but what is important for our purposes is that Olga Viktorovna attributes the return to health of these rehabilitants to their fidelity to God and the techniques of prayer, confession, and communion that reveal this fidelity. By working on themselves with these techniques miracles become possible. But for this to occur there must be serious, frequent, and intense (*intensivno*) work on the part of the rehabilitants. Prayer is not enough on its own. Confession and communion, which in the Orthodox tradition are usually done together, are also necessary. Together these practices constitute the primary Orthodox techniques for ethically working on the self. As such, they reveal the special relationship between the individual sinner and the loving and forgiving God, a relationship of fidelity, hope, and trust, in which, in the Orthodox view, it is possible for a person to change himself into a truly moral person.

Talal Asad argues that in medieval Western Christianity the combination of confession and penance played a significant role in making Christian persons through the processes of moral education and subjectivization.[10] I argue that confession plays a similar role in the rehabilitation program run by the Russian Orthodox Church, but with a significant difference. In medieval Western Christianity public expressions of bodily physical pain by means of penance were central to this process, whereas in the Orthodox Church program public expression takes the form of public confession and penance that relies more on the expression of bodily emotional pain than physical pain for the remaking of moral persons.

The distinction between private confession and public confession is very similar to the distinction Foucault makes between the early Christian practices of disclosing the self by means of *exagoreusis,* the "analytical and continual verbalization of thoughts carried on in the relation of complete obedience to someone else," and *exomologēsis,* the "dramatic expression of the situation of the penitent as sinner which makes manifest his status as sinner." Both of these practices were to varying degrees linked to confession, and it is Foucault's contention that Christianity as a confessional religion set the rules and conditions for the transformation of the self required for salvation. The revelation of the truth of oneself and the renunciation of those aspects of oneself that need purification are primary conditions for Christian salvation. As Foucault put it, "Each person has the duty to know who he is, that is, to try to know what is happening inside him, to acknowledge faults, to recognize temptations, to locate desires; and everyone is obliged to disclose these things either to God or to others in the community and, hence, to bear public or private witness against oneself."[11] This is the practice of confession.

Foucault argues that in Western Christianity *exagoreusis* eventually became more important. Kharkhordin, on the other hand, convincingly shows that in Russian Orthodoxy *exomologēsis,* as both public confession and penance, remained significant until the Revolution.[12] This is true despite the fact that, as in the West, private confession became increasingly important beginning in the medieval period, when it became a sacramental obligation that was to be performed at least once a year. This obligation appears to have been adhered to by most practicing Orthodox in the eighteenth and nineteenth centuries,[13] even after the Petrine Reforms stipulated that priests break the confessional code to report any confessions of acts against the state. It is unclear how common private confession and public penance and confession were during the Soviet period, although it seems unlikely that the latter was very common. In the post-Soviet period, however, private confession is once again a significant aspect of Orthodox spiritual and moral practice.[14] At the same time, public confession and penance have become much less important, though in the Church program both public and private confession are important ethical techniques.

Private Confession

For many of the rehabilitants and ex-rehabilitants in the Church program, practicing Orthodoxy is a completely new experience. Although prayer and services were hardly ever experienced by most of those I came to know, these practices did not evoke the kind of response confession did. These other practices were most likely first done in a social setting, which provided the comfort of being with, following, and learning from others; confession, however, at least in its private form, was hardly comfortable for those who were being introduced to it. For many, this unnerving feeling remains for some time, even after years of confession with the same priest. Fear was one of the most common emotional responses reported to me by many with whom I spoke, and especially for those rehabilitants relatively new to The Mill.

Still, it is well-known that confession is expected by those who attend The Mill, and it is this expectation, bordering on unofficial requirement, that leads many to confess for the first time in their life to Father Maxim. The reaction to this experience is mixed. Many say that after confessing they experienced an overwhelming feeling of lightness or of having finally thrown off an unbearable burden, and yet it was not uncommon for them to also admit that they were uncertain if they would confess again. The fear and uncanniness is just too much for many.

For example, Olya, a very friendly and outgoing twenty-two-year-old who always showed a big smile despite having lost several of her teeth to the ravages of heroin addiction, once told me about her fear of confessing a second time to Father Maxim. She had recently returned to The Mill from the city, where she spent about a week for medical attention. While there she spent an evening with her boyfriend. When she returned to The Mill Father Maxim, in the midst of asking her about her health and the treatment she received in the city, asked if she had seen her boyfriend. Taken by surprise at the unexpected question, Olya could not hide that she had. Father Maxim simply responded that they should meet for a confession sometime soon. When I asked her if she would, she replied that she knew she should, but that she was scared. "I can't get myself to do it," she told me. The fear of exposing oneself is not only difficult to overcome, but it also impedes the process of coming to embody the need to confess. For like prayer, confession too must be utilized in such a way so that its performance in time becomes a cultivated embodiment of the very process of disclosing the self to oneself and others.

This can be seen in the words of Katya, a twenty-four-year-old ex-rehabilitant who had recently returned to the city from a parish and who gave a talk at The Mill one evening during a group therapy session. The point of her talk was to tell about her experiences at the parish and in so doing help others see the benefits of deciding to go. She also spoke about her experience of confession.

> I had this problem with confession for the longest time. I just did not go and that's it. And here [The Mill] I confessed once and just superficially, strictly speaking just for show. But when you go to a parish you have your worldview changed for you and your moral foundations are changed through confession and spiritual literature. Let's say that if you do something, for example, let's go back to the main problem of young people—sex. Say, you like, you sleep with a person and the next day you are not so comfortable about it, in principle something is wrong and you cannot understand what it is because this has become totally normal. Confession teaches us, that is, you morally begin to understand that if you confess your sins this means that you are doing something wrong. And with the help of this you slowly start understanding that this is fundamentally wrong, and it is so with absolutely everything. You understand that your main problem is not drug addiction, but your moral attitude toward life and it is a wrong moral attitude, and that it started way back and only later grew into drugs. . . . And your whole life is outlined in front of you, and you have tons and tons of time to think about it. Nobody bothers you. And you already

learn to be one-on-one with yourself. And you understand where it all came from and where the beginning is. And confession is just like, well, not just, but it is, say, when you got mad at someone and then confessed about it. You just got mad and confessed and you understand that you did something wrong, confessed once, twice and the third time you realize there is such a thing as meekness in you. And that's that, and you are unlikely to get mad in a situation like that again.

Here we see the narrative description of a person's experience of cultivating her ethical sensibility by means of confession. But confession itself is something that had to be cultivated. As Katya says, for a long time while at The Mill she could not confess, and when she did it was only for show. Only after continued efforts in the parish, where confession is obligatory, was she able to come to embody the need to confess. Similar to some of the women in the Egyptian piety movement Mahmood writes about as having to force themselves to act out shyness in order to cultivate it as an embodied virtue,[15] Katya had to force herself to confess so that in time she could come to "realize there is such a thing as meekness" in her. This meekness, in time, allows her to better control her reactions in certain ethically challenging situations. That is, by means of forcing herself to confess and eventually learning the benefits of this practice, Katya was able to cultivate an embodied ethical sensibility of self-discipline and control that helped her to live more morally in the social world.

How was this done? It was done through the laborious and reflexive process of coming to know herself as a sinner. In the example Katya gives, one feels uncomfortable after having slept with someone, or as it is called within the Church, fornication. This bodily response to one's actions is, Katya suggests, most often ignored since the act is considered normal by most youth today. But through the act of confession one learns that this bodily response of discomfort is in fact an indication of the immorality of the act, which in turn points to the immoral foundations of the person. Through the process of confession one comes to better understand oneself. That is, the confessing person is more clearly able to interpret her own bodily—emotional and physical—responses to how she acts in the world. Confession, then, by forcing one to reflect upon one's own actions and responses to these actions, reveals one to oneself as a sinful and immoral person.

Having been revealed by means of confession as a sinful and immoral person, the confessing person can begin to utilize the technique of confession to overcome this nature and more solidly set herself on the trajectory of sobriety, faith, and morality. This can come only with time and continued practice. As Katya put it, a person "confessed once, twice and the third time" she realized that there was "meekness" in her. Through the continued and refined practices of confession the sinful person is able to come to know herself as a meek person. Afterward the particular sinful act confessed is unlikely to happen again.

This, of course, is an idealistic account of the process of confession. It is doubtful that transformations are so easily and schematically accomplished. What is important about Katya's account, however, and this is particularly important in the context of where these words were spoken, is that in time confession comes to be considered an especially strong technique for interpreting one's acts, thoughts, and emotional world, and learning to control them. For at The Mill one of the most important messages provided to rehabilitants is that they must take control of their acts, thoughts, and emotional worlds. That is, the immoral foundations that are considered the root cause of their addiction must be overcome by means of an intentional, reflexive, and purposeful exercise of self-discipline and control. Only in time and with much practice and care can this control eventually reach the hoped-for stage of unreflexive and unintentional embodied morality. Confession is vital to this process.

This process was described to me several times as a process of cleansing the soul. Here is how Aleksei described it to me:

In order for values to find a spot in a drug addict's soul, in order for there to be a place for them to stay, this vessel of the soul first needs to be purified [ochistit'] in confession. And the more and deeper you go into confession the more you get and receive of these spiritual values. All of this is founded on the idea that you are completely infested. And this infestation makes your soul ugly. Just imagine what will happen with a rubber vessel if we keep stuffing rubbish into it! It is, you know, all deformed. So the human soul is deformed too by these sins, passions and transgressions. . . . Rehabilitation [with the Church] leads the person to a realization of the need for self-cleansing, for confession. And through confession you come to a deep repentance and then begin to preserve the Lord inside as something sacred. You long not to insult the Lord with sins and passions, not in thought, not in feelings, and this is very, very hard.

The immoral and sinful soul/person is metaphorically represented by the image of the overstuffed garbage bin. Only confession can clean and purify this soul so that space becomes available for moral and spiritual values. Interestingly this process is articulated as a zero-sum game. That is, spiritual-moral values cannot fit into the soul as long as the limited space of the soul is taken up with the rubbish of sin. The latter must be removed to make room for the former.

It is also interesting that Aleksei speaks of God as entering one's soul once sin is removed through confession. It is this presence of God within one, so Aleksei seems to be saying, that motivates one to continue ethically working on oneself through confession and other means. Not wanting to insult God, one begins the difficult process of watching one's acts, thoughts, and emotional world so as not to sin. God's presence within oneself, in Aleksei's conception, discloses the embodied nature of the ethical technique of confession. That which becomes the primary motivation for not sinning is found within one's very own body/soul— within oneself.

Similarly Misha described going to confession as going to the *banya* (sauna): it washes you and rids you of impurities. He said, "Confession is like *banya*. Another example is when a person does not wash for a while and then you approach him and he smells bad. Spiritually speaking when a person does not confess for a while, then what goes on inside? And imagine a person who has never gone to confession. It's a total nightmare!" In the examples from Aleksei and Misha confession is described as a cleansing of the soul. But it is more than that; it is also a metaphorical description of the process of leaving behind or getting rid of the sinful, immoral person and revealing or making space for the spiritual and moral person. Thus whether by metaphorically throwing out the trash or sweating out the impurities, confession is vital to the process described as "stepping over" oneself. That is, confession in the Orthodox view is a necessary technique for the trajectory of morally remaking oneself. It is for this reason that private confession is introduced to rehabilitants at The Mill and emphasized, even if this emphasis falls on uncomfortable and fearful ears, as an important part of the rehabilitation process.

Public Confession and Penance

Private confession, even if it is hesitatingly accepted by many of the rehabilitants, constitutes a central part of the ethical process of remaking moral persons in the Church-run program. Those who spoke the most about confession's importance in their rehabilitation process were those who had returned to the city after having spent six to twelve months at a parish, monastery, or nunnery after first rehabilitating at The Mill. In other words, for those who have most successfully worked through the Church-run rehabilitation program, confession is central to their narratives of remaking themselves.

Private confession, however, was talked about in a much less positive manner by those just beginning the rehabilitation process. For most of them private confession remained an uncomfortable process that evoked such negative emotions as embarrassment and fear. Many avoided private confession when they could. What they could not avoid, however, was the various forms of public confession and penance that take place at The Mill and other Church programs. These practices were spoken of in more positive terms than private confession. One reason this is so, I suggest, is because for many persons in the Church program these practices are not recognized as confession. However, I suggest that many of the therapeutic practices that take place in the Church program can in fact be interpreted as forms of public confession and penance.

According to Kharkhordin, there is precedence from the Soviet period of the Orthodox tradition of public confession and penance, or *exomologēsis*, taking different forms and being practiced in nonreligious ways.[16] Because these nonreligious practices were not recognized by those who performed them as having roots in the Orthodox tradition, the new forms went unquestioned and were easily adopted. Kharkhordin argues that the Orthodox practice of *oblichenie,* of "publicizing sins and accusing the sinners," was first adopted by nineteenth-century Russian revolutionaries, then was systematized by Lenin as a means for workers to disclose the social injustices they experienced, and eventually was adopted as the main form of public and self-criticism in the Soviet Union. As a result of this, Kharkhordin argues, *oblichenie* was central to the Soviet project of subjectivization and individualization. In fact although the word is the noun form of the verb *oblichit',* meaning "to reveal or expose," Kharkhordin draws from the definition given by Vladimir Dal', whose famous nineteenth-century dictionary is widely considered the authoritative source on the Russian language, and claims that *oblichenie* is better defined as "en-personation" (*ob-lichenie*), that is, the process that endows one with personhood.[17] This is both a public and a critical process.

In early Christianity and, according to Kharkhordin, up until the nineteenth century in Russian Orthodoxy, *oblichenie* took the form of public confessions, exposure, revelation, and penance, which for the person who underwent this ordeal was "an essential step toward liberating the self from [sins] and, in a sense, [acquiring] a new, true self imbued with Christian conscience."[18] Similarly during the Soviet period public forums for self-criticism and exposure by others within one's community or *kollektiv,* for example during the purges, self-criticism sessions, and even the late Soviet educational practice of the Lenin Pass, were all significant practices for one to make oneself into a Soviet person. By meticulously examining and publicly exposing the deeds and acts of individual persons, Soviet *oblichenie* practices, argues Kharkhordin, brought about a change similar to the Protestant Reformation. That is, through the process of the public revelation of the questionable and "sinful" person, *oblichenie* allowed for the making of new persons by means of subjectivization and individualization. In the West this was done primarily through private and personal confession brought about by the Reformation; in the Soviet Union it was much more of a public and penitent-based process.

New forms of *exomologēsis* were easily integrated into the secular and atheist Soviet practices of disclosure and subjectivization without being recognized as having religious roots, and a similar process is occurring in the Church program for drug rehabilitation and HIV prevention and care in the St. Petersburg area. I suggest that public confession and penance are a vital part of this program and at the same time *not* recognized as forms of *exomologēsis*. In fact I contend that the practices are also not recognized as such by the staff of the program. Instead staff and rehabilitants consider *exomologēsis* practices to be secular therapeutic practices based on a scientific psychology and in no way related to Orthodoxy. And though Foucault claimed that psychoanalysis and other therapeutic practices are closely linked to Christian confession,[19] this is strongly denied by the Russian Orthodox Church. It is my contention that these public therapeutic and disciplinary practices are closely linked not only to Orthodox *exomologēsis*, but also to Soviet practices of *oblichenie*. Indeed it is the background understanding and acceptance of these Soviet practices, as well as the acceptance of these therapeutic practices as borrowed from Western psychological models, that helps cover over the roots of both of these practices in *exomologēsis*. Here we see, then, three distinct discursive sources that contribute to the unique ethical assemblage that partially constitutes the therapeutic process in the Church-run program.

One evening a week rehabilitants at The Mill meet in a small room in the main building to participate in a group therapy session that, as I suggested earlier, is similar to Soviet techniques of self-cognition and evaluation. This session is also a form of *exomologēsis*, as were many of the Soviet techniques of self-cognition and evaluation. In the session rehabilitants place a number on a wall chart next to certain self-characteristics that they wished to work on. Examples of such characteristics are responsibility (*otvetstvenost'*), confidence (*uverennost'*), and laziness (*len'*). After the person publicly evaluates herself in front of the group, the group tells the person how they think she has fared in this particular work on the self for the past week. The process thus combines self- and group criticism.

The process is also a form of public confession and penance in that the conversations often focus on particular acts the person performed in the past week, particularly those that hindered the progress of her working toward achieving her ethical goals. For example, a young man who had already been at The Mill for about a month spoke about his progress in working toward overcoming what he viewed as his laziness and accepting more responsibility. For the past week he had given himself a seven out of ten for responsibility and a five out of ten for laziness. In explaining his self-analysis to the group he said that although he had accomplished all of his responsibilities for the past week, he had at times taken a few more cigarette breaks than usual and in general had not felt like doing his work. While this was generally accepted by the group, a young woman asked him why he ranked his sense of responsibility higher than his laziness, for if he had been particularly lazy in the past week hadn't he also been lacking in responsibility? The young woman wondered how he could make a distinction between the two. In her conception, if one is lazy, then one is also lacking responsibility. Others in the group made some noises indicating that the young woman made a good point; the young man gave no defense against her questioning, changed his seven to a five for responsibility, and sat down.

Here we see a clear instance of a public confession and what could best be described as a form of public shaming penance. The young man readily confessed his "sin" of laziness, which was committed not only by means of bodily actions (i.e., taking extra cigarette breaks), but also by means of his emotional acts (i.e., he did not feel like doing his work). This confession was nearly accepted without confrontation until the young woman raised her question. She called into question the validity of his confession; that is, she wondered if his confession had gone far enough since he had not also confessed what she saw as a lack of responsibility. But in doing so she also leveled on him a form of public penance. In raising this question she effectively shifted the group's interpretation of his actions and their interrelatedness, thus causing the young man to change his own self-analysis. The penance, then, came in the form of group criticism that led the young man to publicly admit to having "sinned" even more than he had originally been willing to do, and thus undergoing a kind of public shaming that resulted in his having to lower his self-rating for responsibility. In other words, by means of public penance the young man was compelled to make a second confession by equating his lack of responsibility with his laziness. Having done so, the young man was able to quietly sit back down. His "sins" had been publicly washed away, for by undergoing the public confession and penance he was able to once again return to the group and continue on his trajectory of working on the self. He was able to continue on the process of "liberating the self from [sins] and . . . [acquiring] a new, true self imbued with Christian conscience."[20] This kind of confrontation is not untypical of what happens during this particular group therapy activity.

A similar form of *exomologēsis* can be seen in various other group therapy activities in the Church program. After the prayer that opens every meeting of the Sunday Club in the Aleksandr Nevsky Lavra, the first activity calls on everyone to introduce themselves and say a little about who they are and why they are there. This is not unlike the opening of many secular and semisecular therapeutic meetings of a similar kind, for example, 12-step programs. For many of the regulars of the Sunday Club this is an opportunity to speak about something they may have done or encountered during the week that troubled them. Often what is said concerns some way the person acted that has left him feeling unsettled. For example, it is not uncommon for persons to confess that they strongly desired to use heroin recently or had an argument with a parent.

Perhaps the most common confession is the desire to meet a woman to marry (most of the attendants at these meetings are men), and at times the confession includes the desire to fornicate. It goes without saying that the desire to fornicate, let alone the act itself, is a sin. The Church and all those in attendance at the meetings would certainly support the institution of marriage, but what is being confessed here is the desire—the longing and impatience that many rehabilitants and ex-rehabilitants told me they feel to meet someone they can marry, someone to share their life with, someone who can help them remain off drugs. This desire is perhaps even more overwhelming since many of them are concerned they will never find a partner who will want to be with an HIV-positive person.

This public confession is usually met with sympathy. However, occasionally the response is a form of public shaming penance. This is especially so for those few persons who repeatedly confess the same desires. In these cases other regular attendees of the meetings who are familiar with the frequent confession, as well as Aleksei, who runs the Club, will lightly but openly chastise the person for repeatedly having sinful desires. Such responses by the group include "I understand you, but we have told you several times you need to remain patient with this and not worry so much [*tebe nuzhno poterpet i ne volnovatsia tak silno*]" and "Last week you told us the same. God will provide you with a wife when it is time [*Bog tebe poshlet zhenu, kogda pridet vrema*]" and "When you have this desire you need to pray [*Kogda voznikaet eto zhelaniye nado pomolitsia*]." The confessing person in these instances always responds with something like the following: "Yes, I know we have talked about this before, but it is difficult. I will try not to concern myself with it so much [*Ya znayu, chto my govorili ob etom ranshe, no eto trudno. Postarayus ne silno ob etom bespokoitsia*]."

In this way the confessing person publicly reveals his innermost desires and in so doing seeks to leave them and the person who has them behind. This process of working to move beyond the desiring self to a more controlled self is supported by the public shaming offered in response by the group. The moral subject in this context is partly constituted by means of suffering a public penance and being publicly disciplined to enact and embody self-control.

Public penance can also take a more obvious disciplinary form. This is quite clear in the extra work doled out at The Mill when a person breaks a rule. It is not uncommon to see someone performing an unusual cleaning or other task that is clearly marked off as having been assigned as penance for a particular "sinful" transgression. These extra tasks include cleaning with a toothbrush between the wooden boards that make up the floor just inside the front door of the main building and neatly stacking the wood beside the *banya*. These tasks are very public since they take place in some of the most central areas of The Mill, and everyone understands them as obviously disciplinary. In fact other rehabilitants often ask the person working what he did to receive the "penance." I never saw

a case when the question went unanswered. Thus, this disciplinary practice works in the reverse order of what we saw in the earlier examples;
that is, in these cases the public penance of the disciplinary task evokes
singular acts of public confession repeated several times to each person
or small group of persons who ask what the "sinner" had done.

Although the order of the public confession and penance duality is
reversed in these cases, the effect is the same. In the Church program
exomologēsis practices are techniques of ethical training by means of publicly revealing the sinful self so as to move beyond that self and in so
doing work to create a new moral person. Although those who work in
and attend the Church program understand these practices as secular
therapeutic activities and not necessarily religious forms of discipline,
they are rooted in early Christian and Orthodox practices of *exomologēsis*,
and were covered over as such by their secular transformation
during the Soviet period. Therefore what many consider to be adopted
secular techniques of therapy and discipline may in fact be the return
of practices of *exomologēsis* to Russian Orthodox institutions that see
as their main task the transformation of individuals into Orthodox
moral persons.

Just as private confession is a central technique of subjectivization in
the Church program, so too is public confession and penance. The only
difference is that while the former is recognized as such, it seems as
though there is little or no recognition that the latter is taking place. This
is so because the public confessional techniques are so closely linked to
adopted secular therapeutic techniques. Vinh-Kim Nguyen shows how
"confessional technologies" imported by NGOs to Ivory Coast AIDS
prevention programs have similarly worked as public techniques of
subjectivization for the cultivation of sexual identities.[21] I suggest that
because these public confessional techniques are performed much more
often because of their link with therapeutic practices and, in the case of
rehabilitants at The Mill, with less hesitancy, this unrecognized practice of public confession and penance is more vital to the rehabilitation
process than that of private confession. Subjectivization in the case of
this particular Russian Orthodox institution is clearly more of a public
and social ordeal than a private one.

ENCHURCHMENT

Several times I was told that in addition to helping persons stop using drugs, the goal of the Church program is to set the person on the path of enchurchment (*votserkovleniya*). *Votserkovleniya* is the concept used by the Church to describe the *process* and *goal* of becoming a true Orthodox person. It is a process because one must incrementally transform oneself into what the Church calls a spiritually moral person. *Votserkovleniya* is also a goal because it describes the being of a person who has become spiritually moral. That is to say, enchurchment also describes the state of having embodied the Orthodox way of life. To become enchurched is to embody the social body of the Church and the sacred body of Christ.

Just as rehabilitation is a lifelong process, the process of *votserkovleniya* is a lifelong endeavor, for to have reached the goal of fully achieving enchurchment is to have realized the likeness of God within oneself. Although this potential stemming from the image of God is within all humans, it is rarely achieved, yet according to Orthodoxy it is what all persons should strive for in this life. It is the intention of the Church program to begin teaching individuals the techniques necessary to set them on the trajectory of this lifelong path. By providing the context in which persons can begin to ethically work on themselves by means of integrating prayer and confession into their everyday lives, the program does more than attempt to make healthy the individual and social body; it also attempts to make healthy the individual and social soul.

If the goal of *votserkovleniya* is the embodiment of an Orthodox spiritual morality, then the process of doing so is also a process of bodily techniques, that is, interrelated physical, emotional, and intellectual techniques, meant to cultivate this particular kind of sensibility. I have been arguing that in the Church-run program prayer and confession are the two central Orthodox ethical techniques for remaking the moral person, the primary techniques of enchurchment. But while enchurchment may be the ultimate goal of the therapeutic process in the Church-run program, the cultivation of a normal life is, if not the minimum goal as Father Maxim describes it, also the foundation for the capacity of further cultivating enchurchment. Therefore, while prayer and confession are central to the therapeutic process, the cultivation of what Russians call a normal person capable of living a normal life constitutes the majority of the therapeutic regime of the Church-run program. To a great extent much of this cultivation process is related to Orthodox moral theology and human rights. For our purposes it will perhaps be more interesting to note how they also contribute to the cultivation of normal persons as responsible subjects capable of living in a new Russia increasingly defined by a neoliberal discursive regime of radically decentralized self-responsibility and discipline.

EIGHT Cultivating a Normal Life

One afternoon in May I was walking with Sasha, a volunteer, through
one of the fields back to the main building of The Mill. We had been
looking at the three small houses being built by rehabilitants intended
to house visitors who come to The Mill for occasional seminars and
conferences held on drug rehabilitation and HIV/AIDS. As we walked,
Sasha and I were talking about how good the houses looked considering none of the rehabilitants had ever built anything before, let
alone a house. "That is what happens here [at The Mill], people get
the chance to have a lot of experiences they never had before, to learn
things they never imagined," he said. "You know, most of the people
who come here will return to the city and start using again. Everyone
knows this. So more than anything, in my opinion, what is possible here
is the chance to live a normal life, even if for only a few months. And

if you are lucky, you learn some things and can continue this normal life back in the city." I asked Sasha what he meant by "this normal life." "A normal life like everyone else gets to live. To work, to eat three meals a day, to have some friends and talk [*obshchat'sya*]—a normal life."

Although the phrase and concept "normal life" (*normal'naya zhizn'*) is quite common in everyday Russian discourse, very little has been written on it. Aleksei Yurchak is one of the few who has considered a "normal life," and the related concept of a "normal person," in some detail.[1] His analysis, however, focuses on the use of these concepts in the late Soviet period, and although he provides interesting insights, I consider his work primarily in order to contrast it with what I suggest is meant by this concept in contemporary Russia, particularly among those with whom I did research in the St. Petersburg area. Although it may be possible to contrast the content of a "normal life" between these two historical periods, what might be called the *form* of this life has remained more or less the same. To make this statement more understandable, let me first turn to Yurchak's description.

In his analysis of everyday relations to the authoritative discourse of the late Soviet period, Yurchak provides a deeply interesting and subtle perspective on why the Soviet Union collapsed.[2] Drawing from Austin's theory of performatives, Yurchak makes a distinction between those few who understood the authoritative discourse of the late Soviet period as a constative truth, and the majority, who had a meaningful and performative relationship with the discourse. The former were primarily those at the two extremes of Soviet life: the Party activists and the anti-Party dissidents. Yurchak claims, however, that the vast majority of the Soviet people peformatively reproduced the authoritative discourse, but did so in a way that enabled "the emergence of various forms of meaningful, creative life that were relatively uncontrolled, indeterminate, and 'normal.'"[3] It was this performative reproduction of the authoritative system and its discourse and representations, Yurchak argues, that led, paradoxically, to its collapse. This is so because this performative stance allowed for a kind of normal life that was at one and the same time within and outside the authoritative discourse.

What is important for our purposes is Yurchak's point that a normal life in the late Soviet period was primarily defined in terms of having a particular kind of meaningful and practical relationship with authoritative discourse and practice. A normal person living a normal life in the late Soviet period stayed away from the extremes of identifying himself too closely with politics, the state, and its authoritative discourse and practices. Neither dissidents nor Party activists were normal people. Indeed one of Yurchak's informants told him that he and his coworkers considered one of their coworkers who was reading a dissident article to be "abnormal" (*nenormal'nye*), which echoes Joseph Brodsky's claim that those normal people who avoided dissidents were the "healthy majority."[4] Similar attitudes were conveyed to Yurchak about activists.

If a normal life and a normal person in the late Soviet period were defined in terms of a performative stance toward authoritative discourse and practice, and the avoidance of those who identified with and found meaningful truth in this discourse, then a normal person living a normal life in contemporary Russia, as described to me, also has a particular kind of stance toward the current authoritative discourse, but a stance in direct opposition to that of the late Soviet period. Today rather than a performative stance toward authoritative discourse, a normal person has a constative stance toward it. That is to say, if we assume the authoritative discourse today is primarily of a neoliberal consumer-capitalist type—that is, a discourse primarily focused on money, consumption, and decentralized responsibility—then a normal person is one who has a kind of relationship with this discourse that sees it as providing the kind of life a normal person should live.

Other than a concern with having a family and the kind of close friends with whom one can engage in intimate conversation and sociality (*obshchenie*), which are both considered important to a normal life, the primary focus of every discussion I had with my interlocutors about a normal life was about money, materiality, and the kind of lifestyle that allows for and enjoys them. I suggest in Russia today a normal life is more or less what an American might call a middle-class lifestyle.[5] Over and over again I was told that a normal life, or the life rehabilitants hoped to have, consisted of having a steady job with a good income, one's own home with a good television, computer, and other modern technical equipment, and the ability to share these both physically and emotionally with friends and loved ones.

This normal life was also often described as "a life like everyone else. Just normal." As in Yurchak's description, a normal life is not lived at the extremes of a relationship to the authoritative discourse and practices, but rather *not* at the extremes. At one extreme is the life they lived as a drug user: poor, involved in criminal activity, and having few if any good relations with other persons. This is not a normal life. But neither is the life of an overly wealthy person. Many in Russia today consider the wealthy to be morally questionable, and thus not normal people who live normal lives. As Zhenia once told me, "Of course I will never be rich, and I wouldn't even want it because you don't get rich just like that, you know, but I just want to be comfortable—to have enough [*dostatochno*] money, and of course a family."

Zhenia's comments about not being rich, and the moral evaluations that go along with it, were echoed by a factory manager with whom Caroline Humphrey did research. He told Humphrey, "I am a normal, law-abiding person. I try to carry out my work, I try to do my thing honestly [*chestno*], so there should be a result. I don't want to be a rich person, I don't want to be poor. I just want to be a normal [*normal'nym*] person."[6] As does Zhenia, the factory manager defines a normal person and life as, first, someone living between the extremes of rich and poor and, second, in moral terms of being honest, hardworking, and law-abiding. It is clear that both the factory manager's and Zhenia's comments are not meant to be critical of the dominant discourse and way of life of neoliberalism. Rather, like Yurchak's informants in the late Soviet period, they are pointed at the extremes of the discourse, for example those who immorally take advantage of discursive possibilities in order to get rich.

The factory manager's articulation of a normal person and Zhenia's desire for a comfortable life also echo Yurchak's formal description of a normal life during the late Soviet period. Yurchak claims that one of the reasons people avoided dissidents and activists is because they threatened "the stability of normal life."[7] This stability was characterized as maintaining a performative stance toward the authoritative discourse and practices, and it was this stability that provided normal life with meaningful possibilities of creativity. Similarly I suggest that a normal life today, as Zhenia so clearly put it, is largely defined by material comfort and monetary stability.

Humphrey describes the desire for a normal life by late 1990s Russian entrepreneurs as a desire for the respect and observation of laws, which would make a normal and stable life possible.[8] A decade ago Humphrey saw this desire for a normal life as a desire for a "future new society," and to some extent it has been realized in the Russia of today. But if a normal life during the late Soviet period was characterized by an apolitical distance that allowed for everyday joys, friendship, and creativity, then so too today a normal life remains largely apolitical. This is so, however, primarily because the current Putin-Medvedev regime is seen as being responsible for bringing about the conditions that make possible this stable, normal life.[9] This apolitical distance, I suggest, is produced by means of the very disciplining techniques meant to produce normal persons. In other words, normal persons in contemporary Russia are by definition apolitical.

One significant aspect of being a normal person who lived a normal life during the late Soviet period was the ethics of responsibility one had for those within one's social network.[10] To live a normal life during this period meant to be within a social network of *svoi* (us/ours), or "those who belong to our circle," which is distinguished from the kind of sociality represented in Soviet authoritative discourse.[11] A normal person had a responsibility to others within her *svoi* not to upset the stability and comfort of their normal life. Often this responsibility required the performative enactment of those very authoritative discourses and practices the dissidents and activists viewed as representing truth. As Yurchak puts it concerning Komsomol assignments and meetings, "The terms *svoi* and 'normal people' [implied] that one understood that the norms had to be followed at the ritualistic level, that this was no one's personal fault, and that one should participate in these routine rituals to avoid causing problems,"[12] that is, to avoid disrupting one's own and others' normal life.

I suggest a similar sense of responsibility applies today to the concepts of a normal life and a normal person. Similar to what Yurchak describes, today a normal person also has responsibility to those within her social network not to disrupt the stability and comfort of their normal life. However, this network has been reduced to, on the one hand, one's family and a few very close friends and, on the other hand, one's workplace and those within it. In today's consumer- and market-driven Russia a normal person is primarily responsible for the economic well-being of her family through a demonstrated responsibility to her workplace and, as Humphrey's factory manager told her, a work ethic of honesty and hard work.[13] Whereas a normal life during the late Soviet period may have demanded a moral responsibility to one's *svoi* not to cause potential political harm to others, in today's Russia the moral responsibility of a normal life entails supporting the very economic survival of one's family, as well as the emotional sociality between family members and intimate friends.

Clearly, although the form may be very similar, there has been a significant shift in the content of what constitutes the concepts of a normal life and a normal person between the late Soviet and post-Soviet periods. The Church-run program attempts to prepare rehabilitants for this post-Soviet version of a normal life, which many of them have never experienced as adults. If, as I have been arguing throughout, the Church-run program is primarily concerned with making new moral persons through the therapeutic process of working on bare life, then the new persons it attempts to make are what most in Russia would call normal persons, and what I as an anthropologist call *responsibilized subjects*.

NORMAL LIFE AND RESPONSIBILITY

No matter what life trajectory a former drug user ends up on within the range of possibilities available in post-Soviet Russia, responsibility has become one of the moral sensibilities increasingly necessary to live that life.[14] In this sense, contemporary Russia has squarely entered what many describe as the neoliberal world. Neoliberalism can be seen as a paradoxical form of governance in which the government actively creates the conditions within which appropriate kinds of behavior and activity are more easily enacted, and at the same time encourages a radical decentralization of responsibility requiring the institutional and personal cultivation of autonomy and discipline.[15] One aspect of this decentralized governance is the necessity of individuals to govern themselves; thus radical decentralization has become individualized.

An important component of this decentralized person is the cultivated sensibility of self-discipline that has as its primary characteristic responsibility.[16] This is not only responsibility for others but, perhaps more important, self-responsibility. The former in fact relies upon the latter. Neoliberal persons can be said to be constructed as both individual and collective subjects. This may also have been the case with what we might call a modernist subject, but in neoliberalism the relationship appears to be reversed. If the modernist is a collective subject first—a human subject or a national subject prior to a local subject—then the neoliberal is an individual first. Only after the neoliberal person is properly cultivated can she legitimately and effectively participate in and be responsible for collectives. Indeed this participation is also reversed: the neoliberal person is first responsible locally—at work, in the family, in the community—before she is responsible to the nation or humanity.[17]

It is precisely this trajectory of personhood and responsibility that the Church-run program offers by providing a context in which moral, normal, and responsibilized persons can be cultivated. As I argued in part I, the Church, according to its recent adoption of a human rights discourse, understands this context as structured according to a notion of rights meant to help realize the inherent dignity of all persons and guided by moral standards. In other words, the Church-run program is not only a paradigm of the kind of society the Russian Orthodox Church would like to establish based on their notion of rights, but is a space of inclusion-exclusion intended to actively encourage the cultivation of these new moral persons. In this sense the Church-run program fits precisely with one aspect of neoliberal governance. As Graham Burchell has argued, neoliberalism can partially be defined as the active encouragement on the part of government for individuals and collectivities to take responsibility for the kinds of issues government agencies once managed.[18] The specific task of providing the conditions for the cultivation of appropriate morality and the responsibilization of persons has thus been radically decentralized. It is my contention that the Church-run program, unbeknown to them and contrary to their intentions, is an example of this neoliberal form of governance.

It would be a mistake, however, to claim that the notion of self-responsibility is an exclusive value of neoliberalism or did not exist in Russia until only recently. In fact, as Stephen Collier argues, neoliberalism and Soviet modernity share a number of values.[19] The difference is primarily in the mechanisms by which neoliberalism rationalizes and reconfigures the institutions and persons that embody these values; as Collier puts it, the neoliberal reforms in Russia "seek to re-inscribe existing values."[20] Just one of these values is that of responsibility.

This is clearly seen in Kharkhordin's analysis of Soviet processes of working on the self. From Stalinist-era practices of self-criticism to the annual late Soviet Lenin Pass rituals of high school students, these forms of "collective deliberation on the individual" were meant to judge and cultivate responsibility within individual persons.[21] Similarly Fitzpatrick suggests that self-criticism practices before the collective were one means by which individuals could take responsibility for their actions and "admit fault."[22] These practices of responsibility-taking before the collective were meant to help cultivate new forms of moral personhood. Kharkhordin points out, however, that in the early Soviet and Stalinist periods an ambiguity existed between the primacy of the collective and the individual in terms of to whom the *self* in self-criticism referred, whether the individual or the collective.[23] This ambiguity may actually have helped to strengthen individual responsibility, for if the collective required more in-depth self-criticism and the cultivation of more responsibility, then I myself as a member of the collective must go through these very same processes.

Although this mutual relationship existed between the collective and the individual in the pre- and postwar Soviet Union, Yurchak argues that it certainly did not exist, at least in any substantive form, in the late Soviet period. Despite the lack of a substantive and meaningful interconnection between individuals and formal collectives, the latter remained important social contexts for cultivating a certain kind of responsibility in the late Soviet period. In this period, Yurchak argues, many of the collective rituals that may have once symbiotically cultivated responsibility in both the collective and the individual became meaningless performances of authoritative discourse. Yet these performances continued to cultivate responsibility in individuals by creating new and meaningful moral relationships between persons within one's intimate social network.[24]

Because nearly everyone recognized the performative nature of the Komsomol meetings, Yurchak argues, participants wanted to simply get through them without causing themselves or others within the group any problems. Therefore protocol was generally followed without question. This was so, Yurchak argues, because by means of the very recognition and participation in these meetings *as performances,* a sense of responsibility was cultivated toward the others in the group, or the *svoi,* who recognized the performative but yet necessary nature of the meetings.[25] Thus although these Komsomol meetings failed to produce the "truth" of collectivity and the kind of responsibility that goes with this truth that Soviet authorities expected, they nevertheless helped produce another form of responsibility. This new form of responsibility also relied on the integral relationship between the collective and the individual. But in this case the relationship was between individuals and an informal collective formed in the recognition of the illegitimacy of the meetings, rather than a formal collective finding legitimation in the state. It is important to recognize, however, that individual responsibility, as in Stalinist times, remains primarily with the collective. That is, a responsible person is first of all one who supports the collective in its success. Collective success in this late Soviet case meant the continued ability to enact Komsomol meetings as performances and thus not to cause unnecessary problems for one's *svoi.*

Thus the moral concept of responsibility is not new to Russia, as it was central to both the formal and informal rituals of Soviet collective practices. If it is true that the modernist subject was cultivated as a collective subject first, then Soviet ideological practices attempted to construct the modernist subject extraordinaire. A Soviet subject was not only an exemplary person, but also an exemplary member of the collective, whether that collective was the Komsomol, the Party, the state, or humanity, and was to take the shape of the New Soviet Man. If reality did not always match this ideological aspiration, the results nevertheless produced subjects who felt a sense of self-responsibility because they felt a sense of responsibility toward the collective. Neoliberal discourses and practices in post-Soviet Russia, then, should not be seen as introducing the moral concept of responsibility. Instead it is more appropriate to view it as continuing and intensifying the decentralization of responsibility that Yurchak shows began in the late Soviet period.

Neither should it be thought that the concept of responsibility has a tradition only within the political discourses and practices of Russia, for moral responsibility has also been central in Russian Orthodox Christian moral theology. In the Orthodox tradition moral responsibility (*nravstvennaya otvetstvennost'*) is the necessary consequence of humans possessing a God-given moral conscience, which unites all humans with the same moral foundation. This unity of moral being is an important aspect of the dignity and respect due to all human persons. Therefore all persons are morally responsible for their actions not only toward others, but to the social world in which they live, as well as to themselves.[26]

This notion of moral responsibility continues to be a central theme of contemporary Russian Orthodox discourses of morality, and it is particularly linked to intersubjective relations between persons within and across societies. In fact this has been the focus of several of Patriarch Kirill's speeches and media interviews given while he was still a metropolitan, and there is a strong sense in Moscow that his position on this and similar social issues was central to his being chosen patriarch and the Church's increased concern with such issues.[27] For example, in a newspaper interview Kirill raised the question of whether human freedom, at both the level of the individual and society, can exist without moral responsibility. He claimed that freedom is possible not because one's own freedom does not restrict the freedom of others, as he characterized the liberal view of this concept; rather freedom is truly possible only when society and every individual respects the God-given dignity of every other person. This respect is enacted by means of moral responsibility.[28] He has made similar arguments concerning the relationship between human rights and moral responsibility.[29]

For Kirill, as well as Philaret and other moral voices within the Orthodox tradition, moral responsibility consists of embodying and enacting the God-given moral law inherent and localized within all human persons as moral conscience. Freedom and human rights founded upon this moral responsibility are limited by the parameters of the Orthodox notion of God's moral law. Moral responsibility in the Orthodox view, then, is a limiting of freedom and rights within the social world so that such social relations as family, labor, and health can be lived according to Orthodox morality.[30]

I would suggest that what may appear to be quite different notions of responsibility in the Russian Orthodox Church and the neoliberal perspective contain deep similarities in both expected dispositions and referential contexts. This is true despite the differences of the foundational assumptions for valuing responsibility. Both are concerned with *limiting* individuals' acts, thoughts, emotions, and relations in such a way that they adhere to a particularly defined authoritative and disciplinary moral tradition. In other words, both neoliberalism and Russian Orthodoxy share the notion that responsibility is about cultivating and enacting limits rather than enabling the expansion of moral possibilities. Similarly, although this cultivation of limitation may find differing discursive and disciplinary foundations, they both tend to reference the same social contexts in which it should be enacted. Thus both neoliberalism and Russian Orthodoxy emphasize the importance of enacting responsibility within the heteronormative family, the labor market, and on and within the individualized body as the marker of health, illness, and potential suffering and as the locus of a self-disciplined social and emotional person.

NINE

Normal Sociality

Phenomenological anthropology and its study of intersubjective experience are often misunderstood as focused on individuals. But as should be clear from the analysis so far, the anthropology of intersubjective experience is not a focus on individuals isolated and autonomous from one another. Neither does it focus on abstract, deterministic, and structuring structures that for a long time have been the focus of social scientific and anthropological research and analysis. Instead phenomenological anthropology is concerned with the *relationships* between persons, institutions, and discourses that mutually shape and reshape one another. A focus on intersubjective experience is a focus on sociality as a mutually constituting process rather than society as a determining structure. Referencing Sartre, the phenomenological anthropologist Michael Jackson describes this dialogical intersubjective sociality in the following way:

What is possible for a person is always preconditioned by the world into which he or she is born and raised, but a person's life does more than conserve and perpetuate these pre-existing circumstances; it interprets them, negotiates and nuances them, re-imagines them, protests against them, and endures them in such complex and subtle ways that, in the end, human freedom appears as "the small movement which makes of a totally conditioned social being someone who does not render back completely what his conditioning has given him."[1]

The intersubjective and ethical experiences that I am describing can be seen as examples of persons actively remaking themselves in the context of a Russian Orthodox Church drug rehabilitation and HIV prevention and care program. But this context is not deterministic, despite the discourse of the Church and its staff that would like to give the impression that the rehabilitation process can successfully occur only within the program by following a certain standard procedure, and doing so with a particular emphasis on the religious practices of prayer and confession. Rather the program is an assemblage constituted by a range of possibilities within which rehabilitants can interpret, negotiate, and imagine various ways of remaking themselves in order to attempt to overcome their addiction. What is of particular interest is the range of possibilities that exist in the program that are not a part of the official therapeutic program: those experiences of sociality created by the rehabilitants themselves that are vital to their own rehabilitation.

One of the ways this kind of experience is often described by the rehabilitants and the staff at the Church-run program is as *obshchenie*. *Obshchenie* can simply be translated as "communication" or "association" or even "social intercourse," but in everyday usage it tends to have a much stronger and intimate meaning than any of these suggest. Unlike a simple conversation (*razgovor*), *obshchenie* is an intimate and dialogical sociality during which the participants become in some sense different persons. Anna Wierzbicka has argued that this process of *obshchenie*, or what she translates as "communing talk," allows individuals to mutually develop each other and themselves, in effect creating each other anew in the process.[2]

This is so because *obshchenie*, which is closely related to *obshchestvo* (society or company, as in a company of friends), as well as a number of other *obshch-* words indicating sharing, commonality, and being together with, is more than the exchange of words; in fact it may not always entail speaking at all, but is instead a kind of dialogical being-together-with that results in the creation of new, even if ever so subtle persons. Indeed often what is simply translated into English as "dialogue" or "dialogical" in Bakhtin's work is in fact in the original Russian dialogical (*dialogicheskoe*) *obshchenie*.[3] Bakhtin recognized that this kind of dialogical *obshchenie*, or this kind of intersubjective experience, is necessary for the self-development not only of the characters in Dostoevsky's novels, but in social life as well.[4] Much of the Church-run program is spent in the midst of this kind of *obshchenie*, an intersubjective experience that is vital to the rehabilitation process because it is primarily during this time that rehabilitants engage in the kind of everyday sociality that is vital to the ethical cultivation of normal persons.

"OBSHCHENIE" AS ETHICAL PRACTICE DURING FORMAL ACTIVITIES

"When I first got here I didn't trust anyone in my life, but now I've begun to learn how to trust." So Masha once told me while she smoked a cigarette on the side porch of the main building of The Mill while taking a break from ironing clothes. Twenty-one-year-old Masha had been at The Mill nearly three months by this time; she had been using heroin since she was fifteen and had come to think of other people as only a means to getting drugs, most commonly through stealing or sex. When I asked her what she was doing at the rehab center that allowed her to begin to trust others, she told me it was simply a matter of the *obshchenie* she is able to have at the center. "You know, before I didn't have a normal life, I didn't just hang out with people, we always had something else to be concerned with. But here we can have this, here we can get to know other people and communicate [*obshchat'sya*] with them." Like Masha, for many of the rehabilitants their time at The Mill is the first opportunity, or at least the first in a long time, to have the kind of intersubjective experiences that most people take for granted in everyday social life. It is these kinds of intersubjective experiences that help rehabilitants learn how to interact with others in the give-and-take of everyday social life, and in doing so work on themselves to become more trusting and open persons. The dialogical experience of *obshchenie* that becomes possible for them at The Mill is a central component of the rehabilitation process of making new moral and normal persons.

Opportunities for *obshchenie* are everywhere at The Mill. Perhaps the most obvious are those formally offered within the structure of the daily schedule, particularly the evening group activities. The art therapy sessions are indicative of how these group activities can often turn into moments of ethically constructive, intersubjective *obshchenie*. These therapy sessions occur once or twice a week and are always led by Lena. According to Lena, art therapy is a particularly useful form of individual and group therapy because it stimulates both individual imagination and social interaction, two "skills" she believes all rehabilitants need in order to overcome their addiction.

How is this done? Each session begins with everyone sitting at one of the large tables in the dining room, and Lena sitting at the head of one end. She passes out paper and colored pencils and crayons, then turns on a recording of classical music and asks everyone to close their eyes. After allowing everyone to sit quietly for about a minute she says something like the following: "I want you to try to find a quiet place where you find something that you are scared of or worried about or care about. Try to see it and feel it. Maybe it is a person or a memory that goes by or just some image or colors that you feel. Now at the count of three open your eyes." For the next five minutes or so everyone draws what they saw.

Two things from Lena's instructions seem particularly important. First, her instructions are vague and open-ended. She does not ask them to imagine any one thing in particular, such as a particular moment in the past or a hoped-for future. Instead she leaves it up to individual rehabilitants to imagine what is important to them at this particular moment in their rehabilitation process. Or perhaps from a less agentive perspective, she allows for the possibility of nonconscious fears, concerns, and hopes to disclose themselves in the meditative moment. In any case, Lena's instructions are intentionally vague to allow for individual expression in the therapeutic process.

The second thing that is particularly important about Lena's instructions is her focus on the emotional world of the rehabilitants. A central theme of many of the therapies offered in the Church-run program is to provoke the rehabilitants to become more aware of their own and others' emotions and to learn how to express or empathize with these emotions socially. In fact according to most of the rehabilitants and staff members with whom I spoke, *obshchenie* is not possible without the sharing, at least to some extent, of each other's emotional worlds.

After everyone is finished drawing, each takes a turn showing what she drew and says something about it. Ideally this is meant to provoke a conversation among the rehabilitants and Lena. More often a give-and-take occurs between Lena and the person who is showing her drawing, with occasional side comments by others. For example, one young man once showed a drawing of himself on a boat sailing away from an island toward the horizon and the sun, and said, "This is just something about my future." Lena immediately interpreted his drawing as a metaphorical or symbolic representation of his hoped-for future and said, "The sunset and water represent movement. The sun is also love." Lena wanted to engage the young man in what the various aspects of the drawing meant to him and his future. That is, she was asking him and the others to consider the drawing in terms of a *kind* of future he could have, not in terms of a specific future. She further implied this interpretation when she asked him, "Is there anything outside the picture?" He replied, "There is no limit." He too, then, at this moment was willing to interpret his own image in symbolic terms.

But then another rehabilitant asked him a very literal question: "Where is it?" "I don't know," he replied, "but I always wanted to go someplace warm and to the sea." "Me too," a third person interjected. "That would be cool [*kruto*]," the original questioner replied. After a few moments of silence Lena thanked him for sharing his drawing and asked the next person to begin. If her initial symbolic interpretation was helpful for initiating an imaginative view of a possible kind of future, then this literal interpretation of the drawing was helpful for imagining a particular and specific future that others could share. I suggest that both are important for the therapeutic process.

By focusing on symbolic interpretations, Lena hopes to allow rehabilitants to draw a connection between their "internal" and "private"
emotional world and the kind of ethical work they are doing at The Mill,
as well as the hoped-for result of this work. She wants rehabilitants to
see that ethically working on their emotional worlds by means of these
therapies and the public expression of these worlds is just as significant
to their goals as is the other work they do at the center. A more literal
interpretation of the drawing, which is much more commonly given by
the rehabilitants, builds on and helps concretize the connection made by
the symbolic perspective. In this case, the future hoped for as a result
of the ethical work done at The Mill is not a matter of "movement" and
"love," but the realization of a long-held desire to vacation at the sea
and to feel the warm sun on one's face. This possible future envisioned
as the result of the ethical work done in rehab was the shared hope of
at least three rehabilitants at the table that night, and as such helped to
bring them together in the recognition of a mutually held desire.

At first glance it may be difficult to recognize this therapeutic exchange
as an instance of what I described as *obshchenie*. After all, if *obshchenie* is
supposed to be the kind of intersubjective interaction that allows individuals mutually and creatively to develop each other into new persons,
shouldn't we expect these interactions to be more extensive, or more
intense, or more intimate? This interaction lasted only about a minute,
with several long pauses between utterances. Can we really believe it had
such an effect? I suggest that it did. First, we should recall that *obshchenie*
as it was described to me by many rehabilitants in the program need
not consist of words exchanged; it can also simply be time spent
together. As such, *obshchenie* should not be defined or identified by
words or the number of utterances exchanged. Instead it is about the
outcome of the interaction.

The real question, then, is how did this interaction affect the persons
involved? One possible answer is that it helped at least three rehabilitants
at the table that evening to recognize the person in the other. Ozawa-de
Silva has argued that one of the main goals of Japanese Naikan therapy,
which has its foundations in Buddhism and is commonly used in drug
rehabilitation programs in Japan and elsewhere, is to teach persons to

see others in their life as unique persons who have their own loves, fears, desires, and concerns, just as they themselves do.[5] This is brought about by the imaginative exercise of seeing oneself from the perspective of others in one's life. I suggest that in this moment of intersubjective *obshchenie* at least the three rehabilitants who spoke were able to, even if ever so slightly, recognize the unique person in the other. That is, they could see that the others also have dreams for the future and most likely fears about how and if this future will ever occur, and perhaps most important, that these are dreams and fears that they themselves also have. It was a moment that pulled each of them outside themselves and allowed them, for a very short time, but from the therapeutic perspective hopefully an enduring moment, to see themselves in another.[6] This moment was made possible by Lena's initial symbolic interpretation, for by setting the image of a possible kind of future, she opened the imaginative space for others to begin to concretize this imagined future with real possibilities: vacations, the sea, and all that they entail.

Aleksei, the leader of the Sunday Club at the Aleksandr Nevsky Lavra, agrees with this view of *obshchenie*. This is how he described it to me when I commented that *obshchenie* seems to be vital to the rehabilitation process: "*Obshchenie* is more than just talking, it is understanding one another and feeling what the other feels and sharing emotions. Something should come out of it. It is not just chatter."

To see *obshchenie* utilized in a more intense and focused intersubjective manner, however, consider an example from one of the therapeutic activities led by Aleksei at the Sunday Club. One Sunday in October Aleksei asked half the group to stand in a circle and face outward. The other half of the group stood on the outside of the circle, each person facing someone in the circle. Aleksei asked a question, and each person on the outside of the circle had thirty seconds to answer to the person he was facing, while that person stood silently and listened. After thirty seconds each person on the outside of the circle moved to the next person and answered another question. This continued until everyone had returned to their original position, at which time those who had made up the circle moved to the outside while those on the outside formed a new circle, and the cycle was repeated. Some of the questions we had to answer during the exercise were What is your favorite band or music and why? What has been worrying you recently? What did you do that was interesting this past week? What goal do you want to accomplish this month? What is your favorite movie and why? What is your favorite food and why?

Afterward Aleksei explained to the group that this was an exercise in *obshchenie*. He began by saying that it was an exercise to help us listen to others. He said that drug users, and in fact all people, have a very hard time just listening to others. He also said that this was an exercise about learning not just how to listen, but how to speak to others about personal things, to open up and not to be closed (*zakrytyi*). At this point he demonstrated the posture of a closed person (arms crossed or hands in pockets with head down) and an open, communicating person (hands out and moving and head up while looking at the other person). *Obshchenie*, then, as Aleksei described it to the group, is an embodied dialogical process that necessitates not only an open speaker, but also an open listener.

Aleksei then asked the group what they thought of the exercise. Several people agreed that it was important for them to learn how to communicate with others and to open themselves up more, but the overwhelming response was that it was very difficult. The most common responses were about the difficulty of listening to the other silently, and most found it especially difficult to look the others in the eye. Some also expressed the difficulty of speaking for so long. Each of these responses suggests the real difficulty many of the members of the group still have with intersubjective *obshchenie*.

Both of these examples of *obshchenie* as it is practiced within the formal activities of the Church-run program point to the real emphasis put on rehabilitants working on themselves to become more open and social persons. From the perspective of the program a rehabilitated person is a socially engaged person who can express herself and her "private" world to others, as well as listen to and understand the personhood of the other. Like all disciplinary ethical techniques of the self, one becomes an *obshchitel'nyi* person by means of working on the practice of *obshchenie*. As Mahmood puts it concerning the ethical practice of shyness among women in an Islamic piety movement in Egypt, a practice that also has to do with the moral disposition of intersubjectivity, "It is through repeated *bodily* acts that one trains one's memory, desire, and intellect to behave according to established standards of conduct."[7] That is to say, there is nothing natural about being a particular kind of moral person; it is something that one must work on repeatedly and in various ways in order to cultivate it over a lifetime.

The recognition of this effort has led to the integration of these *obshche-nie* practices, as well as other ethical techniques, into the formal structure of the therapeutic program. As Lena put it to the group at the end of the art therapy session, "By doing this activity we are getting to know ourselves. And from a Christian point of view we are all made in the image of God and the closest we get to this image is when we are creative, so think about that in your free time and see how creative you can be." In pointing out that creativity is the closest one can be to God, Lena reiterates the Orthodox moral theological perspective that the sole purpose of a human life is to continually work on oneself to move toward God-likeness and moral perfection, the intentional recreating of oneself toward moral perfection.

These *obshchenie* practices also emphasize the link between the inherent worth of each person and his capacity to be moral and normal. The Church-run program is a space in which Orthodox human rights provide the context for the enactment of morality, while at the same time works upon the bare life of rehabilitants to enable the embodiment of this morality. In linking this ethical goal to the *obshchenie* activity they just completed, Lena reiterates the need for each rehabilitant to continue to ethically work on himself and to carry this work with him beyond the formal structure of the group activity.

"OBSHCHENIE" AS ETHICAL PRACTICE DURING FREE MOMENTS

One morning in May I arrived at The Mill to spend a few days. After settling in and speaking with Oleg in the staff office for a few minutes, I set out to find some work to do and people to talk with. During the day The Mill often has the feel of an abandoned old farm; you can stand anywhere on the property and not see another person in any direction for ten, twenty, even thirty minutes. But then off in the distance you will make out a few rehabilitants squatting in the field weeding, or someone will step out of the barn or garage. On this day I saw a group of four guys standing around the woodpile outside the *banya*. They were taking a rest from chopping wood, so I went over to help and to talk.

I walked into the middle of a conversation about football (soccer). Since it was Thursday morning, and no radio or televisions are allowed at The Mill, they were eager to ask me the scores of the matches from the night before. By this time I had learned that it was one of my unstated duties to bring news of football results with me each time I came, so I was well prepared. Dima, in his ever present Manchester United jersey, was happy to hear about their latest victory, but soon the conversation turned to the daunting task of the Russian national team having to play the English national team to qualify for the European Championship. And so it went for some time, five young men standing around talking about football, women, the weather, and nothing at all, as some smoked cigarettes and all took a turn chopping wood for a few minutes. Then, from some hiding place I did not see, one of them took out a *Playboy* magazine and began passing it around. When it got to me I took a look and asked jokingly if this was "spiritual literature" given by the staff. A few laughed politely, but one nervously asked me not to tell Father Maxim about it, revealing the still ambiguous position I held for many of the rehabilitants at The Mill. I assured him I would not.

Moments like these at places like the wood pile, far from the gaze of the staff office, are reminiscent of the free places in total institutions Erving Goffman describes as "bounded physical spaces in which ordinary levels of surveillance and restriction [are] markedly reduced." He contrasts these with what he calls off-limits space, where the presence of all or certain patients are not allowed, and surveillance space, where patients expect and are aware of being "subject to the usual authority and restrictions of the establishment."[8] The Mill has all three of these kinds of places.

I suggest, however, that at The Mill it is not so much places that are free, as moments. At a center that consists of over ten hectares of land

and only about twenty-five rehabilitants, one or two volunteers, and one staff member at any one time, free places are not difficult to come by. One never knows, however, when a free place will become a surveillance place, for the staff member, or a volunteer, who has much less authority but nevertheless stands in a place of authority over rehabilitants may happen along. Thus it is not uncommon for Oleg to unexpectedly take a look in the barn, or Lena to have a smoke on the porch, or Fathers Maxim and Aleksandr to take a walk through the kitchen, suddenly shifting the social context from that of a free moment to one of surveillance. In fact it is in these surprise shifts of authoritative moments that most of the disciplinary cards are given out by staff. The Mill can at times have a panoptical feel to it, although not in visual or spatial terms, but in temporal terms.

I have no doubt that my own presence, although often ambiguous, was also often felt by rehabilitants to be an intrusion into their free moments. This was true at the wood pile, where at first I was welcomed into the group of young men as a source of football information and an interlocutor and participant in other "manly" conversations and tasks, but was quickly shifted by what I intended as a joke meant to further bring me into their fold but was interpreted, by at least one rehabilitant, as a potential danger to his and their freedom.

The danger in losing these free moments is not simply a matter of finding oneself, once again, under direct surveillance, or possibly being disciplined for minor offenses. There is also the real danger this loss of freedom can have to the rehabilitation process, for these free moments, during which a significant amount of intersubjective *obshchenie* takes place, are vital to the rehabilitation process at The Mill. Just as *obshchenie* is a central aspect of the therapeutic program at The Mill, it is also true that the vast majority of it takes place in these free moments outside of the official program and the surveillance of the staff. Everyone, staff included, recognizes this. In a very real way, then, it is possible to say that a significant amount of the rehabilitation process at this rehab center is, I hesitate to say individual because *obshchenie* is always done with others and as such is a social process, but it is certainly at the same time a self-induced rehabilitation. That is, the bulk of the rehabilitation takes place outside the official program and particularly in these free moments.

Perhaps one of the most common activities performed during these free moments is looking at personal photographs. Nearly every day I was at The Mill over the course of the year I saw people huddling together looking at and talking about photographs. Whether it was people sitting at a dining-room table after a meal passing around photographs, or two guys standing in the barn while cows mingled about, or a few young women taking a break from kitchen duty, photographs seemed to bring people together. Perhaps most interesting is that this form of sociality occurred not only around new photographs that had recently been developed or sent from relatives or friends from the city, but also around photographs that everyone had already seen several times. It seems that looking at photographs with others is not (always) about the novelty of the image, but is sometimes about being with others and dialogically opening oneself to them. The photographs act as a kind of material link between persons that invite them to engage in intersubjective *obshchenie*.

Because the photographs they looked at could depict nearly anything—activities at The Mill; a recent trip taken by some of the rehabilitants to a monastery; a birthday party; a friend who had died from an overdose; relatives, a girlfriend, or a child back in the city; a drunk friend at a party five years earlier; or a holiday in Ukraine—they are a unique source for stimulating the kind of intersubjective communication that opens interlocutors to one another. Once I was looking at photos with four rehabilitants; one of the photos was of Klara's mother holding Klara's child. This stimulated a conversation that went well beyond the photo. It began with a straightforward question to Klara about the child and who will take care of her when she returns to the city. Soon another young woman began telling us about her own child. Then Dima started talking about his desire to have a child one day. After a few minutes Klara began to talk about her relationship with her mother, and this set everyone on this topic for the next several minutes. The photograph itself was no longer important; intersubjective *obshchenie* had begun and the sociality was now about the persons there intersubjectively together and not the image. The photograph may have been the impetus, but now the activity had shifted to a group of persons intersubjectively coming to understand one another as actual persons with feelings, pasts, hopes, pains, and joys, and in the process themselves growing into more *obshchitel'nyi* persons. This free moment of ostensible photograph sharing may have been the most significant therapeutic aspect of this particular day for those involved, for in those ten minutes or so all involved most likely opened themselves more and opened themselves to others more than in any other activity in which they participated that day.

Smoking is another free moment when *obshchenie* is commonly practiced, in particular the smoking that takes place on the side porch of the main building. Because smoking is not allowed in the building, this is where everyone who is in the building must go to smoke. It serves as the main congregating place for smokers, though rehabilitants working in the field, at the *banya,* or just about anywhere else will also smoke in those places. Often individuals will walk from where they are working to the side porch in order to smoke with others. What might begin as one person sitting there smoking a solitary cigarette can turn into a group of four or five within minutes.

These free moments of sociality can at times be little more than persons sitting and standing together saying very little to one another, or randomly making comments about the weather or the old decrepit dog who looks like she should have died years ago and often lies on the porch with the smokers. But they can also turn into more obvious moments of intersubjective *obshchenie,* when persons engage one another in meaningful and creative ways. On the smoking porch I've heard and took part in such conversations as whether or not to go to a parish, feelings of fatigue and other symptoms from HIV-related illnesses, what they really liked about the film they watched the night before in contrast to what Father Maxim had them discuss, beginning university when one returns to the city, or that a rehabilitant feels abandoned by her mother because she hasn't called in over a month. These are conversations that go well beyond the weather and the dog and serve to bring people together in a closer relationship of understanding one another as real persons, in the process helping each of them come to a better understanding of themselves as well. Again, if one of the main therapeutic goals of the Church-run rehabilitation program is to remake rehabilitants into normal social persons, then such *obshchitel'nyi* moments are vital to the success of the program even if they are taking place in free moments.

Smoking on the side porch should be considered a free moment in the strictest sense of its being always open to the risk of shifting to a surveillance moment. Not only can one of the staff members or a volunteer walk out the main door of the building, which leads directly onto the porch, at any time, but Lena, the only staff worker who smokes, or a volunteer can also join the smokers on the porch at any time. This shift does not necessarily entail a change of conversation, especially if it is a volunteer or one of the former drug-using staff members who comes to the porch, but it does alter the feel of the moment. For example, once I was on the porch with three female and two male rehabilitants and we were making fun of one of the guys who had had to work in the kitchen the day before because several of the women had been ill and unable to work. We were making jokes about his wearing an apron and his inability to peel potatoes when Lena came out the door and lit a cigarette. After a brief pause and an exchange of greetings with her, the joking continued but at a much less intense level. Even Lena joined in on the jest. But something had changed. The laughter was less free, the pauses were longer, eyes looked to the ground more often. A feeling of restraint overtook the five rehabilitants on the porch, and even I felt as though I should watch my words.

This example shows precisely how power relations often work at The Mill. There was nothing about this joking moment that Lena or any of the other staff members would have had a problem with. There was no *Playboy* magazine, or smuggled bottles of vodka, or sex talk. This was precisely the kind of intersubjective *obshchenie* the staff encourages. Nevertheless the staff's very presence hindered this intersubjective therapeutic experience. In these cases of shifts from free to surveillance moments, power stands in the way of the very thing it hopes to support.

Such relations, however, are not so problematic during the smoking breaks at the Sunday Club because Aleksei, the leader of the Club, does not smoke, so he stays inside and prepares tea while the majority of those attending go outside to smoke. Also, because the Club is a post-rehabilitation club, surveillance and authority are much less central to the process. The smoking break, however, is important for what happens at the Club, for it is during this time that attendees can socialize and engage in *obshchenie* outside the official parameters of the program.

Just outside the door of the main entrance to the largest building in the central square of the Lavra anywhere from five to fifteen attendees of the Club, almost always male, smoke and talk for about fifteen minutes, marking the halfway point of the meeting. They talk about what they did over the past week, make plans to do something together in the upcoming week—such as walk down Nevsky Prospect together or watch a movie—talk about movies and music, and exchange CDs and DVDs that they had promised to bring the week before. While the official therapy of the meeting helps the attendees work on certain *obshchitel'nyi* skills that can in time become embodied, it is during the smoking break that these very same skills can be used and practiced in the process of coming to cultivate them as one's own.

This smoking time is particularly important for many rehabilitants because in their attempt to stay away from their old drug-using social context and networks they rarely have an opportunity to socialize with others. Many of them still do not have jobs and have very few friends, and their relatives still have a hard time trusting and opening up to them, as do they to them; therefore, for a significant number of these attendees freshly back in the city from rehabilitation, the smoking break and the walk back to the metro after the meeting are the only opportunities they have for sociality and *obshchenie*. They must make the most of this time and they know it. Isolation and loneliness threaten their very sobriety. Fortunately many of them are able to make friends in these free moments and are able to carry those friendships into their everyday lives. *Obshchenie* and friendship are vital for ex-rehabilitants back in the city and for their quest to remain drug-free and to continue to cultivate themselves into new moral persons.

"OBSHCHENIE" AS ETHICAL PRACTICE BACK IN THE CITY

So far we have seen how *obshchenie* is a central aspect of the rehabilitation process both in the context of the official structure of the Church-run program and in the free moments found around the edges of this structure. *Obshchenie* is also an important part of staying drug-free back in the city. It is vital to the necessary task of finding a new set of friends so as to avoid returning to the old social network of drug users, and these new social networks often replace the authoritative surveillance of the rehabilitation program with a form of mutual surveillance. How are these dual and seemingly contradictory roles of *obshchenie* played out back in the city?

One place this occurs is at the Tuesday reception at Botkin Hospital. While the reception is an official part of the Church-run program, the ex-rehabilitants, who regularly attend the reception and socialize among themselves as Oleg interviews prospective rehabilitants, have a position outside the program at this point. They are visitors who are no longer subject to the authoritative structure of the program. They are there by their own choice and with the main purpose of meeting with other ex-rehabilitants in order to socialize, gossip, joke, and make plans to get together elsewhere. This visitor status is clearly seen not only in the way that Oleg openly interacts with them as he never does with anyone at The Mill, let alone with any of the applicants at the reception, but also in the way the ex-rehabilitants interact with the applicants.

As I described in part I, from three to seven ex-rehabilitants sit along one side of the small room in which Oleg conducts interviews with applicants and generally chat quietly among themselves, drink tea, and eat cookies, pastries, and fruit. Occasionally, however, they become involved in the interviews as unofficial commentators. For example, overhearing Oleg make an amusing comment to an applicant they may respond with laughter and perhaps a comment or two of their own, as the applicant smiles awkwardly. They may warn or scold an applicant about her obstinacy. Once a young woman came with her husband to apply for admission to The Mill. This was her first time at the interview.

Throughout the short interview she gave vague answers to Oleg's questions, several times belittled her husband when he attempted to help her answer, and showed obvious disrespect for several of the program's main tenets that Oleg was attempting to communicate. This continued despite several attempts by Oleg to warn her that this attitude would not help her gain acceptance to The Mill. It was only when the ex-rehabilitants began to talk audibly among themselves about her attitude that she began to rethink it. Finally she asked the group what they were saying about her. A young man replied that even if she was lucky enough to actually be accepted to The Mill, she would never last because she would never be able to do what was expected of her. A young woman told her that there is hard work to be done at The Mill and no one, not the staff or other rehabilitants, would put up with this kind of attitude. Hearing these comments the applicant obviously reconsidered her attitude and spent the rest of the short interview attentively listening and answering.

Although this example may be out of the ordinary because of the applicant's particularly strong attitude, such commentary and surveillance are not at all uncommon. What is ostensibly meant to be a gathering of ex-rehabilitants coming together for *obshchenie*, that is, to socialize, meet old acquaintances, drink some tea, and hear some gossip, can at times turn into a moment of surveillance not unlike how staff and volunteers at The Mill once watched them. Those who were once kept under a disciplinary eye have now become those who discipline. And in this context these disciplinary eyes have a power often beyond that held by Oleg, for in this reception the applicants still know very little about the Church-run program. They know that Oleg is the key to their acceptance, but the ex-rehabilitants have been there and are seemingly successful. They are the people the applicant wants to become, and their authoritative gaze and words hold much persuasive power.

This gaze is at times also turned onto other ex-rehabilitants. Over the course of a year I twice witnessed the group calling into question the sobriety of one of their members. In both cases the person admitted to having used recently. This is precisely why making new friends and *obshchenie* with other ex-rehabilitants is in some sense always a relationship of mutual surveillance, for as it was told to me several times, "We know all the signs of someone using." In both of these cases the person had slipped and used once or twice in the previous weeks but had not done so that day, nor had they returned to a regular regimen of heroin use, which they call "the system." Yet the others could see. They know what using looks like when it walks in the door, and within minutes they had taken the person out to the hall to talk with him away from Oleg. From what I know neither person started using again. The mutual surveillance made possible in this context of *obshchenie* seems to have worked for now. But, as the saying goes, "Heroin can wait," so this "for now" is often an anxiety-ridden present for the newest of ex-rehabilitants returning to the city.

A similar kind of mutual surveillance can be seen among relationships of ex-rehabilitant friends in the city. These small networks of friends are formed when ex-rehabilitants first meet at the Sunday Club or at the Tuesday reception; some met at The Mill or one of the parishes or monasteries and remained friends back in the city. At the Sunday Club there are two main groups of friends made up of six or seven regulars; the occasional attendees remain either completely outside these two networks or on the edge of them. These two groups of friends have very few people outside of the group whom they would call friends, and therefore the vast majority of their social life is spent with other members of the friendship network. They talk on the phone with one another, they walk on Nevsky Prospect together, they watch movies or television or listen to music together, they help each other find work, and they provide financial help if one of them cannot find work.

One of these networks—Max, Misha, and Sasha—spent a significant amount of their free time together. In fact Max and Sasha eventually moved into an apartment together, and they sometimes talked about founding a commune for ex-rehabilitants in the city. Misha and Sasha had become very close while living together at one of the parishes. They met Max at the Sunday Club, found that they had much in common because of their shared experiences living at a parish, and soon became close friends. They attended church services together each Sunday before attending the Club together; they attended several weekend Church retreats together; on Tuesdays they attended a weekly meeting at the

Lavra for Church palliative care volunteers; and other nights of the week they would spend together watching movies or television. For a few months they also worked together remodeling one of the floors of the hospital where Max works. They were in every sense friends and spent much time together learning, growing, and having fun with one another in a very close *obshchitel'nyi* relationship.

I say "were" because in time this tight friendship network eventually lost Misha. Zhenia became part of this network, and very soon afterward she and Misha became a couple. This came as no surprise to anyone, and certainly not to me, since I had known both of them before they met one another, and both had for some time been telling me how important it was to them to find someone to marry. In their desperation they were perfect for one another.

At first they were a couple within the group, spending all their time together with either Max or Sasha or both. But soon they began to spend more and more time alone. Max and Sasha began to worry about Misha, and once even confronted him about how fast things seemed to be moving. Misha did not respond well to this, declaring his love for Zhenia. After this Max and Sasha rarely saw Misha, but they continued to call him. At times their phone conversations were like old times, comfortable and fun, but at other times not so much. Max and Sasha began to worry that Misha and Zhenia were using together. Then came the news that Zhenia was pregnant and that Misha had married her. Max and Sasha were not invited to the small ceremony. They continued to call, but more and more Misha would not answer. Once when he did answer Max asked him straight out if he had started using again. After some silence Misha said no and found a way to get off the phone soon afterward. He never answered his phone again when Max or Sasha tried to call, nor did he or Zhenia ever again attend another Sunday Club or palliative care volunteer meeting. They both disappeared.

Two things are clear about this group of ex-rehabilitant friends. First, for over a year the three men were a close group who provided each other with a new network of friends back in the city who were not part of their old drug-using network, but perhaps more important, they provided each other with the opportunity to be new social and normal persons and in doing so also new moral persons. That this was happening for over a year is in no way diminished by the unfortunate place in which Misha found himself, for breakdowns occur in everyone's life, and fighting addiction with heroin makes this ever more likely and more noticeable when it occurs. I point this out simply because it should not be thought that those rehabilitants and ex-rehabilitants who end up using heroin again have not changed themselves in any way. This is clearly not true, especially since the process Misha and others like him are going through is best understood as a process of working on the self and not curing the self. Yet the unfortunate truth is that when an addict has a breakdown it is more public and potentially dangerous than the breakdowns of most others.

The second thing that is clear about this group of friends is that in addition to providing a network of intersubjective *obshchenie* for one another, they also provided a relationship of mutual surveillance for one another. I suggest that this is partly why they spent so much time together. If the only time they were apart from one another was when they worked, and remember they also worked together for several months, they had very little opportunity to feel the loneliness and social isolation that many drug users report feeling, let alone the opportunity to give in to temptations of using. It should be noted that Misha began using again only when he spent time away from the group. This is important because there is no doubt that Misha and Zhenia also had a relationship of *obshchenie*; the difference is that there seems to have been a lack of mutual surveillance that is more easily and efficiently enacted within a larger group.

This danger was immediately noticed by Max and Sasha. They warned him about moving too quickly with Zhenia. They continually asked him to spend more time with them, and invited Zhenia along as well. As Max and Sasha saw it, the danger was not that Misha and Zhenia were starting a relationship, but that this relationship was too quickly isolating both of them from a larger support network. When it became obvious that Misha was not communicating with the group anymore, they kept calling him to try to keep him in the network, to try to maintain a relationship of *obshchenie* between them. They saw what was happening, but if he was no longer physically with them, they could no longer help him. Surveillance became increasingly difficult with this distance despite their best attempts, until finally Max had to confront Misha about using. And it was this verbal expression of the mutual surveillance, this verbal disclosure of what everyone already knew was there that finally lost Misha to the group.

For over a year Misha mutually engaged in this group disciplinary support with Max and Sasha, and for a year it went unsaid and it worked. But when *obshchenie* breaks down and disciplinary tactics are disclosed, the sociality that was at the heart of this ethical relationship was no longer possible. Everyone in the Church-run program is aware that there are certain moments of authoritative surveillance that they must accept in order to be in the program. Even though Max, Misha, and Sasha all knew it was also a part of their friendship, indeed it was part of why they had formed the close-knit group in the first place, it could not be said. This is so because although all intersubjective relations are characterized by power differentials, in order to have a truly *obshchitel'nyi* relationship these power differentials must be covered over. When power is revealed within a relationship, *obshchenie* ends and simple conversation begins.

"OBSHCHENIE" AS ETHICAL PRACTICE IN THE CONTEXT OF THE CHURCH'S DRUG REHABILITATION PROGRAM

In an important article on the pragmatic usage and metalinguistic view of language in the context of an American drug treatment program for homeless women, E. Summerson Carr claims that the "talking cure is based on the assumption that words can do much more than refer to sick selves; they can also produce healthier ones."[9] Using the terminology of a moral rather than a medical approach, I would agree with Carr in that talk in its various forms in the Church's drug rehabilitation and HIV prevention and care program is central to the production of new moral persons. While the therapeutic emphasis on talk in Carr's

American program is on the honest revelation of one's true self through "truthful" speech-acts, I have suggested that in the context of the Church-run program in the St. Petersburg area the emphasis is on the dialogical opening up of oneself with others in a mutual process of cocreating and recreating each other's moral personhood, or *obshchenie*. This is a difference between the disclosure of an individual, foundational, and true presence that was always already there but covered over with addiction, and the mutual creation of an entirely new personhood that is possible only with others. It is certainly true that from the perspective of the Russian Orthodox Church this mutual creation is possible only because of the inherent foundation of the image and likeness of God found in all human persons, yet this image and likeness are simply the potentiality that allows for the dialogical process of ethical self-recreation.

This difference is at the level of the respective metalinguistic view held by the two treatment programs. Borrowing from the work of Jane Hill, Carr argues that local "regimes of personhood select some speech acts as exemplary of 'healthy' human agency," and that these reflect a local language ideology.[10] As I have argued elsewhere, *obshchenie* is considered by some Russians to be an important component to the constitution of one's own moral personhood, as well as the resolution of particular ethical dilemmas.[11] Similarly Eugene Raikhel reports that some Russians have argued that Alcoholics Anonymous programs are particularly well-suited for the Russian context because it relies on "heart to heart [*po dusham*] conversations" between persons.[12] These heart-to-heart conversations are another way of describing the process of *obshchenie*. While I hesitate to make any general claims about a so-called Russian language ideology, it is clear that this view is also central to the therapeutic approach of making new moral persons at the Church-run program.

This is where it is necessary to remember the connection between *obshchenie* and *obshchestvo* (society), as well as the other *obshch-* words, and it becomes possible to see the essential social nature of the rehabilitation process in the Church-run program. Although many of the staff and rehabilitants describe the process as individually focused, that is, emphasizing the necessity of individuals working on themselves and their particular needs, the centrality of *obshchenie* in this process reveals that such ostensibly individual ethical work is in fact always done with others. In Carr's example this is also true, but the emphasis on referential language covers over the social nature of the process because it tends to limit "the reach of words to the contents of individual psyches."[13] On the contrary, in the Church-run program the emphasis on intersubjective, dialogical *obshchenie* discloses the necessity of individuals who are working on their particular needs to always do so with and among others. That is to say, it is recognized that an individual can become a new moral person only through the process of being social. In other words, the Church-run program works on the assumption that being a moral person and being social are not mutually exclusive, but in fact are mutually constituting, and that it is only this mutual constitution that can produce normal persons.

In her comparative study of consumption practices in postsocialist Russia and Vietnam, Vann has argued that individual consumers in these countries are not being transformed into the autonomous individuals that might be expected to follow the neoliberal reforms that drove the postsocialist changes. Rather the reasoning process and identity that have accompanied these reforms are better viewed as social and collective, reflecting traces of the socialist legacy on neoliberal values that I discussed in the introduction.[14] I'm not entirely convinced that the post-Soviet identities being cultivated in contemporary Russia are quite as social and collective as Vann would have it. Nevertheless the distinction I have been drawing between what Carr calls the "language ideologies" of the United States and Russia does suggest real differences in the kinds of neoliberal subjects cultivated in each context. The importance of *obshchenie* in everyday relations and in the therapeutic process of making new moral persons suggests that there is a stronger emphasis on sociality in the Russian version of the neoliberal person than that of the American. In this sense I agree with Vann that we need not think of the neoliberal project as uniformly imposing a certain model wherever it may be applied. Rather, as neoliberalism increasingly becomes one more if not the dominant aspect in a local assemblage it is shaped in certain ways to more easily and seamlessly become a part of that specific local assemblage. Many of the values, reasonings, and practices may be quite similar across many global assemblages, but the kinds of persons and the processes by which they come to embody them locally may be quite different. For this reason it may be more appropriate to speak of neoliberalisms.

FROZEN FEELINGS

I have been arguing that a good deal of the Church's rehabilitation process focuses on remaking rehabilitants into new moral persons who are able to engage in normal forms of sociality, and that much of this is based on the ability to engage in relationships of *obshchenie*. Much of this depends on what many of those involved in the Church-run program call "the thawing of frozen feelings." One of the most common ways drug addiction was described to me was as a disease of frozen feelings (*bolezn' zamorozhennykh chuvstv*). Rehabilitants told me that they need to learn how to feel again or how to control their emotions;[15] staff told me that many of the therapeutic activities are aimed at allowing and teaching rehabilitants how to emote properly; and ex-rehabilitants often said that the world became a different place once they and their feelings began to thaw (*ottaivat'*).

This image of drug addiction as a disease of frozen feelings suggests that drug users have no feelings at all, that they are emotionally incapable of relating to themselves or the world and people around them. Once the rehabilitant begins to thaw, the image suggests, emotive movement is once again possible. To an extent this image is supported by the way some spoke to me about their experience as drug users. For example, I heard many stories about those who did not care and had no emotional response to a sister dying from cancer, the increasingly obvious health problems resulting from their own heroin use, their own and others' HIV status, whether or not they were hurting their friends and family members, and their own acts of stealing and prostitution. Each of these stories supports the image of a person emotively frozen and cut off from their own ways of being in the world by suggesting that there simply was an absence of an emotional world.

I want to offer another interpretation of this idea of frozen feelings: that what those involved in the Church-run program call frozen feelings in fact indicates the predominance of what might be better described as asocial feelings, or feelings that hinder what is considered appropriate forms of sociality. In other words, the rehabilitation process can be understood not as a process of "thawing" a person so she is able to once again have an emotional world, but as a process of remaking oneself into the kind of person who is able to control her own emotional world and do so in a more socially appropriate way. It is a process of becoming persons who can emotively express themselves in ways that support rather than hinder their intersubjective sociality.

Anthropologists have described the social nature of emotions.[16] Far from being a sign of the internal and private world of individuals, as in the predominant Western view, emotions can be seen as an "interpersonal process of naming, justifying, and persuading by people in relationship to each other," and are central to the construction of persons.[17] In this view emotions are not so much internally contained within individuals, although because they become most clearly manifest in and on the bodies of persons it may at times appear as though they originate there; rather emotions are one aspect of characterizing being in particular intersubjective relations. Changing and working on the emotional world of persons is a matter of altering the way a person is in her social world.

This is the approach taken by the Church-run program in their attempt to "defrost" (*razmorozit'*) the emotional world of rehabilitants. Although much of the talk I heard regarding this process focused on individuals and the need for them to alter their own internal and private emotional worlds, the kind of work and exercises done in the program, much like the *obshchitel'nyi* exercises, were actually aimed at changing rehabilitants' emotional worlds by changing the way they engage in social relations. It has been argued that the focus of both Russians and non-Russians on the emotional worlds of individual persons neglects the political-economic context that plays a significant role in shaping these worlds.[18] In contrast, in the Church-run program the discursive emphasis on individuals, though not specifically addressing political-economic issues, masks their practical emphasis on social relations.

In fact this way of discursively focusing on the emotional worlds of individuals, while at the same time emphasizing the social nature of these emotional worlds, is characteristic of Russian Orthodox writings on the subject. It is also central to the way the Church views drug addiction. As Father Maxim puts it in his thesis on the Christian view of drug addiction, drug users are under the influence of many passions.[19] As I described in part I, passions are embodied and nonconsciously enacted sin; they also suggest the necessary relation between the individual (consisting of both body and soul) and her social world. For example, in one of his most important works on moral transformation St. Theophan the Recluse, a highly influential nineteenth-century bishop, provides a categorical schema of the main passions against which persons must struggle as they ethically work on themselves.[20] In his categorization of the passions he makes a distinction between the passions of the body (e.g., sexual lust, love of pleasure, adulterous feelings, and willfulness in everything) and the soul (e.g., self-will, possessiveness, envy, hatred, and anger), and yet this distinction is not so clear-cut. Bodily passions of love of pleasure and adulterous feelings are intimately entwined with the emotional world of a person, just as such passions of the soul as anger and possessiveness are inseparable from the body. The emotional world of the passions as described in this classic Orthodox work on moral theology is clearly not simply an internal and private affair of individual persons, but instead is a public and embodied way of being.

As such, this embodied and public emotional way of being is also a way of being in the world. Each of these passions, and there are more (e.g., opportunism, ungratefulness, revenge, judgment, depression, and ambition), depends on a person's being in a social world in a particular way. Metropolitan Philaret argues that in order for a person's emotional world to develop in a spiritually and morally appropriate way, he must be socialized by his parents from childhood in an appropriately Orthodox way. In particular it is important to "come into contact with people's needs and wants, and to give [him] the opportunity to help." In doing so he will develop what Philaret considers the "elevated feelings of sympathy, mercy [and] compassion"; if not, he will develop the passions listed by St. Theophan.[21]

This link between the embodied emotional world of individual persons and their social world was made explicit to me several times. For example, Olga Viktorovna, the head of the orientation department for the Church-run program, was explaining the process of orienting the new rehabilitants to the social world of the rehabilitation center when she made this link between their emotional world and their being in the social world:

> Here we need to explain to the person what awaits so he does not become afraid because he is used to living in destructive relationships. . . . Because when they come to us they usually have a number of psychological traumas and they kick off like a chain reaction. The person experiences a lot of pain and fear and he goes through a lot and there is much resentment about what is happening. He experiences a deep feeling of loneliness and of course he thinks nobody understands him. He does not trust anyone because recently he has only been around drug addicts, where he has been cheated and he cheated himself. . . . He lost the ability to *live* in this world. He is disorganized. He lost touch with reality and being responsible, he is filled with all-out protest, fear, horror, misunderstanding, pain, desperation and spite. And when they are here [in the Church-run program] they begin to understand that they do not want to live with this and we show them that they have an opportunity to be filled with something else.

Clearly Olga Viktorovna sees an intimate connection between the embodied emotional world of drug users and their social way of being in the world. Indeed part of the process of her orientation is to prepare the new rehabilitants for the new social reality into which they will enter, a social world she would describe as a family of mature and spiritual love, what the Russian Orthodox Church's view of human rights sees as a social context that allows for the training and enactment of morality. This new social world of the rehabilitation center is far from the way she describes the social world to which the drug users have become accustomed, a world of cheating, pain, and loneliness, which dialogically contributes to the embodied emotional world of fear, horror, and desperation, and which feeds back into their social world in a circle that can be ended only with the loving social world of the Church-run program.

Just as the old social world of the drug user plays a significant part in the dialogical relationship between person and world, so too, Olga Viktorovna claims, this necessary dialogical relationship will continue in the context of rehabilitation. But in this context the loving and familial social world slowly but surely begins to alter the rehabilitating person and his emotional world: "We show them that they have an opportunity to be filled with something else." At the Church-run program the rehabilitants are thrown into a new world founded on relationships of "love, mature love, spirituality, where you need to learn to be truly humble and tolerant, to respect one another." By offering a new social world, a world that I have suggested can be considered an Agambian paradigm of the kind of world the Church would like to establish with its view of human rights, the program claims to offer the opportunity for a new life, that is, a new way of being a moral, responsibilized, and normal person in the world.

Related to both this necessary connection between a person's emotional world and her social world and the idea that drug addiction is a disease of frozen feelings is the view that drug users are egoists. I was told several times by staff, rehabilitants, and ex-rehabilitants that all drug users are characterized by egoism, that is, a self-centeredness that disconnects them from their social world and, ironically, eventually from themselves. Oleg once told me, "What makes a drug addict different is that he is deceitful, irresponsible and absolutely egocentric, and all these qualities lead to his disability." In Oleg's formulation these asocial qualities add up: deceit and irresponsibility lead to absolute egoism, which is one of the main reasons one uses heroin. Similarly Father Maxim once told me that there are many reasons why a person begins to use heroin, but they can all be reduced to the fact that drug users are egoists. Both Oleg and Father Maxim went on to tell me that one of the main tasks of The Mill is to help rehabilitants overcome their egoism by teaching them how to be with, care for, and become responsible for others. Father Maxim expressed this in terms of teaching them how to work together as a *kollektiv*, and Oleg expressed it in terms of allowing them the opportunity to open themselves up to others and have others open themselves up to them in *obshchenie*.

This was echoed to me by Nika, a twenty-two-year-old professional DJ who had been using heroin for five years and almost gave up her opportunity to go to The Mill because it meant turning down an opportunity to deejay at a very popular Russian rave festival. She told me that the staff often tells rehabilitants that drug users are characterized by frozen feelings. When I asked her what she thought this meant she told me, "Well, I think they are right, you know, because drug addicts are all egoists. We don't care about anyone else or what we do to them, we only care about one thing: getting that next fix. And you know, I don't know how this will turn out, but I've really liked being here and being able to feel something again." I asked her what kinds of things she has felt at The Mill that she liked, and she said, "Everything! Of course I like to laugh with others and feel some kind of joy, but I also like that I cry. I do that a lot now. I cry for myself and I cry when I hear about other people's lives."

Nika's claim that staff tell rehabilitants that drug users are characterized by frozen feelings is in line with Hunt and Barker's observation that treatment agencies and clinics often attempt to redefine persons as addicts by stripping them of previous identity characteristics or telling clients what defines an addict.[22] If the purpose of rehabilitation and treatment is to create new persons, then rehabilitants and clients must learn who they are before they can overcome themselves on the way to a new moral personhood. The way they can begin to work to overcome their egoism is, to use a bit of Heideggerian language, to be thrown into an entirely new social context where they must engage with, work with, be responsible to, and care about others.

This therapeutic strategy is closely linked with Orthodox moral theological views of overcoming passions and sinfulness. In the Orthodox view egoism is the foundational cause of all passions, and therefore it is egoism that must be overcome by means of ethical work on the self in order to become a passionless person and fight against sin.[23] In other words, the moral transformation of a person begins with fighting egoism. Metropolitan Philaret claims that the root cause of an emotionally underdeveloped person, similar to those with frozen feelings, is the egoism caused from not being raised in a properly social environment, and Patriarch Kirill in his speech on human rights and responsibility warns of the moral danger of individual egoistic interests over those of society, family, and nation.[24] The self-sacrificing love that Kirill advocates instead of egoism is very similar to Philaret's claim that "feelings of sympathy, mercy, compassion, etc. must be developed in the heart of the Orthodox Christian.[25] Clearly the approach of the Church-run program is significantly influenced by these Orthodox conceptions of the passions of drug use and the egoism that is the foundation of these passions.

But the Russian Orthodox Church is not alone in viewing asocial emotions and egoism as characteristic of drug use. Various public discourses of addiction and treatment characterize drug use in very similar ways. Laurie Drapela argues that there is a relationship between such negative emotions as despair and increased drug use among high school dropouts in the United States, and Antonio Verdejo-García et al. argue that negative emotions and impulsivity, two characteristics they believe are closely related, are risk factors in the development of alcohol and substance abuse dependence.[26] Similarly H. C. Fox et al. claim that the inability of persons seeking treatment for their cocaine addiction to manage and control their emotions is a significant factor in their relapse, and An-Pyng Sun reports that women who completed substance abuse treatment programs believed "negative emotions and interpersonal conflict" were major factors in their relapse.[27]

In the context of rehabilitation and treatment programs, working with clients to overcome their negative, or what I call asocial, emotions is considered an important aspect of the therapeutic process.[28] In her study of identity transformation in the context of a rehabilitation center, Frankel argues that one of the central precepts of this process is cultivating sociality among rehabilitants, and that a fundamental aspect of this sociality is learning how to "face and share [one's own] genuine feelings." Because of this much of the formal therapeutic activity is aimed at "circumventing the defensive maneuvers individuals employ to avoid facing or expressing negative feelings of hate, fear, anger, guilt, and pain."[29] Frankel notes that this leads to group therapy activities primarily being an opportunity to reward the expression of negative emotions to the detriment of the expression of positive feelings, a strategy that she questions.

As I have been arguing, the Church-run program also sees over-coming asocial emotions, what it calls frozen feelings, as central to the therapeutic process. However, it does not conceive of this process as the revelation of "genuine" feelings and the real person, as both Frankel and Carr described the process in American rehabilitation programs.[30] Similar to what I described as cultivating an *obshchitel'nyi* disposition, at The Mill and the other Church programs the process is focused instead on helping rehabilitants cultivate the ability to manage and control their emotional worlds, and to do so in such a way that they are able to become more social persons. While the Church program certainly recognizes that many of the rehabilitants struggle with sadness, depression, loneliness, and anger, among other asocial emotions, it does not believe that these must be completely eliminated or replaced with so-called positive emotions such as joy and happiness.

Rather the Church program suggests that if one can *manage* and *control* these asocial emotions in ways that allow one to engage in more inter-subjective relations such as *obshchenie*, then one can begin to cultivate oneself into a more social person who can find within this new person-hood moments and dispositions of positive emotions. Thus this process is not about the revelation of a genuine person already there in waiting with positive emotions, but the cultivation of a new, self-controlled social person through the very process of sociality.

THAWING OUT IN REHAB

I have already shown that group therapy sessions at both The Mill and the Sunday Club are meant to cultivate new dispositions of *obshchenie*, as well as at times performances of public confession. They are also meant to help rehabilitants and ex-rehabilitants manage and control their emotions such that they are able to engage appropriately in intersubjective sociality. It should not be surprising that in one group therapy session participants are able to work on various aspects of themselves. This is just one of the ways the therapeutic process entails what I called the temporal expansion of particular activities, and as such is able to initiate multiple and yet interrelated trajectories of working on the self, each focusing on a particular aspect of a single individual. Thomas Csordas describes a similar phenomenon in Catholic charismatic healing, where images are used to focus therapeutic attention: "Images as symbolic signs may initiate the elaboration of alternatives by directing the attention of the patient toward a particular aspect of her life experience that can be taken up into the therapeutic process of ritual healing."[31] In charismatic healing, as well as at the Church-run program, this aspectual focus can shift throughout the therapeutic process, and in doing so phenomenologically multiply its potential effectiveness.

One afternoon in December I was talking with Zhanna in the dining room of The Mill as we ironed and folded clothes together. She seemed to be in a particularly good mood on this day and I asked her about it. She told me that the evening before, during the group therapy session, she had experienced a shift in her emotional world that caused her to begin to think that she could possibly overcome her addiction after all. I asked her how this came about. She replied that nothing in particular happened, but she simply realized that being together with others helped her experience her emotional world in a way that she never had before. As she put it, she experienced an overflow of emotions (*emotsii menya perepolnyayut*). She went on to tell me that as a user you forget what "simple human communication [*prostoe chelovecheskoe obshchenie*]" is, and that being at The Mill and participating in the group sessions allows them to have these experiences. Thus, similar to Masha's comments about *obshchenie* on the smoking porch, Zhanna explicitly links the importance of intersubjective sociality with her own emotional world, and in turn to her continued ability to ethically work on herself.

Unfortunately I was not at the therapy session to witness what caused this overflow of emotions, but as Zhanna described it, it was more a matter of being together with others than any one of the particular activities done. Others described the same experience. For example, Aleksei from the Sunday Club once told me that just attending the Club makes his mood (*nastroenie*) better regardless of the particular activities done that week. He sees the same effect in others at the Club as well ("Ya vizhu kak u drugikh rebyat tozhe"). For many it is the opportunity to be together with others, to interact with them, and to open up and experience the opening up of others to them, and not any one of the particular activities, that helps them begin to experience and manage their emotional worlds. This seems to support the metaphorical image of a melting ice cube that several used to describe the process of thawing their frozen feelings. Like an ice cube that slowly and imperceptibly melts, so too, I was told, the frozen feelings of a rehabilitating drug user gradually and over time melt and her emotional world once again begins to flow.

The therapeutic activities are meant to instigate this process, even when the activities are not specifically focused on the cultivation of emotional worlds. For example, participants in the *obshchenie* exercise around the circle at the Sunday Club discussed earlier primarily responded to the exercise by articulating their emotional reaction to it. However, other group therapeutic activities specifically focus on the cultivation of rehabilitants' emotional worlds. This can be seen in the following example from The Mill.

One evening in November everyone gathered around one of the large tables in the dining room for one of Lena's art therapy sessions. This evening the session was to focus on the emotional world of the rehabilitants. Specifically, Lena asked them to draw three different images: one image representing what they consider to be one of their own negative emotional characteristics, another that represents one of their positive emotional characteristics, and a third representing how the two can be brought together. There are a couple of important implications that come from Lena's instructions that are important for understanding the Church-run program's approach to working on emotional worlds. First, although it is understood that negative emotions are just that, and primarily so because they impede proper sociality and moral relations, positive emotions are also to some extent questionable. That is to say, positive emotions must also be controlled. Just as asocial emotions must be managed and controlled so as to allow for sociality, so too positive emotions should not hinder appropriate and moral social relations. Thus in this exercise the rehabilitants must show how both the negative and the positive can become one moderate and controllable emotion.

Second, this exercise is not about revealing a genuine feeling that lies hidden and must be disclosed through therapeutic work, nor is it about ridding oneself of the negative emotion. Rather it is about beginning the process by means of imagination of ethically working on oneself to become a new moral person who has cultivated the capacity to manage and control the various aspects of one's emotional world. All people, according to the Church-run program following Orthodox moral theology, have negative emotions and overly positive ones as well; the ethical key is to control and manage them. When one has cultivated the capacity to experience a negative emotion and, in that very social context and moment, can change it into a less negative emotion that does not hinder one's sociality, then one has become a more morally disciplined person. The process of becoming a new moral person is in part a process of the ethical transformation of the internal disciplinary management of one's emotional world. This can be seen in the way Lena responded to two of the rehabilitants' images.

Boris is twenty-five and has been shooting heroin for ten years. He arrived at The Mill about a month prior to this session, and it was well-known that one of his main concerns was meeting a woman to marry. He had come to believe that his only chance to stop using was to find a wife. He raised this topic for discussion in several group sessions and seemed particularly concerned that no woman would love him because he is HIV-positive, which is a very common concern among rehabilitants. Needless to say, his zeal for finding a wife did not go unnoticed by the female rehabilitants, most of whom eventually avoided being around him.

Therefore no one was surprised at Boris's three images: three wavy lines with the word *fear* written underneath (he told us the lines indicated the shaking of his body that was sometimes caused by his fear), a heart with the word *love* written underneath, and a heart with a crack in it with the words *broken heart* (*razbitoe serdtse*) written underneath. He explained that although he has many fears in life that stop him from doing things he would like to do, he most fears the rejection of women. This fear is compounded, he said, because he has a lot of love that he wants to show to someone but is afraid it will not be reciprocated. His fear combined with his love leave him with a broken heart.

Lena was not happy with Boris's drawings and explanation. In her view, he did not properly follow the instructions of the exercise. Instead of imagining and then drawing how one can train oneself to manage, control, and alter one's emotional world, Boris drew representations of his currently experienced emotional world. He did not imaginatively find a way to manage fear and love into a new and workable emotion, but instead revealed the way various aspects of his emotional world actually work together and the result they leave him with. This failure to follow the instructions was further compounded by the fact that the resulting broken heart is just the kind of negative and asocial emotion one is supposed to attempt to manage.

After explaining all this to Boris, Lena then interpreted his images in a way that she thought would be more useful for him according to the parameters of the exercise. She acknowledged that both fear and love were appropriate images that, as far as she knew him, represented important aspects of his emotional world. But she suggested that patience would be a better way to reconcile the two than with a broken heart. "You already know what that is like," Lena told him in reference to the broken heart. "Why don't you try patience?" She explained that love is a powerful emotion, and in some sense fear is an appropriate counter-emotion, but when fear gets in the way of love it becomes a problem. This is why the broken hearts occur, she told the group and Boris. But if fear can be combined with love by means of patience, then broken hearts need not occur. With patience one can slowly but strongly build a relationship that will result in mutual love for one another.

In the context of an American drug treatment program, Carr explains, therapists engage in much hermeneutic work in their sessions with clients.[32] Much of this work focuses on what the client doesn't say. Lena's work, though certainly a case of hermeneutic analysis, is of a different kind. Instead of asking probing questions and waiting for "true" rev-elations, Lena actively suggests and authoritatively shows why another imaginative possibility is a better approach for the ethical purposes of the exercise she is leading. As I argued earlier, unlike the attempts in the American context to reveal the true and genuine self covered over by addiction, in the Church-run program the attempt is to create new moral persons. This is precisely what Lena is doing in her interpretive therapeutic work. After pointing out the negative cyclical nature of Boris's emotional world, she shows him how another option will more productively help him achieve his goal of finding a loving wife. If a rehabilitant is unable to do the imaginative work Lena deems necessary, she will step in to authoritatively discipline him in the expectation that eventually he will begin to get it right himself.

In the same therapy session, in fact only about ten minutes after the exchange between Lena and Boris, Kristina presented her three images. Kristina is twenty-two, has been using heroin on and off since she was sixteen, and has a three-year-old daughter whom Kristina's parents have mostly raised. This is the second time Kristina has been a rehabilitant at The Mill. As she told me, she did not take her first time in rehab very seriously, thinking that just spending time away from the drug and the city would be enough, and she began using heroin again within a week of returning to the city. Now, six months later, she claims to understand what she needs to do and intends to live in a nunnery after her three months are over. The staff agree that this time Kristina is certainly working much harder on herself than she had the first time.

Kristina's three drawings were a giant eye looking at a dollar sign, clothes, and other consumer products, with the word *envy* written underneath; the word *humility* with no image (she said that she could not think of an image that represents it); and two people facing one another and smiling, with the word *well-wishing* (*dobrozhelatel'nost'*) underneath and the phrase "I am calm" (*Ya spokoina*) written on the body of the figure representing herself. Kristina explained that she is often envious of what other people have in their life—such as money, a good job, nice clothes, and a family—and this leads her to feel bad about herself and want to get high. She said that sometimes she can also be very humble, which she agreed is generally a good thing to be, but if one is too humble it too can lead to feeling bad about oneself. Interestingly both Kristina's negative and positive emotional characteristics potentially lead her to have negative attitudes and relations with herself. This, however, is reconciled in the third image and the emotional characteristic of well-wishing, which is represented by her calmly being with another person. For Kristina the two emotions are imaginatively managed by means of intersubjectively being with others in a way that does not lead her to feel bad about herself.

Lena was quite pleased with Kristina's images and explanation, so much so that she had very little to say in response. What she did say, however, is very important for understanding the Church-run program's approach not only to working with rehabilitants' emotional worlds, but to the therapeutic process in general. Lena simply commented that she liked the image of the giant eye because it represented the self-centered nature of negative emotions, which are to a great extent driven by egoism. She said that the last image represented very well what is hoped will be the outcome of the therapeutic process at The Mill: people who are able to engage in normal relations (*normal'noe otnoshenie*) with other persons. Indeed, as the words "I am calm" inscribed on Kristina's imagined body suggest, this therapeutic training of emotional management is primarily about controlling the bodily intersubjectivity between persons, and in doing so cultivating the embodied ability to live a normal life.

Lena did not say much in response to Kristina because in her view Kristina had already done the appropriate work on herself in the process of imagining, drawing, and explaining the images and emotional characteristics. This is generally Lena's therapeutic strategy: to authoritatively correct and discipline when a rehabilitant is not doing the proper work, and to authoritatively acknowledge and support when the work is being done properly. In other words, when ethical work on the self is done well, nothing much more needs to be said; it simply needs to be acknowledged as such. But what had Kristina done well? And how was it different from Boris's work?

Kristina recognized that both of her emotional characteristics—envy and humility—potentially led her to feel bad about herself. This is so because, in Lena's interpretation of Kristina's self-analysis, both of these are driven by egoism and self-love. The giant eye suggests an overinflated self-image looking out at the world and comparing oneself with others. In the case of envy, this comparison reveals the lack of certain material objects and social relations in the life of the self-centered person. In the case of extreme humility, the person is potentially led to disengage from social relations because such extreme forms of humility can result in a kind of self-love that isolates one from other persons. But with what Kristina calls "well-wishing" she opens herself up to others in intersubjective sociality that is characterized by emotional and bodily calm. Thus what Kristina recognized and Lena authoritatively supported was that when emotions—both negative and positive—are not properly managed and controlled they lead to asocial behavior, and when they are properly managed and controlled they lead to normal social relations.

Boris, on the other hand, did not recognize this important distinction. All three of his images focused on himself and asocial behavior. Although Lena did not say it, his images were, for lack of a better word, inspired by egoistic concerns about finding a wife. In Lena's interpretation even Boris's "love" is a matter of wanting someone to love him, rather than his being able to love others. Her recommendation of patience is an option that would allow him to engage in proper social relations with others and to build a strong and lasting loving relationship. Boris failed to work on himself in this therapeutic activity because he was unable to escape the self-centered focus of his emotional world.

This example shows the importance the Church-run program puts on the distinction between asocial and social emotional worlds. In particular it highlights the centrality to this distinction of the problem of egoism. Outside of the formal therapeutic program at The Mill I observed rehabilitants during free moments either working on themselves to overcome their own asocial emotional world or disciplining others for their asocial emotional worlds.

THAWING OUT IN FREE MOMENTS

Earlier I mentioned that I once heard a conversation on the smoking porch in which a rehabilitant felt abandoned because her mother had not called her in a month, and that this was an example of the kind of *obshchenie* that occurs in the free moments at The Mill. This particular instance also revealed how rehabilitants can discipline others and their asocial emotions as they are manifested in intersubjective relations. It

was a Tuesday afternoon in late October and several persons were standing on and around the porch smoking. Packages sent by parents and
relatives had just arrived from the city, which occurs every Tuesday
when a volunteer drives to the city to pick up medicine, these packages,
and assist Oleg at the Tuesday reception at the hospital. Rehabilitants
usually look forward to this day since for most of them it means the
arrival of, among other things, new packs of cigarettes, candies, and
photos. Since Zhanna's arrival, however, she had not received any packages from home. So while everyone on the porch on this day was talking
about what they received, Zhanna sat silently. By now it was well-known
that Zhanna was not receiving any packages or phone calls from home
and was beginning to feel quite depressed about it. For the most part
people tried to be respectful about her feelings, but on this day it seemed
to have been forgotten as people spoke all around her about their packages. Zhanna was looking increasingly depressed.

Suddenly a rehabilitant who had just arrived that past Thursday and
who apparently knew nothing about Zhanna's situation asked her why
she looked so sad. At first Zhanna tried to avoid the question by giving
a quick smile and taking another drag on her cigarette. But he per-
sisted. "What's wrong with you?" he asked. Others took notice and gave
him dirty looks. "What did you get in your package?" he asked Zhanna.
She replied, "I didn't get anything. I never get anything." He said,
"Well I didn't get anything either, why be so upset about it?" With this
Zhanna began to cry and told him and everyone listening that she
felt abandoned, that her mother had not called since she arrived, that
she got no packages, and that she felt completely alone. Then she fell
silent and cried. Two of the female rehabilitants rushed over to her
and put their arms around her, whispered something in her ear, and
led her inside.

The rest of us stood silently for a few moments, not knowing what to
say. The new rehabilitant awkwardly took a drag from his cigarette. Suddenly Ksusha began to explain to him not only Zhanna's situation but,
more important, why he acted inappropriately even though he didn't
know her situation. "Couldn't you see she didn't want to speak? When
you are here you have to learn how to think about others' feelings, you

cannot think only about yourself." Then Aleks interjected, "You didn't receive a package because you just arrived, but she hasn't gotten one for a month. It is completely different, but you tried to make it the same."

Both Ksusha and Aleks authoritatively disciplined the newly arrived rehabilitant. They recognized that he was new and did not know Zhanna's personal situation, but more important, they interpreted his actions and words as manifestations of his self-centered and egoistic emotional world. This was most clear in Ksusha's words. She chastised him for thinking only about himself and told him that in rehabilitation he will need to learn to "think about others' feelings." She articulated the common discourse that drug users are self-centered egoists who think only of themselves and that rehabilitation is a process of controlling and managing these asocial emotions, and in doing so being able to engage in social relations. From the perspective of those on the porch, the new rehabilitant could do neither: not only could he not control his own asocial emotions, but because of this lack, he caused Zhanna to lose control of her asocial emotions.

This is an example of how rehabilitants can sometimes help discipline one another in their quest to become new moral persons. Although this is a particularly obvious example, there are numerous others that could serve just as well. For example, I once witnessed Boris being admonished by a female rehabilitant for not thinking of the feelings of the women at the center in his seemingly never-ending quest for a wife. Another time I watched as two male rehabilitants told a third that his recent depression was beginning to affect his work and that this made more work for them; they told him he needed to start dealing with it better so as not to affect others as much. In each of these examples rehabilitants took the Church-run program's perspective that asocial emotions result in asocial behavior, and thus must be controlled and managed. They disciplined their fellow rehabilitants by encouraging them to work on themselves, thus also serving to bring about a more supportive context for their own work on themselves. They encouraged a therapeutic context in which each rehabilitant must cultivate the self-discipline necessary to manage her own emotional world, and in so doing exhibit a sense of responsibility not only for herself but for the therapeutic community.

I also witnessed rehabilitants working in free moments on their own emotional worlds. Anger is the most common asocial emotion with which people at The Mill try to work. Anger erupts often there, in many different contexts and for many different reasons. For example, rehabilitants become angry at other rehabilitants because they think that the other has in some way insulted or disrespected them, or because they think the staff is not treating them fairly in terms of work assignments, or because they hear that a boyfriend has started using heroin again and has left their child at a parent's house, or at nothing in particular or their life situation in general. Anger, in various manifestations and degrees, is not difficult to find at The Mill.

However, it is far from the case that rehabilitants at The Mill immediately work on their anger, or any other asocial emotion, or immediately discipline it in others. It is much more common that anger and other asocial emotions are expressed without any public attempt to ethically work to control or manage it. Indeed The Mill is a place where the public expression of asocial emotions is quite common. However, on occasion rehabilitants consciously make an effort during free moments to ethically work on their emotional sensibilities in ways that accord with the approach of the Church-run program.

For example, I once witnessed Katya, a twenty-two-year-old from a St. Petersburg suburb, who had been at The Mill nearly two months, react with anger toward Klara, who had told her that for the third day in a row the staff had scheduled her to work in the kitchen. Most try to avoid this work assignment because it means beginning work one hour earlier and finishing over an hour later than everyone else. Katya's first reaction was to begin yelling at no one in particular, "Why? Why always me?" After a few seconds of this she fell silent and put her arms on her waist, took a few audible deep breaths, and smiled at Klara. "Okay, what can I do?" she simply said, and Klara responded with a nod of her head, as if to agree that nothing could be done, and therefore the anger was only hurting herself.

Of course I cannot know why Katya became so angry. It could have been from a feeling of injustice at what she viewed as the unfair scheduling of kitchen duty. It could also have come from what the staff would label egoistic feelings that led her to think she should not have to do such work. The cause of Katya's anger is not important for our purposes; what is important is that she was able to catch her anger in the moment of its manifestation and bring it under control so that it did not lead to potential further troubles, such as offending Klara. (I have seen this cycle of anger and offense occur several times at The Mill.)

It is particularly interesting that Katya used a technique taught by the Church-run program to rehabilitants to be used in just this kind of situation. Vladimir Alekseevich, the psychologist who runs the orientation meetings, explained this technique in terms of training the rehabilitants in moments of anger to "pause yourself [*sdelai pauzy*]" and to "figure out what is behind the anger." It seems that this is precisely what Katya did in this situation, and in doing so was able to maintain a good sense of sociality with Klara. More important, she was able to ethically work on herself so as to better control her anger. It is this kind of ethical work, so rehabilitants are taught and most try to enact, that must be repeated over and over outside of the formal programs of the rehab center, which potentially lead to the cultivation of the kinds of sensibilities and dispositions deemed necessary for living a normal life.

TEN

Disciplining Responsibility

LABOR AND GENDER

Prayer, confession, *obshchenie,* and managing one's emotional world may all be vital to the process of making normal persons, but ultimately the Church-run program recognizes that a normal person must also, as Oleg once put it to me, "contribute to society." Two aspects of the therapeutic process at The Mill closely related to the idea of a normal life as a contribution to society were expressed to me many times throughout the course of my research: a normal life in relation to work and a normal life in relation to family, particularly in terms of relations between genders. Both of these hold a primary place in the therapeutic process.

LABOR THERAPY AND THE ETHICAL DISCIPLINE OF WORK

Earlier I argued that in contemporary Russia a normal person living a normal life is primarily characterized as a financially self-sufficient

working person who enjoys, to varying degrees, the comforts of consumer and material products and whose primary responsibility is to
his family, his closest friends, work, and himself. What might be considered the foundation for this kind of normal responsibilized person
is the ability to engage in appropriate forms of sociality and maintain
self-discipline and control over his emotional world. The image of this
normal person and life can be seen on television commercials and programs, in magazines, and on the streets of most major cities in Russia.
It can also be heard in the words of many of the rehabilitants in the
Church-run program. As Roma explained, "[A normal life] means that
I make enough money to fully provide for myself in terms of housing
and food and some small trivialities [melochei, which in this context refers
to unnecessary but pleasurable consumer products]." When I met Igor
at The Mill he was twenty-two and there for his second time. On that
day, wearing an apron and working in the kitchen because most of the
women were sick, he said, "[A normal life is] a life where my desires, not
dreams, but ordinary grounded desires will come true." When I asked
how this would come about he told me, "What can I do? I can get a job
and I will buy myself everything I want." Now an ambulance driver back
in the city, Igor is attempting to construct this normal life for himself in
just the way he described it.

While the Church-run program may not endorse such a consumer-
oriented lifestyle, it does support and encourage what it considers to
be a normal life, which is very similar to that described by many of
the rehabilitants. For example, once while I was talking with Natalia
Aleksandrovna about the ultimate goal of the program, she told me that
it goes unquestioned that the primary goal of rehabilitation is eternal
salvation, and this requires sobriety. But as she went on to tell me, each
person has his own will and can choose the level of his participation
in the Church. Since the majority of those who rehabilitate with the
Church-run program do not choose to participate in church life to the
extent that is hoped, Natalia Aleksandrovna considers a return to normal
life a marker of success. Or as she put it, this return to normal life is
characterized by rehabilitants' "social adaptation, return to their family,
or creation of their own [family]. It is also getting a job or returning to

school." Her words echo those written by Father Maxim in his thesis on the Church's view of drug addiction: "Bearing in mind that not everyone is able to answer the call of God and the Gospel of Christ, a minimum goal is also set . . . [the return] of the person to normal life in society."[1]

With that minimum goal, which is perhaps the main goal of most of the rehabilitants, much of the therapeutic process in the program can be viewed as disciplinary training for this kind of life that most rehabilitants have never experienced as adults. Indeed, as much theoretical and empirical research has argued, whether or not one is a rehabilitating drug user the very process of coming to live a normal life in either an industrial or postindustrial consumer-driven society is a disciplinary process of ethically making oneself into a new kind of person.[2] This has been particularly the case in postsocialist Eastern Europe, where both local and global investors, entrepreneurs, and business managers have considered the creation of a new class of self-regulating, responsible, and disciplined workers to be essential for a successful transition to a market-based economy.[3] Perhaps unique about the context at The Mill is that while much of this kind of neoliberal discipline has been imposed on those who have already been a part of the labor market in Russia, the vast majority of those at The Mill have never had or never successfully held a job. In a sense, then, the labor therapy and training at The Mill must begin from the very beginning in training rehabilitants to become productive members of the new post-Soviet working class.

THE DAILY SCHEDULE

To begin with, it is important to consider the center's daily schedule, which, at least theoretically, is exactly the same every day, Monday through Friday. It looks like this:

7:00 Wake up
7:15 Exercise
7:30 Prayer service
8:10 Breakfast

9:00 Beginning of the working day

2:00 Lunch

3:00 Continuation of the working day

6:00 End of the working day

6:10 Spiritual conversations and fitness

7:00 Dinner

7:30 Group activities

10:30 Evening prayer service

11:00 Lights out (first attempt)

11:30 Lights out (final)

Every morning, including Saturday and Sunday, wake-up is at seven, and those who are working in the kitchen and on the farm that day wake up at six. I have never seen anyone exercising in the morning, other than playing Ping-Pong, and until a new rule was imposed in January forbidding smoking until after breakfast, the time between waking up and morning prayer was usually spent smoking on the side porch. The morning prayer service, as is the evening service, is led by the staff member working that day; it is held in the church and lasts until about eight.

Like all meals, breakfast begins with everyone standing, facing an icon, and praying, after which the men sit at one table, the women at another, the volunteers at a third, and the staff at a table of their own. The food is served one bowl at a time by the two women who have kitchen duty for the day. It is expected that there will be no talking, a rule that is followed when Father Maxim is on duty and is followed to varying degrees with the other staff. During each meal one of the rehabilitants stands at a podium to the side reading biblical stories from a book for children or stories of the lives of saints. After everyone is finished eating, which is more or less when the staff member finishes his or her meal, everyone stands once again for a prayer spoken in unison. On most mornings and after most meals there is a break of about twenty to thirty minutes before the next scheduled activity, during which time most rehabilitants smoke and sit around chatting. It is against the rules for anyone at any time of the day to go back to bed. These disciplinary practices of prayer and spiritual readings frame each day, meal, and activity for the rehabilitants and are closely related to those in a monastery, thus placing the rehab center within an authoritative disciplinary structure.

At nine the workday begins and continues until six, with an hour break for lunch. Keep in mind, however, that the two women working in the kitchen and the several men working with the farm animals have been working since six in the morning. Every evening the staff member assigns each rehabilitant a certain job for the following day, so that to some degree work duties rotate daily. The women tend to work in the kitchen, do laundry, clean all the buildings, and in season work in the gardens and greenhouses. The men, who also work in the gardens and greenhouses, work with the farm animals and in the garage and wood-working shop, maintain the *banya* on Thursdays, cut down trees and chop wood, and build anything that needs to be built. Work is clearly conceived and doled out along traditional gender lines and thus reveals the way the Church-run program conceives of a normal life and the kinds of jobs and gender relations of which it consists.

Between six and dinner, which is often before seven, there is free time for rehabilitants to relax, exercise, read, or chat with one another or with a staff member. After dinner the group therapy sessions begin and continue until about ten. The evening prayer service is more or less the same as the morning service. After prayer there is usually a small amount of free time, during which everyone relaxes, talks, and prepares for bed. When Father Maxim and the deacon are on duty, lights out is usually held to as the official schedule dictates; however, when Lena and Oleg are on duty lights out can go up to an hour later than scheduled. This is just one of the many examples, including talking during meals, of how the disciplinary atmosphere is quite different based on which staff member is working. The next morning the same schedule is repeated. The only exceptions are on weekends: the first half of Saturday is a working day and the rest of the day is free of labor, and Sundays are entirely free of labor and there is an expanded morning church service.

This is the disciplinary schedule kept by all rehabilitants at The Mill for the three months of their rehabilitation. Through its daily, weekly, and monthly repetition, it is meant to mold rehabilitants into persons who are able to live within a temporal structure that mimics that of normal life. Because the vast majority of rehabilitants have never worked or studied, they have no, or very little, experience living within such a temporality. Indeed the schedule and the long days are the focus of most of the complaints I heard from recently arriving rehabilitants, as well as the theme of a lot of the advice given to them by those who had already been there for some months.

Such a schedule is not uncommon in therapeutic institutions, and in fact seems to be an essential part of the therapeutic process.[4] In his ethnography of a shelter for homeless persons in Boston, Robert Desjarlais argues that "a system of values was embedded in the uses of and calibrations of time" within the shelter. While Desjarlais is right to point out that the use of a strictly regulated daily schedule promotes a hierarchy of power relations between staff and therapeutic clients, for our purposes it is important to note how in doing so it also ethically trains rehabilitants for a normal work life. Just as the homeless shelter maintains a daily schedule to help clients "learn how to act and think in better accord with the rhythms of time inherent in work settings and mainstream American capitalist culture," The Mill attempts to prepare rehabilitants for a similar capitalist labor culture waiting for them in post-Soviet Russia. Rehabilitants are expected to embody the same morality of "responsibility, self-discipline, reliability, and personal integrity" that the homeless shelter attempts to establish.[5]

If one of the main goals is to prepare rehabilitants for a normal life in contemporary Russia, then it is not surprising that ethical training of regulated temporality is a significant part of the process, for the restructuring, fragmentation, and regulation of time is a significant aspect of the industrial and postindustrial world. It has been argued that the post-Fordist economy that defines much of contemporary capitalism is characterized by a temporal compression that demands flexibility.[6] The kind of manual labor jobs The Mill prepares rehabilitants for, however, are still primarily structured by more modernist conceptions of time and the kind of responsibility and discipline associated with it.[7] By disciplining persons in the rhythms of a workday and workweek, with its standard schedule of eight to ten hours, five days a week, accompanied by leisure time in the evening and weekends, the temporal training at The Mill resembles the kinds of temporal adjustments needed in the daily lives of young women working in factories in Malaysia rather than the flexible and transnational temporality of financial traders or quasi-full-time workers at such corporations as Walmart.[8]

The temporal structure of the day and its repetition over weeks and months is a significant aspect of the therapeutic process of ethically training rehabilitants for a responsible normal life in contemporary capitalist Russia. Simply by their very presence at The Mill, rehabilitants over time come to embody the temporal rhythms necessary for living a normal life in contemporary capitalist Russia. Within this daily schedule further ethical training becomes a process of disciplining responsibility.

DISCIPLINING RESPONSIBILITY THROUGH LABOR

Notwithstanding the occasional weekend seminars on how to use computers, the vast majority of the work done at The Mill is manual labor. Thus the Church-run program is preparing rehabilitants to enter Russia's lower class of manual laborers. If this is so, then it is certainly understandable that the ethical cultivation of responsibility is at the center of the disciplinary goals of this therapeutic process. For although responsibility and self-discipline are necessary at all levels of the neoliberal capitalist workforce, it could be argued that it is particularly important to the workings of this economic system that they be part of the very foundation of this system's labor market, that is, the manual laboring class. Therefore, if labor therapy at The Mill can be considered a kind of career training, then it is not so much a particular labor skill that is central to this training, although many of the rehabilitants return to the city to find jobs utilizing these very skills, but rather the embodied responsibility that will prove necessary to successfully enter the labor market and live a normal life.

One aspect of this ethical training of responsibility is cultivating a kind of Levinasian responsibility to the other.[9] As Father Maxim explained as we drove along the dirt road leading to The Mill on my very first visit, "Labor therapy is meant to teach them how to be responsible." This was important, he said, because the work done by rehabilitants is what kept The Mill running, for the vast majority of the food, furniture, and buildings, as well as all repairs, are produced by rehabilitants. When Father Maxim explained labor therapy in terms of responsibility, he was speaking in this context of responsibility to others and to the rehab community (*kollektiv*). In this sense labor therapy is a process of learning that in order for the community or group or family to do well, each individual person must do what is required of her. Many of the rehabilitants who have been at The Mill for some time recognize this, as can be seen when they discipline new or less responsible rehabilitants about their lack of work ethic.

This lesson of the responsibility one has toward others was clearly learned by some of the more successful ex-rehabilitants, that is, those who have not started using again. For example, Sasha once told me that the most important thing he learned in rehab that helped him overcome his addiction is that he has to be responsible for something: "I learned that I cannot just care about myself, and I couldn't even do that before really, but I need to have something to care about [*zabotit'sya*], something to be responsible for [*otvetstvennym*]." When I asked him what he meant by this, he told me that to be responsible for something meant that an other relied on him. To be responsible for and care about something or someone is to embed oneself in a relationship of mutuality, a relationship that is constituted in the very expression of responsibility. Neither the responsibility nor the relationship can exist without the other. What Sasha learned, and what has helped him remain heroin-free for nearly two years, is that he must engage himself in a network of social relations in which he feels significantly responsible for that network's very survival. He found just such a network of social relations in his friendship with Max, his volunteer work with the Church's palliative care program, and his previous friendship with Misha and Zhenia.

Aleksei, one of the ex-rehabilitants and palliative care volunteers I met at the Sunday Club, made an interesting connection between the labor therapy he did at The Mill and his volunteer work. I asked him about his time at The Mill and what he thought was particularly helpful for him there. He replied that he thought working with the animals on the farm was the most important thing he experienced at The Mill: "Before this I never had the experience of being responsible for another person or animal. And with this work I learned that I could really care about and love another thing and not just myself, and more important that my love for this animal was what kept it alive. That was powerful for me. So I have tried to use that lesson in my life here in the city, and now I work as a palliative care volunteer and try to help people with HIV and other illnesses stay alive or at least feel that they are not alone."

Aleksei was able to cultivate a morality of responsibility for others in the context of working with farm animals, and then transfer that sensibility into relations with other persons. His newfound responsibility has become manifest in his volunteer work at one of the AIDS centers in St. Petersburg and in his marriage to a woman he met at the Sunday Club. He has integrated himself into various sets of social relations in which he takes responsibility for the care of others and, in doing so, shows them that they are not alone in this world. Further he has learned that he too is not alone in the world. For both Sasha and Aleksei responsibility for others is not simply a matter of giving themselves over to another; more important for their very survival as former drug users, responsibility for others entails that they embed themselves in networks of social relations that depend on them enacting responsibility for others. In other words, the kind of responsibility for others cultivated at The Mill is a responsibility of sociality.

But it would be misleading to say that this is the only kind of responsibility worked on at The Mill, for inextricably linked to responsibility for others is self-responsibility, or what might be called self-discipline. We have already seen how this self-responsibility as self-discipline is worked on by rehabilitants in terms of controlling their emotional worlds. It is also worked on at The Mill in the context of labor therapy through disciplinary strategies enacted by staff, volunteers, and senior rehabilitants meant to cultivate the kind of self-discipline and responsibility thought necessary for the making of new moral and normal persons. The reflexive aspect of responsibility is perhaps more clearly seen in the Russian word *otvetstvennost'*, which has as its root *otvetit'*, the verb meaning "to answer." *Otvetstvennost'* is probably better translated as *answerability*, which more clearly reveals this concept's reflexive nature. To be responsible often entails being answerable to an other; to be answerable in the first place means being answerable to oneself and one's acts, thoughts, and emotions. It is just this sense of self-responsibility, or self-answerability, that is worked on at The Mill, particularly during labor therapy.

One afternoon I was with Oleg as he walked around The Mill, as he does every few hours to see how the day's work is progressing and to keep an eye on the rehabilitants. Two young women were preparing dinner in the kitchen and a third young woman, Natasha, was ironing and folding laundry on one of the dining-room tables. When we arrived in the dining room Natasha was just exiting the kitchen and sitting back down in front of the laundry. Unfortunately for her, no one except the daily cooks is allowed in the kitchen. As he walked past her he nonchalantly said with a smile, "That is a card."

On the wall in the staff office is a list of all the names of the rehabilitants currently at the center. Under their names are spaces to place small colored cards; a green card is a reward for having done something positive or out of the ordinary, a blue card is given for breaking a rule, three blue cards result in a red card, and one red card plus one blue card almost always lead to being expelled. The vast majority of blue cards are given for transgressions against disciplinary rules in the context of labor therapy, as in this case with Natasha. For getting caught in the kitchen she received a blue card. She protested, explaining that she was trying to pass on a message to someone in the kitchen who couldn't hear her, but Oleg pointed out that instead of going into the kitchen she could have just stuck her head through the service window between the two rooms and told the woman. As he said this he stuck his head through the window and, wearing a big grin, made a sarcastic remark to the two women in the kitchen. Everyone, including Natasha, laughed and Oleg and I continued our walk.

Notwithstanding the lighthearted nature of this disciplinary encounter, the fact remains that Natasha was punished for her transgression of disciplinary boundaries. As the laundry person for the day, her duties were to take laundry in and out of the machine, hang it to dry, and sit in the dining room and iron and fold. She is, of course, allowed to take toilet breaks and occasional smoke breaks, but other than this she should be working in her designated space. This regulation of space and time is not unlike the kind of governance one would experience in any other workplace, and it is the assumption of the staff that the rehabilitants must learn how to live within this disciplinary regime. Therefore when Oleg found Natasha outside the bounds of her designated spatial limits he immediately and, from his perspective, with justification assigned her a discipline card.

While this was clearly a punitive encounter characterized by clear power distinctions, the role of humor cannot be passed over. In his important work on ethical subjectivity the philosopher Simon Critchley argues that humor can play an important role in the shaping of new moral persons, or what he calls ethical subjectivities, in that it allows for the sublimation of the anxiety of the constant demand to work on oneself.[10] I have seen some rehabilitants angrily argue with Lena after receiving a disciplinary card and others humbly accept one from Father Maxim, even if they later grumbled about the injustice of the punitive action. Oleg, however, often uses his humor and lightheartedness to ease such tensions. Natasha may very well have felt that the punitive action was unjust. After all, what harm comes from her briefly going into the kitchen? But Oleg's sarcastic tone and his performative mimicry of how she could have relayed the supposed message to those in the kitchen worked to transform any feelings of injustice into laughter, thus effectively covering over, or sublimating, any anxieties Natasha may have felt.

Still the disciplinary effect was not lost. Later that afternoon I asked Natasha about what had happened. She told me that she knew she wasn't supposed to be in the kitchen but that she really was trying to relay a message from someone who had briefly entered the dining room and tried to shout something to those in the kitchen. She knew the women in the kitchen hadn't heard, so she went in to tell them. In most cases she would have gotten away with this, but unfortunately it was not the free moment she thought it was, and Oleg walked in and caught her. I asked her how she felt about receiving the card. She told me that of course she was not happy to be disciplined, but she had broken the rules and so must be held responsible. Next time, so she told me, she will do as Oleg said and talk to them through the service window. She went on to tell me that Oleg's sense of humor helped her not to react with negative emotions, and because of this she could more clearly see that she had in fact broken the rules, even if for what she thought was a good reason. While Natasha may not have put it in these words, this encounter most certainly had a disciplinary effect on her that the staff hope will help her cultivate a sense of self-responsibility and discipline.

This is so not simply because Natasha claimed that she now understood that she must be responsible for keeping the rules of The Mill. It is quite possible that she told me this only because she thought it was what I expected to hear or because she knew it was what she should say. Disciplinary techniques are rarely so effective that they lead to this kind of one-to-one correlation between the disciplinary act and a change of behavior by means of cognitive understanding. Natasha certainly knew this rule before she broke it, and yet she did break it; knowing a rule has nothing to do with whether one obeys it. It seems more likely that this disciplinary strategy is effective because it places a material limit on Natasha's future behavior. Because she wants to remain at The Mill she will more closely ethically watch herself in moments when the transgression of a rule becomes possible. Thus, this technique of disciplinary cards works to cultivate self-responsibility because it forces rehabilitants consciously and ethically to alter their own behavior so as to remain on the new life trajectory of a self-disciplined, normal, and responsibilized moral person.

If the disciplinary cards were the most common way of training self-discipline and responsibility at The Mill, then labor itself can also be used as a disciplinary technique. Once I arrived at The Mill when everyone was resting after eating lunch—everyone but Nika, who was on her hands and knees just inside the front door of the main building cleaning between the wood planks with a toothbrush. She smiled and gave me an "I can't believe this either" look, and I asked her what she was doing.

She explained that the day before she had tracked in a large amount of mud on her shoes after having worked in the fields all day. Father Maxim had seen this and disciplined her with extra work. She finished the story by telling me, "I should have known to clean my feet before I came in." Thus she understood her transgression and the disciplinary technique was effective in getting her to reflect on her own sense of self-discipline and responsibility for the cleanliness and orderliness of the communal property.

But how do Nika's words fit with her smile and the look she gave me? At first I interpreted the look to mean that she thought the punishment was too harsh; I took it to be an expression of the resigned frustration that many rehabilitants feel at times toward what they view as unnecessary therapeutic procedures and disciplinary strategies. However, after hearing Nika's comment that she should have known better, I believe it is more appropriate to interpret her look as an expression of her frustration with herself, an expression of a person who knows she should have done something differently but didn't, an expression of a person who, although she certainly wished she was not cleaning between the floorboards with a toothbrush, understood why she was doing just that. This look, combined with her acknowledgment that she should have known better, suggests that Father Maxim's disciplinary technique may have had some success in provoking Nika's sense of self-responsibility, as well as her responsibility for others in the *kollektiv*.

The way this disciplinary technique works is the reverse of the way the disciplinary cards work. Whereas the card system puts a material limit on transgressions and thus seeks to shift the ethical work from a cognitive understanding of rules to the intentionally cultivated embodiment of rules, the technique of extra disciplinary labor forces the rehabilitant to cognitively recognize that she broke a rule. Prior to this incident Nika may not have considered that tracking mud into the main building affected others, but after being disciplined into recognizing that someone must in fact clean the mud she tracked in by means of the very tedious process of cleaning between floor boards with a toothbrush, it is unlikely that she will forget in the future. Thus, this labor discipline enacted through the bodily experience of a hurting back, sore knees, squinting eyes, and cramping fingers works to imprint responsibility to others on Nika's bodily memory and cognitive understanding.

There are, however, innumerable examples of rehabilitants who do not understand and refuse to accept discipline and responsibility. As I have already mentioned, it is not at all uncommon for those Lena disciplines to argue back, or for those who humbly accept Father Maxim's discipline to complain about it, sometimes bitterly, in other company. In other words, The Mill is clearly a place of contestation and tension, and there is little doubt that much of this has its roots in the unequal power relations between staff and rehabilitants and the punitive regime of discipline often used for ethical training. But as Eugene Raikhel shows, this punitive approach is common throughout the entire spectrum of post-Soviet drug and alcohol treatment programs.[11] Likewise this disciplinary approach also has clear roots in the Orthodox monastic tradition. Given these local religious and secular traditions, the staff of The Mill perceives this tension simply as the necessary resistance of new initiates to a new life trajectory that promises a normal life requiring just the kind of self-discipline and responsibility they are attempting to provide by means of these disciplinary techniques. Should rehabilitants ever question these techniques, the staff need simply reference the examples of those ex-rehabilitants such as Sasha and Aleksei who claim that above all it was the responsibility they learned at The Mill that helped them to remain heroin-free after leaving. A rehabilitant who wants to live a life free of heroin can say nothing in response. His inability to respond discloses his powerlessness.

DISCIPLINING LIFESTYLE, DISCIPLINING GENDER

Self-discipline and responsibility go beyond the work ethic. As Elizabeth Dunn and Alexei Yurchak have pointed out in the case of postsocialist factory workers in Poland and entrepreneurs in Russia, respectively, a significant aspect of reshaping one's personhood in the context of advanced capitalism is a matter of disciplining one's lifestyle.[12] By consuming the appropriate products, dressing in the appropriate manner, and spending one's free time in appropriate spaces doing appropriate activities, one is able to fashion oneself into the kind of person who is publicly recognized as normal and potentially successful.

The same transformative process is under way at The Mill. Although it is well understood that the vast majority of rehabilitants will not advance to the level of middle management or entrepreneurship that Dunn and Yurchak primarily focus on, the staff at The Mill continually focus on rehabilitants' public self-presentation as an important aspect of remaking themselves into new moral and normal persons. Therefore, staff emphasize the importance of how rehabilitants look and dress. Most important, they remind rehabilitants to keep their clothing clean and to wear different clothes each day. Although work was manual labor, rehabilitants were expected to maintain a fresh and clean appearance, which the staff considers important not only for how one appears to others, but how one sees oneself. One's appearance not only reflects one's personhood to others, but reflexively turns back in on oneself to dialogically construct the new inner person. If physical and material cleanliness is important to this process, then so too is moral cleanliness, for any clothing with symbols or words the staff considers inappropriate, such as sexually explicit words or suggestions, are strictly forbidden. Additionally, rehabilitants are encouraged to wear gender-specific clothing.

If clothes are an important sign and mirror of one's new moral personhood, then so too is the body. There is no requirement on how often a rehabilitant must wash herself; however, staff, volunteers, and even other rehabilitants criticized those who did not maintain a clean appearance. Tattoos are also a point of contention. Many of the male rehabilitants have tattoos on their arms, shoulders, and necks, many of which were made while in prison. The staff generally and strongly urged rehabilitants to keep their tattoos covered whenever possible, metaphorically erasing their past self. If these tattoos were acquired when they were drug users, marking their time in prison or with fellow users on their bodies, then the attempt to cover them is an attempt to cover over, erase, or move beyond that time and person-as-drug-user.

Soon after I got one of my tattoos I was at The Mill, walking around enjoying the warm sun with Maxim, one of the volunteers. After some time he asked about the tattoo; he wanted to tell me how stupid I was for getting it. "I have all these tattoos too," he told me as he rolled up his sleeves to show me, "and I regret every one of them. Now all they do is remind me of how much of my life I wasted and can never get back." No matter how much he tries to cover over the markings of his past life, and no matter how much the staff at The Mill tries to cover them, Maxim will never be able to forget who he was and what he had once done. His past is permanently marked on his body.

Hair is also an important external sign of oneself. As with the gender-specific clothing, so too hair is maintained along gender lines. Men must have short hair; in fact most had buzz haircuts. I never met one female rehabilitant with hair shorter than shoulder length, which actually says more about gender-specific performance in Russia in general rather than The Mill in particular. Hair was not much of a disciplinary problem at The Mill; Zhanna, however, caused much tension with her hair. When she first arrived she had long braids down her back, several of which were colored red, green, blue, and black, which contrasted with her naturally light brown hair. From nearly the beginning Father Maxim told her that her hair was a sin and that she needed to get rid of the braids. Zhanna resisted. Increasingly the staff confronted her about changing her hair and made random comments to her in the hall of the main building, on the smoking porch, and during group therapy sessions. Eventually, after Father Maxim arrived one day and saw that she still had not changed her hair after over a month of the staff's "encouragement," he told Lena that he was not happy about this and that it needed to be changed as soon as possible. Zhanna was called into a private meeting with Father Maxim and Lena to discuss the issue. When I saw Zhanna later that evening she no longer had braids and had dyed blonde hair. She gave me a slight smile as we passed each other on the stairs, and I could see that she had recently been crying. I did not ask her about the change, but later Olga told me that Zhanna had been given an ultimatum to get rid of her braids and dye her hair an acceptable color or leave The Mill. In the end simple power differential worked to enact the change on Zhanna. Whether or not she continued to leave her hair in this more acceptable form after she was finally kicked out of The Mill I have no way of knowing. Suffice it to say, I have my doubts.

Although a good deal of self-discipline and responsibility depends on one's appearance, more important is how one manages and controls oneself in relations with others, specifically gender relations. In the Church's view, a central characteristic of a normal life is being married and having children. Although the importance of marriage and family is often reiterated to rehabilitants, relations between rehabilitants are strictly forbidden. In fact such relations are grounds for immediate dismissal from The Mill. There are at least three reasons for this strict policy against relations between rehabilitants.

First, it is widely claimed that such relations impede the necessary concentration one needs to ethically work on oneself. This claim is made not only by staff, but also quite often by rehabilitants, particularly by male rehabilitants. Several young men told me they wished The Mill was an all-male center because the very presence of women sometimes made it too difficult to focus on themselves. Sexual temptation was an obstacle to the ethical work necessary to overcome addiction. Father Maxim went so far as to link sexual temptation with drug use when he told me that giving in to both is a matter of an underdeveloped moral will. It is the strengthening of this will, or what I would call self-discipline, that Father Maxim sees as the foundation of the Church-run program. Second, and related to this, is that such relations go against the general rule of thumb that a former drug user should not be the significant other of another former drug user. In the view of the Church-run program, such a relationship is too dangerous because neither person in the relationship has the sober experience thought necessary to provide strength in times of temptation. For example, when it was widely believed that Zhenia and Misha started using again, several people in the program told me they expected as much because they had both been users. The reality, however, is that every ex-rehabilitant I either knew or had heard had gotten married had married another ex-rehabilitant. This is not surprising considering that the new social networks of most ex-rehabilitants tend to consist primarily of other former drug users, not to mention the ever present stigma they continue to live with as former drug users and, for most, HIV-positive persons. The third reason The Mill has a strict policy against rehabilitants having relations is the danger of what the

Church calls fornication. Because, in the view of the staff, rehabilitants do not yet properly understand what a true and loving relationship in the eyes of God consists of, and because young people can so often confuse sex with love, it is assumed that any kind of relations between genders at The Mill is a sexual relationship. Such a relationship outside of marriage is by definition a sin. Despite the dangers of a coed rehabilitation center and the desire expressed by many to have single-gender centers, the fact is there is no money for two centers. Thus the dangers and temptations brought on by this coed structure are the result of the same socioeconomic constraints that led many of the rehabilitants to begin using in the first place and limit other options for treatment within the city and country.

I have already mentioned how the gendered division of labor at The Mill reflects the Church's vision of the labor force in contemporary Russia. This same division of labor is also representative of how the Church views intrafamilial relations. The Russian Orthodox Church holds a very conservative view of gender relations within the family. (Indeed this may also describe the predominant conception of the family in contemporary Russia.) Therefore the gendered division of labor can be seen as ethical training for how persons are expected to behave within the traditional family.

According to the Church's institutional position on social relations and society, marriage between a man and a woman is not only a natural relation of harmony, but a fulfillment of God's plans for the unification of the "two different modes of existence of one humanity [*dva razlichnykh obraza syshchestvovaniya v edinom chelovechestve*]" that each embodies.[13] Further, Orthodox moral theologians claim that it is a Christian duty to marry.[14] As clearly articulated in the Church's position that there is a biological, natural, and essential difference between men and women, marriage is not only meant to unite these two "modes of existence," but is also vital for the proper upbringing of children. For example, in a recent newspaper interview Father Chaplin, the deputy head of the Department of External Church Relations in the Moscow Patriarchate, said, "Single-parent, half-families will be unhappy and produce increasing numbers of unhappy people."[15]

The internal relations of this Orthodox family are defined by a gendered hierarchy and division of labor. According to Metropolitan Philaret, the husband is the head of the family, taking on the ultimate responsibility for its well-being.[16] Although the Church's *Social Concept* does not make this claim explicitly, it is implied in the gendered division of labor it claims is vital to the family, in which the man has the "supremacy in responsibility [*pervenstve v otvetstvennosti*]."[17] The husband holds responsibility for the overall well-being of the family, although *well-being* is not defined by any of these authors or documents. The wife's main duty, on the other hand, is to care for the children.[18]

Similar gendered distinctions can be said to characterize the public discourses on marriage in contemporary Russia. Sociological research suggests that traditional gender distinctions and inequalities have increased in the postsocialist period, which appears closely related to the widespread view of a natural, biological, and essential difference between men and women.[19] As Michelle Rivkin-Fish has shown in her analysis of sex education courses for medical personnel and teenagers, gender distinctions and roles, as well as gendered familial duties, are increasingly naturalized and discursively tied to biological differences.[20] Thus, although there is still contention and ambiguity about how Russians feel about the "proper role" of the different genders in the family, it seems clear that the traditional family has become the ideal image in post-Soviet Russia.[21]

The early years of the Soviet Union saw several ideological and practical attempts to address the so-called women's issue. To some extent this proved successful in terms of bringing women into the workforce. But critics point out the "double burden" that existed for many Soviet women in the late Soviet period in terms of working in the labor force and still bearing the burden of running the household.[22] Indeed, despite Soviet claims, Sergei Kukhterin argues that the Soviet regime contributed to the preservation of a patriarchal hierarchy by keeping men in the dominant positions in society.[23] In post-Soviet Russia men have continued to expect this dominant position both in society and increasingly within the family, an expectation that many women appear willing to accept if husbands can adequately provide support and lend an occasional helping hand with children.[24]

Whenever I walked into the kitchen at The Mill I felt as though I was in a space where I did not belong. Other than the bedrooms, the kitchen is the only space at The Mill that is off-limits to a gender. Because anyone who is not working in the kitchen that day is not allowed in it, and because men never work in the kitchen, men are essentially barred from the space. This de facto exclusion of men from the kitchen was apparent in the looks of surprise and bewilderment I got each time I entered the kitchen. Despite these looks, I used my ambiguous position within the center to cross this gendered threshold in order to find out just what happens on the other side.

The kitchen was a place for intimate conversation among rehabilitants, since the work and the close environment made for a comfortable setting. There is something about chopping vegetables, peeling potatoes, and drinking tea that makes talk easy. One of the most common topics I discussed with the women who worked in the kitchen was family. Most of them, still in their very early twenties, already had a child back in the city, and most had done hardly anything to take care of the child. After all, how could they? As they pointed out, they could barely take care of themselves. A heroin user on the system (systematic daily use) has only one task: remaining on the system. Child care is not compatible with the system. For this reason, the parents of these young women tended to be the primary caretakers for their children.

It is not what they hope the future will be like. All of these women expressed the hope that they would be able to return to the city and care for their child, and eventually either find a husband or marry their current boyfriend. (Most of the boyfriends are also drug users, and the women claimed they would marry them only if they too went through rehab.) Because of this hope for a family several women told me that one of the most important aspects of their rehabilitation at The Mill is the fact that they will learn some of the skills necessary in marriage. As Klara once put it to me, "I never cooked a meal in my life, and here I am now making a big pot of soup. And yesterday I made cheese and *tvorog* (curd cheese). If I'm going to take care of my baby and have a husband,

I need to know how to cook and how to keep a house. It's good I'm learning that here." Once while Zhanna and I ironed and folded clothes she told me, "My mother always did this. I guess it is good to learn to do it. Someday when I have my own family I'll need to do it too." For Klara, Zhanna, and many other female rehabilitants, to be a wife and a mother is at least partially characterized by a specific gendered division of household labor.

Similar comments were made by male rehabilitants concerning the work they performed for labor therapy: "I may never work construction, but someday when I'm married I'll need to know how to fix things around the apartment"; "I'm going to marry my girlfriend when I get back to the city, and I plan on furnishing our apartment with furniture I make myself"; "Someday I want a nice dacha in the countryside for my family to go to, and I want a *banya* there too. I've spent so much time here preparing this *banya* each week, now I know how to do it." Just as many of the female rehabilitants envisioned their future with their children and a husband, so too many of the young men hope to have a future with a wife and children. And just as the women conceived of this hoped-for family in terms of a gendered division of labor, so too did the men. Wives cook, clean, take care of children, and wash and fold clothes; men repair things around the house and either build the house themselves or provide the means to purchase it. Men also hope to earn enough for luxuries, such as a country home with a *banya* so the family can peacefully relax outside the city. The staff support these images by emphasizing the importance of marriage in a proper Orthodox life, and everyday notions of gendered life in contemporary Russia also support these gender divisions. This convergence significantly narrows the range of possibilities available for gendered identity. There is little wonder, then, that the gendered division of labor at The Mill went entirely unquestioned by any rehabilitant with whom I spoke.

It is not enough that a normal person can engage in open sociality with the appropriate range of emotions, or work diligently while showing responsibility for both himself and others. A normal person must also do these normal activities in the right spaces and while presenting himself properly. These spaces and self-presentations are often very specifically gendered, upholding Orthodox institutional views of gender and marriage as well as a long history of this traditional divide that, despite discursive lip service, was never transcended during the Soviet period. It is little wonder, then, that this conservative gendered divide is being worked onto the bodies of rehabilitants at The Mill and has also come to characterize the lifestyles and division of labor of the increasingly more numerous neoliberal subjects in contemporary Russia.[25]

Some Closing Words

If from the Russian Orthodox Church's perspective HIV can be considered God's blessing, then this book has shed light on the unintended consequences of this blessing. The Church considers HIV a blessing because it believes the illness provides a motivation for persons to change themselves. The Church-run program provides a context in which this change can take place, and the hope, if not the expectation, is that this change will result in an enchurched person. But as we have seen, not only is this rarely the case, but the very ethical practices utilized in the program provide rehabilitants with the possibility to live a normal life in the neoliberal world the Church sets itself against.

Perhaps in these final pages it is appropriate to raise the question that has been an underlying thread to much of this book: How are we to understand the undeniable fact that much of what happens in the

Church-run program is more akin to what we generally categorize as nonreligious or secular therapeutic practices? To put it plainly, is this a sacred or a secular therapeutics? A simple response would be that it is both, and indeed this is how much of the staff characterize what takes place. Staff point out that they often borrow techniques in part or in toto from organizations or disciplines that they characterize as secular, such as Alcoholics and Narcotics Anonymous and psychotherapy. I often had the impression that this was done for the purpose of convincing the American researcher that the Russian Orthodox Church is a quite modern and global institution capable of and willing to borrow those discourses, techniques, and practices that are widely considered to be best practices for drug rehabilitation. If I am right about their motivations, then we can count these staff members among the majority of those in the world today who appear to make very clear distinctions between what counts as religious and what counts as secular. Perhaps even more surprising is their implied belief that the secular is the mark of the modern, and therefore the mark of best practice for therapeutics.

This implication contradicts the official discourse of the Russian Orthodox Church, which clearly articulates an alternative view of modernity that places Orthodoxy at its very center as modernity's only hope for meaning and morality in the contemporary world. And it reveals just how deeply the basic tenets of secularization theory have filtered down into everyday life. This theory's distinction between the secular and the religious in the modern world, with the former being the marker of modernity, progress, and efficiency, has been recently and increasingly criticized.

According to Talal Asad, for example, modernity is not, as is commonly thought, characterized by the dominance of the secular to the exclusion of religion.[1] Nor is it simply true that the secular and the religious cannot be separated. Rather modernity's central characteristic is that what counts as secular and what counts as religion mutually constitute one another. Each depends on the other for its very existence. This is true not only because each is partly defined in opposition to the other, but also because of the various discourses and practices they share in common. Thus for Asad modernity is distinguished by the mutually constituting hybridity of apparently distinct categories, of which the sacred and the secular mutually constitute one another as modernity's definitive distinction.[2]

I suggest that this mutually constituting process is at work in the Church-run program, despite the staff's rhetorical efforts to highlight the secular aspects of the therapeutic process. I further suggest that it is this very tension between the secular and religious aspects of the therapeutics of the Church-run program that helps create a space of inclusion-exclusion for rehabilitants to discover the range of possibilities available to them for living a normal life. Having found themselves in this space of possibility rehabilitants have the opportunity to set themselves on a new life trajectory by means of consciously working on themselves in order to ethically cultivate a new moral personhood.

If neoliberalism is the paradox of the active construction of spaces of inclusion-exclusion for the purpose of providing the context within which self-disciplined and responsibilized persons can be cultivated, then it seems that The Mill and the Church-run program in general are an instance of this new neoliberal space. Further, if Agamben's contention that modernity is at least partly characterized by the increased focus on the bare life of the individual of unalienable worth, and the decentralization of the power that works on this bare life in the hands of bureaucrats, physicians, and priests, then the assemblage of the religious and secular in the form of moral training and human rights as therapeutics in the context of the Church-run program should in no way be surprising. In the space of The Mill and the Church-run program we have all the key ingredients: a separated space for the moral disciplining of a marginal population, decentralized administration of this space by priests, therapists, and nongovernmental (Russian Orthodox Church) bureaucracy, a focus on the cultivation of responsibility and a normal life as good citizenship, and the undeniable truth that the failure of this cultivation and disciplining often leads to the total abandonment of those individuals who cannot be disciplined, and in many cases to their eventual death. Clearly, then, we can view the Church-run program as spaces of inclusion-exclusion par excellence for the subjectivization of modern, neoliberal subjects.

A NORMAL AND SANE LIFE

When Sasha told me that The Mill offers the opportunity to live a normal life and the possibility of continuing this life back in the city, he left unsaid the point that this possibility rests on the cultivation of a sense of responsibility for others that begins with a responsibility for oneself. In other words, echoing what Oleg once told me, The Mill does not offer a place to come and rest for some time; rather the normal life they offer rehabilitants is an authoritative and disciplinary structure within which ethical work must be done in order for there to be any hope that such a life will be possible back in the city.

Throughout this book I have offered examples of what some might call the resistance of rehabilitants to the various techniques meant to cultivate this normal life. Does this mean The Mill is a context of agentive resistance rather than a context of normalization? The answer is that it is neither. In his important critique of the anthropological concept of agency, Asad points out that this concept, and its conceptual partner, resistance, rely on the paradoxical position that "the self to be liberated from external control must be subjected to the control of a liberating self already and always free, aware, and in control of its own desires."[3] This assumed autonomous aspect of the person would need to be free of all influences of power in order to do the work many theorists expect of agency. But as others have shown,[4] and what I have been trying to show here, even in those moments of conscious ethical work that I call the moral breakdown, the ethical subject still finds herself enmeshed in a social world of power, discourses, interest, history, and traditions. An awareness that one is ethically working on oneself should not be misinterpreted as autonomy.

In response to this ideologically driven fascination with autonomy, Asad borrows the concept of sanity from the philosopher Susan Wolf. According to Wolf, to be sane is "a desire that one's self be connected to the world in a certain way—we could even say it is a desire that one's self be *controlled by* the world in certain ways and not in others."[5] Asad elaborates on this and argues that to live sanely in the world "presupposes knowing the world practically and being known practically by it, a world of accumulating probabilities rather than constant certainties."[6] To live sanely in the world, then, is to a large degree to live what Russians call a normal life. But to live a normal life, or a sane life, is *not* to live a life determined by any one discursive and authoritative structure. Rather it is to cultivate a certain sensibility for living within a particular range of possibilities that *counts* as a normal or sane life. Because every society is constituted by a number of competing discursive traditions, this sensibility entails the capacity to negotiate between them and in so doing live a sane life. I suggest that responsibility as I have described it here is a foundational moral disposition that allows for this kind of life in the contemporary world increasingly dominated by a neoliberal discourse.

Ian Hacking argues that with the rise of the statistical analysis of society in the nineteenth century, the concept of normal people came to replace the Enlightenment cardinal concept of human nature.[7] This conceptual shift came about due to what Hacking named "the taming of chance," or the recognition that a world not entirely determined could still be regular and controllable. Statistical techniques, laws, and probabilities became the main tools for taming the sociopolitical world. Out of this conceptual and technical shift came the notion of normalcy, or the adherence to statistical laws and probabilities. As Hacking puts it, "People are normal if they conform to the central tendency of such laws, while those at the extremes are pathological."[8] To be normal is not to adhere to one specific way of living—or one specific disciplinary and discursive tradition—but to live within an acceptable range of what counts as normal. I believe this is what Asad means when he says that living sanely in the world is to know and be known by the world practically, and that this world is constituted of accumulated probabilities and not certainties. In other words, the social world is a range of possibilities, and to live in it sanely is to have the sensibility for negotiating these possibilities. As I have argued throughout this book, the moral disposition of responsibility is the neoliberal virtue par excellence because it allows individuals to "freely" live within this range. In this sense it could be argued that neoliberalism is the ideological expression of an everyday life that has come to be dominated by statistical analysis. Or put another way, it is the metadiscourse for a world increasingly characterized by competing discursive traditions.

Hacking further claims that what counts as normal is affected by individuals attempting to be normal.[9] That is, as persons work on themselves to fit themselves within the range of what counts as normal, this range is itself altered. Unlike unalterable laws of nature, the laws of normalcy are alterable by means of a kind of feedback system between discourse and subjects. It is in this sense that The Mill is neither a context of resistance nor of normalization. It would completely miss the point to claim that rehabilitants' contestations of certain techniques and aims of the Church-run program are examples of their resistance, for more so than any staff member, therapist, or administrator, rehabilitants claimed that their main motivation for entering rehabilitation was to finally have a normal life. But they also know that a normal life is not as narrowly defined as the Church would sometimes have it. Instead they are very aware that a normal life in Russia today is constituted by a range of possibilities that, despite their plurality, provide equal opportunities for living a sane life. It is this knowledge that leads them to contest *certain variants* of a normal life offered by the program, and in the process potentially alter the range of what counts as normal.

For this reason it would be just as wrong to say that The Mill is a context of normalization, if that means the attempt to fit oneself or to have oneself fit into a preestablished normative mold. There is no one normal life. Just as in statistical analysis normal indicates a distribution, so too a normal life can be conceived of as a distribution of possibilities. The main goal of the Church-run program may be to ethically train rehabilitants into a moral way of being for one of these possibilities, yet the fact is the program provides a context in which the ethical skills, the most important of which is the moral disposition of responsibility, are offered so that rehabilitants can potentially return to the city and live out any of these possibilities. This is what Father Maxim calls the minimum goal of the Church-run program.[10]

In fact rather than normalization it may be more appropriate to say that the Church-run program helps rehabilitants cultivate freedom. I intend the concept of freedom in the sense that Barry, Osborne, and

Rose use it in their description of liberalism, that is, freedom as "well-regulated and 'responsibilized' liberty."[11] Freedom understood in this sense is a "formula of rule," a formula for the constitution of persons as at one and the same time subjects and objects of power. That is to say, responsibilized freedom as a "formula of rule" is that which allows persons to negotiate the range of possible discursive traditions, and thus the range of possible ways of living normally in a social world. In this sense it is possible to say that the Church-run program provides the space for the cultivation of responsibilized free persons who, though they may not choose the path of enchurchment, are now better prepared to choose an acceptable life trajectory within the range of possibilities for living a normal life in contemporary Russia. This cultivated responsibilized liberty thus prepares rehabilitants to reenter the market-style neoliberal social context of today's Russia.

It would be a mistake to conclude that rehabilitants seek, and do not resist, a normal life because they are attempting to get away from a life that is so filled with suffering. There is no doubt that the desire to get away from a particular kind of suffering has motivated many rehabilitants to seek a new life, but couldn't the same be said about many others in the world who may or may not suffer just as much? Isn't the factory worker striving for a less strenuous and higher paid position, or the doctoral student hoping for a professorship, or the weekly participant of psychotherapy, the illegal immigrant working three underpaid jobs, even the so-called resisters in third world factories—aren't they all striving for a life of sanity? Aren't they all striving to live a life in which they know and are known by the world practically, a life in which they feel at home? Drug users are no different from the vast majority of human beings; they simply offer a more obvious example of what most of us hope for.

Now, at the end, it is appropriate to return to Andrei, the twenty-year-old whose mother found him dead from choking on his own vomit. No one would disagree that Andrei's life ended tragically, and that the suffering he experienced was shared by several others in his life, not the least of whom is his mother. Andrei did not resist a normal life; he simply was unable to break the hold that heroin had placed on him.

Like most people, Andrei simply wanted to feel at home in his world and know that he was not the cause of his mother's suffering, and for three short months he was able to do this. If it wasn't heroin that hadn't pulled him back in, but some other, more mundane vice or temptation, it is quite likely that Andrei would be alive today. Although everyone at some point experiences breakdowns, unfortunately when a user does it is much more obvious and potentially much more lethal. The heroin user is no different from you and me in his desire to live a normal life or the fact that breakdowns sometimes occur that lead him away from this life. The difference is in the potential consequences. And it is this difference that every rehabilitant is aware of; they all know someone just like Andrei. They all know that heroin can wait. So when Sasha told me, "Most of the people who come [to The Mill] will return to the city and start using again. Everyone knows this. So more than anything, in my opinion, what is possible here is the chance to live a normal life, even if for only a few months," he was not simply expressing the very real difficulties of rehabilitation. More important, he was expressing the very real hope that is offered at The Mill: the hope that another life is possible, and maybe, just maybe, one can find a way to keep heroin waiting just a little bit longer.

BARE LIFE AND RESPONSIBILITY

Andrei's fate is not uncommon among heroin users in Russia today. So it is not surprising that there is often a palpable sense of desperation among rehabilitants at The Mill as they ethically work on and for their very existence as bare life. They know that they too could end up like Andrei. Indeed, on several occasions I was told something like the following: "Everyone I know is either dead or in prison. If I don't change now I will end up like them." The program's staff at all levels of the diocesan organization is keenly aware that the therapeutic process is focused on the bare life of IDUs. I suggest that rehabilitants' desperation over their very survival, and the staff's awareness of this desperation, further solidify and disclose the power differentials I have tried to describe.

I have argued that the Church-run program in the St. Petersburg area, and The Mill in particular, can be viewed as a paradigm of the kind of society the Russian Orthodox Church would like to establish based on their vision of human rights as that which limits and provides the parameters for a proper moral life. This vision is intimately linked with the cultivation of responsibility and self-discipline. If it is true that human rights discourse has now become the world's dominant moral discourse, it still takes various forms and is utilized for different ends in different sociopolitical contexts.[12] Despite these differences, human rights in general, particularly in the sphere of health, have in the age of neoliberal governance increasingly supported disciplinary regimes of responsibilization.[13] As Robins and Biehl have shown for South Africa and Brazil, respectively, this is particularly so regarding the responsibilization that comes with the right to access to antiretroviral treatment for people living with HIV/AIDS.[14] Therefore it should come as little surprise if responsibility has become a central aim of the Church's human rights vision. This is particularly so since responsibility is a central concept in the Church's moral theology and closely linked to this theology's emphasis on the inherent worth of all persons.

Thus, although at first glance the human rights espoused by the Russian Orthodox Church and secular (neo)liberal organizations may appear to be quite different, a closer analysis centered on the notion of responsibility reveals the deep similarities in both expected dispositions and referential contexts of these two discourses. The ease with which the Russian Orthodox view of human rights so easily matches some of the most basic aspects of the secular (neo)liberal view of human rights brings us back to Agamben's analysis of the *homo sacer* and the way it links the sacred and the sovereign, and how this link in turn discloses the centrality of bare life to the work of power. Despite the secular (neo)liberal discursive emphasis on empowerment, which Lupton has argued is a rhetorical strategy for cultivating self-responsibility and self-discipline within individuals,[15] both discursive regimes work directly on fragile bodies in order to *limit* individuals' acts, thoughts, emotions, and relations in such a way that they adhere to a particularly defined authoritative and disciplinary moral tradition, and as such aim to turn those bodies into responsibilized subjects. In other words, neoliberalism and Russian Orthodoxy share the notion that responsibility in its relation to rights is about cultivating and enacting limits rather than enabling the expansion of moral possibilities. In both cases, the disciplinary work of human rights attempts to transform the fragile body of the *homo sacer* into the cultivated body of a normal and responsible subject.

This, however, should not be taken as a contradiction of what I argued in the previous section about the cultivation of sensibilities to live sanely within a moral range of possibilities. In fact when I speak here of Russian Orthodox and neoliberal discursive regimes of human rights limiting moral possibilities, I mean it in the very same way I discussed the cultivation of a sane life. To live a sane or normal life is to live within a certain range of possibilities. And as anthropological research is increasingly showing, the cultivation of responsibility, self-discipline, and self-control, in other words, the cultivation of limits on one's way of being in the world, has become the dominant ethical strategy in much of the world today for living sanely within these possibilities. In other words, there is a constant tension between the creativity and freedom of ethics, and the limitations of morality and its possibilities.

Agamben claimed that the Nazi death camps are the paradigm institution of modernity. But perhaps it is better to think of the work or reeducation camp as the paradigm model instead. The problem with death camps as a paradigm of modernity is that they are a place from which persons do not return. If sovereign power ultimately hopes to have control over the bare life of subjects, then subjects must not simply be killed, but instead must be trained and reeducated. Peter Redfield has argued that refugee camps run by Médecins sans frontières can be viewed as just such a space of inclusion-exclusion that serves to reeducate persons with "less undesirable social norms and political expectations."[16] That Redfield goes on to point out that these social norms can also include those of ethnic resentment and nationalist sensibilities only more clearly highlights the ways such camps help cultivate subjects and objects of power.

This process of reeducation takes place at The Mill and in the Church-run program. By now it is well understood that the work of many international and nongovernmental institutions and organizations can be viewed as a form of transnational governmentality that disseminates and further secures the mechanisms of neoliberal governance.[17] Similarly it has been argued that evangelical faith-based social activism, which is founded on a theology of grace, compassion, and accountability, is well suited to neoliberal forms of governance because of its expectation that recipients of charity are held accountable for changing their sinful behavior as a condition of receiving aid.[18] It may be surprising, however, that the Russian Orthodox Church, which has focused a good deal of its institutional and public discourse on critiquing this new world order, would ultimately find itself working to support it. But this is the ironic fate of the Church-run program, for ultimately it produces responsibilized subjects who are now *better* disciplined to participate in the very Western-oriented neoliberal world from which the Church had hoped to save them. It is perhaps with this ironic twist that the strength of sovereign power's grip on bare life can most clearly be seen, for even when rights are explicitly meant to provide limits, as they are in the Russian Orthodox Church's view, they cannot help but support and strengthen the very sociopolitical regime they are intended to limit.

Notes

1. For an example of the difficulty of transforming one's moral personhood, see Mahmood 2005.
2. McLellan et al. 2000: 1689.
3. Skoll 1984; Frankel 1989; Swora 2001; Carr 2006; Ozawa-de Silva 2007.
4. For studies of drug users, see Waterston 1993; Bourgois 1995; Singer 2006. For a study of a drug treatment program, see Hunt and Barker 1999: 126.
5. Hunt and Barker 1999: 129–30.
6. Asad 2003.
7. Russian Orthodox Church 2008.
8. Foucault 2000b.
9. It should be mentioned that secular (neo)liberal NGOs working on the HIV epidemic in Russia also appear to make this same link.
10. Agamben 1998: 114–5.
11. Ibid., 8.
12. Ibid., 122.

13. Mann, et al. 1999.
14. Agamben 1998: 133.
15. Kistner 2003.
16. Biehl 2005.
17. Comaroff 2007.
18. DeCaroli 2007: 56, 67–69.
19. For a similar understanding of Agambian spaces of inclusion-exclusion, see Hansen and Stepputat 2005: 18.
20. Rivkin-Fish 2005a: 72–73.
21. For example, Martin 1995: 266–67; Bourgois 2000.
22. Agadjanian and Rousselet 2005.
23. Barry, Osborne, Rose 1996: 10–12.
24. Yurchak 2003: 73.
25. On business and administrative relations, see Yurchak 2003; Collier 2005. On consumer practices, see Patico 2008. On medical and welfare services, see Rivkin-Fish 2005b; Teplova 2007.
26. Wolf 1987; Asad 2003.
27. Wolf 1987: 55.
28. Asad 2003: 73.
29. Hacking 1990: 2.
30. Collier 2005: 373.
31. Teplova 2007: 289.
32. Butler 1993; Yurchak 2003, 2006; Mahmood 2005.
33. See, for example, Austin 1962; Bourdieu 1991; Butler 1997.
34. Butler 1993: 95.
35. For an important analysis of how this was done in the late Soviet period, see Yurchak 2006.
36. Yurchak 2003: 75.
37. Deleuze and Guattari 1987: 406.
38. Collier and Ong 2005: 4.

CHAPTER ONE

1. Feshbach 2006: 9–11.
2. UNAIDS 2006.
3. Quoted in Malinowska-Sempruch, Hoover, and Alexandrova 2004: 204.
4. Wallander 2006: 42.
5. Levinson 2004: 53
6. Heimer et al. 2006: 151.
7. Ibid.

8. Malinowska-Sempruch et al. 2004: 196.

9. Feshbach 2006: 24.

10. Brown and Rusinova 2000.

11. Feshbach 2006: 7.

12. Powell 2000: 126.

13. Sontag 1989: 17.

14. Feshbach 2006: 12.

15. Sontag 1989: 18.

16. Meylakhs 2005.

17. Wallander 2006: 48.

18. Both The Mill and Father Maxim are actual names. I have chosen to use them for two reasons: because Father Maxim requested that I use his real name and the real name of The Mill, as did the diocesan director, and because there are no other rehabilitation centers in the region run by the Russian Orthodox Church, nor any other free rehabilitation centers for that matter. Thus any attempt to protect its identity would be senseless. All other names have been changed to protect identities.

19. Krupitsky et al. 2004: 32.

20. Field 2000: 13.

21. Ibid., 18.

22. Malinowska-Sempruch et al. 2004: 204–5.

23. Ibid., 205.

24. Ibid.

25. Ibid., 203.

26. Heimer et al. 2006: 148.

27. Ibid.

28. Robert Heimer, October 19, 2008. personal communication.

29. Pilkington 2006.

30. Ibid., 28.

31. Ibid., 46.

32. Shelley 2006.

33. Kramer 2000: 102.

CHAPTER THREE

1. Russian Orthodox Church 2005.

2. Maria Danilova, "Russian Orthodox Church Launches Campaign to Stop Spread of AIDS Epidemic," Associated Press, September 9, 2005.

3. Ibid.

4. Russian Orthodox Church, www.patriarchia.ru.

5. Russian Orthodox Church 2005: 18.
6. Russian Orthodox Church, www.patriarchia.ru.
7. Russian Orthodox Church 2005: 5.
8. Ibid., 18.
9. Russian Orthodox Church, www.patriarchia.ru.
10. Russian Orthodox Church 2000: 66.
11. Russian Orthodox Church 2005: 6–9.
12. Mefodii n.d.
13. Russian Orthodox Church 2005: 10.
14. Ibid. 8.
15. AIDS.ru, www.aids.ru/aids/pravoslav.shtml.
16. Mefodii n.d.
17. Fassin 2007: 249.
18. Russian Orthodox Church 2005: 18.

CHAPTER FOUR

1. For example, Skoll 1984; Frankel 1989.
2. Csordas and Kleinman 1996.
3. Ibid., 8–11.
4. Csordas 1997: 5.
5. Ibid., 14, italics in original.
6. Zigon 2007, 2008a, 2009b.
7. Zigon 2009c.
8. Ricoeur 1995.
9. Zigon 2007.
10. Foucault 1990, 2000a.
11. Foucault 1990: 29.
12. Voloshinov 2000.
13. Caton 2006: 51.
14. Mauss 1973.
15. Mahmood 2005: 137.
16. Ibid., 138–39.
17. Throop 2010.
18. Critchley 2007: 11.
19. Ibid.
20. MacIntyre 1989, 1991.
21. Rogers 2004: 36.

CHAPTER FIVE

1. Pletnev 2004: 24–28.
2. Avdeev 2005: 183, 197.
3. Russian Orthodox Church, www.pravoslavie.ru/sobytia/narckonf/slovopatr.htm.
4. Pletnev 2004: 30, 31.
5. Ibid., 33.
6. Ibid., 34.
7. Ibid., 34, 35.
8. Ibid., 41–42.
9. Ibid., 57.
10. Ware 1997b: 62.
11. Ware 2001: 62.
12. Ibid.
13. Quoted in Pletnev 2004: 30; *Doroga Domoi,* www.dorogadomoj.com.
14. For a description of this sociality as the basis of prayer, see Ware 2001: 105–28.
15. Vatican, www.vatican.va.
16. Ware 2001: 51.
17. Vatican, www.vatican.va.
18. Russian Orthodox Church 2000, 2005, 2006, 2008.
19. Harakas 2003.
20. Ibid.
21. See Russian Orthodox Church 2000: 21.
22. Kirill 2006b.
23. Philaret 1936.
24. Ibid., italics in original.
25. Ibid.
26. Kirill 2006b; Harakas 1993: 154.
27. Aleksii II 2006.
28. Philaret 1936.
29. Russian Orthodox Church 2001: 21; Kirill 2005.
30. Ware 2001: 59.
31. Philaret 1936.
32. Harakas 1993: 8, 38.
33. Ware 1997b: 222.
34. Ware 2001: 51.
35. Ibid., italics in original.
36. See Kelly and Volkov 1998: 26.
37. Zigon 2009a.

38. Ware 1997b: 62.
39. Payton 2007: 92.
40. Stanley S. Harakas, personal email communication, June 18, 2009.
41. See, for example, Asad 1993: 138–39; Taylor 1989: 127–42.
42. Ware 1997a: 91.
43. Ibid., 92
44. Russian Orthodox Church 2008.
45. Kirill is the former chairman of the Department for External Church Relations of the Moscow Patriarchate and widely considered the moral voice of the Church. He is the main author of several of the Russian Orthodox Church's official documents on moral and social issues, including *Basic Teaching*. In conversations and interviews with priests and other Church members Kirill is often referenced as the Church's moral authority. Since the death of Aleksii II Kirill has become patriarch of Moscow and All Russia. All references in this book to Kirill's writings and speeches are to those when he was still a metropolitan. See several speeches by Kirill on human rights at www.mospat.ru.
46. Agadjanian and Rousselet 2005.
47. See the UN's *Universal Declaration of Human Rights*.
48. Lupton 1995: 59–61.
49. Russian Orthodox Church 2006.
50. Russian Orthodox Church 2008.
51. See Agadjanian and Rousselet 2005: 50.
52. Kirill 2006b.
53. Russian Orthodox Church 2008.
54. Russian Orthodox Church 2006.
55. Kirill 2006a.
56. Russian Orthodox Church 2008.
57. Kirill 2006b.
58. Russian Orthodox Church 2008.
59. Berger 2005: 443.
60. Knox 2008: 285–86.
61. Knox 2005, 2008; Papkova 2008.
62. Papkova 2008: 77.
63. Ibid., 69.
64. Ibid., 72.
65. Agadjanian and Rousselet 2005: 32.
66. Ibid., 47.
67. Russian Orthodox Church 2000, 2005, 2008.

CHAPTER SIX

1.   Raikhel 2006: 259.
2.   Skoll 1984; Frankel 1989.
3.   Swora 2001; Carr 2006; Ozawa-de Silva 2007.
4.   McKinney 2007: 270.
5.   Swora 2001: 64.
6.   Rivkin-Fish 2001: 29.
7.   Fitzpatrick 2005.
8.   Kharkhordin 1999: 231–32.
9.   Ibid., 236–37.
10.   Ibid., 237.
11.   Kelly 2001: 320.
12.   Rivkin-Fish 2001: 30.
13.   Ibid., 30–31.
14.   Fitzpatrick 2005: 13–4; Hoffman 2003: 80.
15.   Kelly 2001: 320–21.
16.   Ibid., 311.
17.   See Fitzpatrick 2005.
18.   Ries 1997: 119.
19.   Pesman 2000: 54 n.
20.   Rivkin-Fish 2005b.
21.   Kharkhordin 1999: 242.
22.   Ibid., 244.
23.   Ibid., 245.
24.   Ibid., 246.
25.   Ibid., 247, 248, 249.
26.   Ibid., 249.
27.   For studies of Catholic and Orthodox monastic discipline, see Asad 1993; Kenworthy 2008.

CHAPTER SEVEN

1.   Kelly and Volkov 1998: 26.
2.   Mauss 2003.
3.   Mahmood 2005: 126.
4.   Robbins 2001, 2004.
5.   Robbins 2004: 275.
6.   Harakas 1993: 61.
7.   Badiou 2003.

8. Zigon 2006, 2008a.
9. Quoted in Harakas 1993: 60.
10. Asad 1993: 101–21.
11. Foucault 2000b: 249, 242.
12. Kharkhordin 1999: 63–71.
13. Scott Kenworthy, personal email communication, April 5, 2008.
14. Zigon 2006, 2008a.
15. Mahmood 2005:156–7.
16. Kharkhordin 1999: 212–30.
17. Ibid., 214.
18. Ibid., 227.
19. Foucault 1990.
20. Kharkhordin 1999: 227.
21. Nguyen 2005.

CHAPTER EIGHT

1. Yurchak 2006. See also Patico 2008, and for other postsocialist societies Rausing 2000; Fehervary 2002.
2. Yurchak 2006.
3. Ibid., 283.
4. Ibid., 106–7.
5. Stephen Kotkin, "Now Comes the Tough Part in Russia," *New York Times,* March 2, 2008; Patico 2008.
6. Humphrey 2000: 187.
7. Yurchak 2006: 107.
8. Humphrey 2000: 189.
9. Kotkin, "Now Comes the Tough Part in Russia."
10. Yurchak 2006: 109.
11. Ibid., 103.
12. Ibid., 110.
13. See Dunn 2004 for a similar argument concerning postsocialist Poland.
14. Rivkin-Fish 2005b; Caldwell 2010.
15. Barry, Osborne, and Rose 1996: 10.
16. Rose 1996: 57–60.
17. Ibid., 57.
18. Burchell 1996: 29.
19. Collier 2005: 373.
20. Ibid.
21. Kharkhordin 1999: 331.

22. Fitzpatrick 2005: 102–3.
23. Kharkhordin 1999: 142.
24. Yurchak 2006.
25. Ibid., 109.
26. See: Philaret 1936; St. Theophan 1996; Russian Orthodox Church 2000.
27. I would like to thank Melissa Caldwell for pointing this out.
28. Kirill 2005.
29. Kirill 2006b.
30. Kirill 2005; Kirill 2006b; Russian Orthodox Church 2006.

CHAPTER NINE

1. Jackson 1996: 30.
2. Wierzbicka 2003: 425–28.
3. Ibid., 425.
4. Bakhtin 1986.
5. Ozawa-de Silva 2007: 435.
6. Ricoeur 1995.
7. Mahmood 2005: 157.
8. Goffman 1961: 230, 227–28.
9. Carr 2006: 645.
10. Ibid., 636.
11. Zigon 2008a.
12. Raikhel 2006: 277.
13. Carr 2006: 634.
14. Vann 2005.
15. Although much anthropological, philosophical, and social scientific discourse makes a distinction between feelings and emotions, I do not make such a distinction here. This distinction between *chuvstva* (feelings) and *emotsii* (emotions) also exists in everyday Russian (as it does in English), although I rarely heard the distinction made among those with whom I did research. Both were used interchangeably, although *chuvstva* was much more commonly used, as was *nastroenie* (mood), although this latter was often used in much more general terms. For this reason I generally use *feelings* and *emotions* more or less synonymously, and to avoid confusion generally refer to *the emotional world of rehabilitants*.
16. For example, Shweder and LeVine 1984; Lutz 1988; Lindquist 2006.
17. Lutz 1988: 3–7.
18. Rivkin-Fish 2005b: 61–62; Lindquist 2006: 2.
19. Pletnev 2004: 37.

20. St. Theophan 1996: 283–84.
21. Philaret 1936.
22. Hunt and Barker 1999: 129.
23. St. Theophan 1996: 220, 284; Pletnev 2004: 30.
24. Philaret 1936; Kirill 2006b.
25. Philaret 1936.
26. Drapela 2006; Verdejo-García et al. 2007.
27. Fox et al. 2007; Sun 2007: 7.
28. For example, Frankel 1989; Huriwai 2002; Baker et al. 2007.
29. Frankel 1989: 172, 173.
30. Carr 2006.
31. Csordas 1997: 108.
32. Carr 2006: 639.

CHAPTER TEN

1. Pletnev 2004: 57.
2. For example, Marx 1887; Thompson 1967; Foucault 1977; Ong 1987; Dunn 2004; Olds and Thrift 2005.
3. Humphrey 2000; Yurchak 2003; Dunn 2004.
4. For example, Goffman 1961; Skoll 1984: 29–40; Desjarlais 1997; Klingemann and Schibli 2004.
5. Desjarlais 1997: 90.
6. See Harvey 1992.
7. See Marx 1887; Thompson 1967; Foucault 1977.
8. Ong 1987: 110–12.
9. Levinas 1969.
10. Critchley 2007.
11. Raikhel 2006.
12. Yurchak 2003; Dunn 2004: 69–72.
13. Russian Orthodox Church 2000: 47.
14. Philaret 1936; St. Theophan 1996.
15. Boris Klin, "Orthodox Church Spokesman on Social Issues, History, Interfaith Dialogue," *Izvestia*, April 15, 2008.
16. Philaret 1936.
17. Russian Orthodox Church 2000: 54.
18. Ibid.; Philaret 1936.
19. Vannoy et al. 1999: 5, 7; Ashwin 2000a.
20. Rivkin-Fish 2005a.
21. Ashwin 2000b: 19; Omel'chenko 2000.

22. Vannoy et al. 1999: 79.
23. Kukhterin 2000: 88.
24. Issoupova 2000; Vannoy et al. 1999; Meshcherkina 2000.
25. See Yurchak 2003.

SOME CLOSING WORDS

1. Asad 2003.
2. Ibid., 182.
3. Ibid., 73.
4. Mahmood 2005; Yurchak 2006.
5. Wolf 1987: 55.
6. Asad 2003: 73.
7. Hacking 1990: 1.
8. Ibid., 2.
9. Ibid. 2.
10. Pletnev 2004.
11. Barry, Osborne, and Rose 1996: 8.
12. Goodale 2006: 25; Merry 2006.
13. Lupton 1995.
14. Robins 2006; Biehl 2007.
15. Lupton 1995: 59–61.
16. Redfield 2005: 346.
17. Hardt and Negri 2000; Ferguson and Gupta 2002.
18. Elisha 2008.

References

Agadjanian, Alexander, and Kathy Rousselet. 2005. "Globalization and Identity Discourse in Russian Orthodoxy." In *Eastern Orthodoxy in a Global Age: Tradition Faces the Twenty-first Century*, ed. Victor Roudometof, Alexander Agadjanian, and Jerry Pankhurst. Walnut Creek, CA: Altamira Press.

Agamben, Giorgio. 1998. *Homo Sacer: Sovereign Power and Bare Life.* Stanford: Stanford University Press.

Aleksii II. 2006. "Patriarch Aleksy Greets Participants in the International Conference on 'Development of Biotechnologies: Challenges to Christian Ethics.'" www.mospat.ru.

Asad, Talal. 1993. *Genealogies of Religion: Discipline and Reasons of Power in Christianity and Islam.* Baltimore: Johns Hopkins University Press.

———. 2003. *Formations of the Secular: Christianity, Islam, Modernity.* Stanford: Stanford University Press.

Ashwin, Sarah. 2000a. *Gender, State and Society in Soviet and Post-Soviet Russia.* London: Routledge.

———. 2000b. "Introduction: Gender, State and Society in Soviet and Post-Soviet Russia." In *Gender, State and Society in Soviet and Post-Soviet Russia,* ed. Sarah Ashwin. London: Routledge.

Augustine. 1953. *Enchiridion or Manual to Laurentius Concerning Faith, Hope and Charity.* London: SPCK.

Austin, J. L. 1962. *How to Do Things with Words.* Oxford: Oxford University Press.

Avdeev, D. A. 2005. *Dushevnye Bolezni: Pravoslavnyi Vzglyad.* Moskva: Izdatel'stvo DAR'.

Badiou, Alain. 2001. *Ethics.* London: Verso.

———. 2003. *Saint Paul: The Foundation of Universalism.* Stanford: Stanford University Press.

Baker, Felicity A., et al. 2007. "Music Therapy and Emotional Exploration: Exposing Substance Abuse Clients to the Experiences of Non-drug-induced Emotions." *Arts in Psychotherapy* 34: 321–30.

Bakhtin, M. M. 1986. *Speech Genres and Other Essays.* Austin: University of Texas Press.

Barry, Andrew, Thomas Osborne, and Nikolas Rose. 1996. Introduction to *Foucault and Political Reason: Liberalism, Neo-liberalism and Rationalities of Government,* ed. Andrew Barry, T. Osborne, and N. Rose. Chicago: University of Chicago Press.

Berger, Peter L. 2005. "Orthodoxy and Global Pluralism." *Demokratizatsiya* 13(3): 437–47.

Biehl, João. 2005. *Vita: Life in a Zone of Social Abandonment.* Berkeley: University of California Press.

———. 2007. "Pharmaceuticalization: AIDS Treatment and Global Health Politics." *Anthropological Quarterly* 80(5): 1083–126.

Bourdieu, Pierre. 1991. *Language and Symbolic Power.* Cambridge, UK: Polity Press.

Bourgois, Philippe. 1995. *In Search of Respect: Selling Crack in El Barrio.* Cambridge, UK: Cambridge University Press.

———. 2000. "Disciplining Addictions: The Bio-politics of Methadone and Heroin in the United States." *Culture, Medicine and Psychiatry* 24: 165–95.

Brown, Julie V., and Nina L. Rusinova. 2000. "Negotiating the Post-Soviet Medical Marketplace: Growing Gaps in the Safety Net." In *Russia's Torn Safety Nets,* ed. M. Field and J. Twigg. New York: St. Martin's Press.

Burchell, Graham. 1996. "Liberal Government and Techniques of the Self." In *Foucault and Political Reason: Liberalism, Neo-liberalism and Rationalities of Government,* ed. Andrew Barry, T. Osborne, and N. Rose. Chicago: University of Chicago Press.

Butler, Judith. 1993. *Bodies That Matter: On the Discursive Limits of "Sex."* New
York: Routledge.

———. 1997. *Excitable Speech: A Politics of the Performative.* New York:
Routledge.

Caldwell, Melissa. 2010. "The Russian Orthodox Church, the Provision of
Social Welfare, and Changing Ethics of Benevolence." In *Eastern Christians
in Anthropological Perspective*, ed. Chris Hann and Hermann Goltz. Berkeley:
University of California Press.

Carr, E. Summerson. 2006. "'Secrets Keep You Sick': Metalinguistic Labor in
a Drug Treatment Program for Homeless Women." *Language in Society* 35:
631–53.

Caton, Steven C. 2006. "What Is an 'Authorizing Discourse'?" In *Powers of the
Secular Modern: Talal Asad and His Interlocutors*, ed. D. Scott and C. Hirsch-
kind. Stanford: Stanford University Press.

Collier, Stephen J. 2005. "Budgets and Biopolitics." In *Global Assemblages: Technology, Politics, and Ethics as Anthropological Problems*, ed. Aihwa Ong and
Stephen J. Collier. Malden, MA: Blackwell.

Collier, Stephen J., and Aihwa Ong. 2005. "Global Assemblages, Anthropo-
logical Problems." In *Global Assemblages: Technology, Politics, and Ethics as
Anthropological Problems*, ed. Aihwa Ong and Stephen J. Collier. Malden,
MA: Blackwell.

Comaroff, Jean. 2007. "Beyond Bare Life: AIDS, (Bio)Politics, and the Neoliberal Order." *Public Culture* 19(1): 197–219.

Critchley, Simon. 2007. *Infinitely Demanding.* London: Verso.

Csordas, Thomas J. 1997. *The Sacred Self: A Cultural Phenomenology of Charismatic Healing.* Berkeley: University of California Press.

Csordas, Thomas J., and Arthur Kleinman. 1996. "The Therapeutic Process."
In *Medical Anthropology: Contemporary Theory and Method*, ed. Carolyn F.
Sargent and Thomas M. Johnson. Westport, CT: Praeger.

DeCaroli, Steven. 2007. "Boundary Stones: Giorgio Agamben and the Field of
Sovereignty." In *Giorgio Agamben: Sovereignty and Life*, ed. Matthew Calarco
and Steven DeCaroli. Stanford: Stanford University Press.

Deleuze, Gilles, and Félix Guattari. 1987. *A Thousand Plateaus: Capitalism and
Schizophrenia.* Minneapolis: University of Minnesota Press.

Desjarlais, Robert. 1997. *Shelter Blues: Sanity and Selfhood among the Homeless.*
Philadelphia: University of Pennsylvania Press.

Drapela, Laurie A. 2006. "The Effect of Negative Emotion on Licit and
Illicit Drug Use among High School Dropouts: An Empirical
Test of General Strain Theory." *Journal of Youth and Adolescence* 35(5):
755–70.

Dunn, Elizabeth C. 2004. *Privatizing Poland: Baby Food, Big Business, and the Remaking of Labor.* Ithaca, NY: Cornell University Press.

Elisha, Omri. 2008. "Moral Ambitions of Grace: The Paradox of Compassion and Accountability in Evangelical Faith-Based Activism." *Cultural Anthropology* 23(1): 154–89.

Fassin, Didier. 2007. *When Bodies Remember: Experiences and Politics of AIDS in South Africa.* Berkeley: University of California Press.

Fehervary, Krisztina. 2002. "'American Kitchens,' Luxury Bathrooms and the Search for a Normal Life in Post-socialist Hungary." *Ethnos* 67(3): 369–400.

Ferguson, James, and Akhil Gupta. 2002. "Spatializing States: Toward an Ethnography of Neoliberal Governmentality." *American Ethnologist* 29(4): 981–1002.

Feshbach, Murray. 2006. "The Early Days of the HIV/AIDS Epidemic in the Former Soviet Union." In *HIV/AIDS in Russia and Eurasia*, vol. 1, ed. J. Twigg. New York: Palgrave Macmillan.

Field, Mark G. 2000. "The Health and Demographic Crisis in Post-Soviet Russia: A Two-Phase Development." In *Russia's Torn Safety Nets: Health and Social Welfare during the Transition*, ed. Mark G. Field and Judyth L. Twigg. New York: St. Martin's Press.

Fitzpatrick, Shelia. 2005. *Tear off the Masks! Identity and Imposture in Twentieth-century Russia.* Princeton: Princeton University Press.

Foucault, Michel. 1977. *Discipline and Punish: The Birth of the Prison.* New York: Vintage.

———. 1990. *The Use of Pleasure.* Vol. 2 of *The History of Sexuality.* New York: Vintage.

———. 2000a. "On the Genealogy of Ethics: An Overview of Work in Progress." In *Ethics: Subjectivity and Truth*, ed. P. Rabinow. London: Penguin.

———. 2000b. "Technologies of the Self." In *Ethics: Subjectivity and Truth*, ed. P. Rabinow. London: Penguin.

Fox, H.C., et al. 2007. "Difficulties in Emotion Regulation and Impulse Control during Cocaine Abstinence." *Drug and Alcohol Dependence* 89: 298–301.

Frankel, Barbara. 1989. *Transforming Identities: Context, Power and Ideology in a Therapeutic Community.* New York: Peter Lang.

Goffman, Erving. 1961. *Asylums: Essays on the Social Situation of Mental Patients and Other Inmates.* New York: Anchor.

Goodale, Mark. 2006. "Ethical Theory as Social Practice." *American Anthropologist* 108(1): 25–37.

Hacking, Ian. 1990. *The Taming of Chance.* Cambridge, UK: Cambridge University Press.

Hansen, Thomas Blom, and Finn Stepputat. 2005. Introduction to *Sovereign Bodies: Citizens, Migrants, and States in the Postcolonial World*. Princeton: Princeton University Press.

Harakas, Stanley S. 1993. *Living the Faith: The Praxis of Eastern Orthodox Ethics*. Minneapolis: Light and Life Publishing.

——. 2003. "For the Health of Body and Soul: An Eastern Orthodox Introduction to Bioethics." www.goarch.org/en/ourfaith/articles/article8076 .asp.

Hardt, Michael, and Antonio Negri. 2000. *Empire*. Cambridge, MA: Harvard University Press.

Harvey, David. 1992. *The Condition of Postmodernity: An Enquiry into the Origins of Cultural Change*. Oxford: Blackwell.

Heidegger, Martin. [1953] 1996. *Being and Time*. Albany: State University of New York Press.

Heimer, Robert, et al. 2006. "HIV and Drug Use in Eurasia." In *HIV/AIDS in Russia and Eurasia*, vol. 1, ed. J. Twigg. New York: Palgrave Macmillan.

Hoffman, David L. 2003. *Stalinist Values: The Cultural Norms of Soviet Modernity, 1917–1941*. Ithaca: Cornell University Press.

Humphrey, Caroline. 2000. "Dirty Business, 'Normal Life,' and the Dream of Law." In *Economic Crime in Russia*, ed. Alena V. Ledeneva and Marina Kurkchiyan. The Hague: Kluwer Law International.

Hunt, Geoffrey, and Judith C. Barker. 1999. "Drug Treatment in Contemporary Anthropology and Sociology." *European Addiction Research* 5: 126–32.

Huriwai, Terry. 2002. "Innovative Alcohol- and Drug-User Treatment of Inmates in New Zealand Prisons." *Substance Use and Misuse* 37(8–10): 1035–45.

Issoupova, Olga. 2000. "From Duty to Pleasure? Motherhood in Soviet and Post-Soviet Russia." In *Gender, State and Society in Soviet and Post-Soviet Russia*, ed. Sarah Ashwin. London: Routledge.

Jackson, Michael. 1996. "Introduction: Phenomenology, Radical Empiricism, and Anthropological Critique." In *Things as They Are: New Directions in Phenomenological Anthropology*, ed. Michael Jackson. Bloomington: Indiana University Press.

Kelly, Catriona. 2001. *Refining Russia: Advice Literature, Polite Culture, and Gender from Catherine to Yeltsin*. Oxford: Oxford University Press.

Kelly, Catriona, and Vadeim Volkov. 1998. "*Obshchestvennost', Sobornost'*: Collective Identities." In *Constructing Russian Culture in the Age of Revolution: 1881–1940*, ed. Catriona Kelly and David Shepherd. Oxford: Oxford University Press.

Kenworthy, Scott. 2008. "To Save the World or to Renounce It: Modes of Moral Action in Russian Orthodoxy." In *Religion, Morality, and Community in Post-Soviet Societies*, ed. Mark D. Steinberg and Catherine Wanner. Washington, DC: Woodrow Wilson Center Press.

Kharkhordin, Oleg. 1999. *The Collective and the Individual in Russia*. Berkeley: University of California Press.

Kirill, Metropolitan. 2005. "There Is No Freedom without Moral Responsibility." www.mospat.ru.

———. 2006a. "The Experience of Viewing the Problems of Human Rights and Their Moral Foundations in European Religious Communities." www.mospat.ru.

———. 2006b. "Human Rights and Moral Responsibility." www.mospat.ru.

Kistner, Ulrike. 2003. *Commissioning and Contesting Post-apartheid's Human Rights: AIDS—Racism—Truth and Reconciliation*. Münster: Lit Verlag.

Klingemann, Harald, and Daniela Schibli. 2004. "Times for Healing: Towards a Typology of Time-frames in Swiss Alcohol and Drug Clinics." *Addiction* 99: 1418–29.

Knox, Zoe. 2005. *Russian Society and the Orthodox Church: Religion in Russia after Communism*. London: Routledge Curzon.

———. 2008. "Religious Freedom in Russia: The Putin Years." In *Religion, Morality, and Community in Post-Soviet Societies*, ed. Mark D. Steinberg and Catherine Wanner. Washington, DC: Woodrow Wilson Center Press.

Kramer, John M. 2000. "Drug Abuse in Post-communist Russia." In *Russia's Torn Safety Nets: Health and Social Welfare during the Transition*, ed. Mark G. Field and Judyth L. Twigg. New York: St. Martin's Press.

Krupitsky, E., et al. 2004. "The Onset of HIV Infection in the Leningrad Region of Russia: A Focus on Drug and Alcohol Dependence." *HIV Medicine* 5: 30–33.

Kukhterin, Sergei. 2000. "Fathers and Patriarchs in Communist and Post-communist Russia." In *Gender, State and Society in Soviet and Post-Soviet Russia*, ed. Sarah Ashwin. London: Routledge.

Levinas, Emmanuel. 1969. *Totality and Infinity*. Pittsburgh: Duquesne University Press.

Levinson, Lev. 2004. "Russian Drug Policy: Stating the Problem and Revealing the Actual Picture." In *War on Drugs, HIV/AIDS and Human Rights*, ed. Kasia Malinowska-Sempruch and Sarah Gallagher. New York: International Debate Education Association.

Lindquist, Galina. 2006. *Conjuring Hope: Healing and Magic in Contemporary Russia*. New York: Berghahn.

Lupton, Deborah. 1995. *The Imperative of Health: Public Health and the Regulated Body*. London: Sage.

Lutz, Catherine A. 1988. *Unnatural Emotions: Everyday Sentiments on a Micronesian Atoll and Their Challenge to Western Theory.* Chicago: University of Chicago Press.

MacIntyre, Alasdair. 1989. *Whose Justice? Which Rationality?* Notre Dame, IN: University of Notre Dame Press.

———. 1991. *Three Rival Versions of Moral Enquiry: Encyclopaedia, Genealogy, and Tradition.* Notre Dame, IN: University of Notre Dame Press.

Mahmood, Saba. 2001. "Feminist Theory, Embodiment, and the Docile Agent: Some Reflections on the Egyptian Islamic Revival." *Cultural Anthropology* 16(2), 202–36.

———. 2005. *Politics of Piety: The Islamic Revival and the Feminist Subject.* Princeton: Princeton University Press.

Malinowska-Sempruch, Kasia, J. Hoover, and A. Alexandrova. 2004. "Unintended Consequences: Drug Policies Fuel the HIV Epidemic in Russia and Ukraine." In *War on Drugs, HIV/AIDS and Human Rights,* ed. Kasia Malinowska-Sempruch and Sarah Gallagher. New York: International Debate Education Association.

Mann, Jonathan, S. Gruskin, M.A. Grodin, and G.J. Annas, eds. 1999. *Health and Human Rights: A Reader.* New York: Routledge.

Martin, Emily. 1995. "From Reproduction to HIV: Blurring Categories, Shifting Positions." In *Conceiving the New World Order: The Global Politics of Reproduction,* ed. Faye D. Ginsburg and Rayna Rapp. Berkeley: University of California Press.

Marx, Karl. 1887. *Capital.* Vol. 1, Ed. Friedrich Engels. Moscow: Progressive.

Mauss, Marcel. 1973. "Techniques of the Body." *Economy and Society* 2: 70–88.

———. 2003. *On Prayer.* Oxford: Berghahn.

McKinney, Kelly. 2007. " 'Breaking the Conspiracy of Silence': Testimony, Traumatic Memory, and Psychotherapy with Survivors of Political Violence." *Ethos* 35(3): 265–99.

McLellan, A.T., Lewis, D.C., O'Brien, C.P., and Kleber, H.D. 2000. "Drug Dependence, a Chronic Medical Illness: Implications for Treatment, Insurance, and Outcomes Evaluation." *Journal of the American Medical Association* 284(13): 1689–95.

Mefodii, Father. n.d. "Mysli o VICH/SPIDe i Protivodeistvii Emu." Unpublished manuscript.

Merry, Sally Engle. 2006. "Transnational Human Rights and Local Activism: Mapping the Middle." *American Anthropologist* 108(1): 38–51.

Meshcherkina, Elena. 2000. "New Russian Men: Masculinity Regained?" In *Gender, State and Society in Soviet and Post-Soviet Russia,* ed. Sarah Ashwin. London: Routledge.

Meylakhs, Peter. 2005. "The Discourse of the Press and the Press of Discourse: Constructing the Drug Problem in the Russian Media." In *Critical Readings: Moral Panics and the Media,* ed. Chas Critcher. Maidenhead, UK: Open University Press.

Nguyen, Vinh-Kim. 2005. "Uses and Pleasures: Sexual Modernity, HIV/AIDS, and Confessional Technologies in a West African Metropolis." In *Sex in Development: Science, Sexuality, and Morality in Global Perspective,* ed. Vincanne Adams and Stacy Leigh Pigg. Durham, NC: Duke University Press.

Olds, Kris, and Nigel Thrift. 2005. "Cultures on the Brink: Reengineering the Soul of Capitalism—On a Global Scale." In *Global Assemblages: Technology, Politics, and Ethics as Anthropological Problems,* ed. Aihwa Ong and Stephen J. Collier. Oxford: Blackwell.

Omel'chenko, Elena. 2000. "'My Body, My Friend?' Provincial Youth between the Sexual and the Gender Revolutions." In *Gender, State and Society in Soviet and Post-Soviet Russia,* ed. Sarah Ashwin. London: Routledge.

Ong, Aihwa. 1987. *Spirits of Resistance and Capitalist Discipline: Factory Women in Malaysia.* Albany: State University of New York Press.

Ozawa-de Silva, Chikako. 2007. "Demystifying Japanese Therapy: An Analysis of Naikan and the Ajase Complex through Buddhist Thought." *Ethos* 35(4): 411–46.

Papkova, Irina. 2008. "The Freezing of Historical Memory? The Post-Soviet Russian Orthodox Church and the Council of 1917." In *Religion, Morality, and Community in Post-Soviet Societies,* ed. Mark D. Steinberg and Catherine Wanner. Washington, DC: Woodrow Wilson Center Press.

Patico, Jennifer. 2008. *Consumption and Social Change in a Post-Soviet Middle Class.* Washington, DC: Woodrow Wilson Center Press.

Payton, James R. 2007. *Light from the Christian East: An Introduction to the Orthodox Tradition.* Downers Grove, IL: InterVarsity Press.

Pesmen, Dale. 2000. *Russia and Soul.* Ithaca, NY: Cornell University Press.

Philaret, Metropolitan. 1936. *Konspekt Po Nravstvennomu Bogosloviyu.* www .dorogadomoj.com/ml111nra.html.

Pilkington, Hilary. 2006. "'For Us It Is Normal': Exploring the 'Recreational' Use of Heroin in Russian Youth Cultural Practice." *Journal of Communist Studies and Transition Politics* 22(1): 24–53.

Pletnev, Maxim. 2004. "Khristianskii Vzglyad Na Problemy Narkoticheskoi Zavisimosti." Thesis, Department of Theology, Russian Orthodox Church, Moscow Patriarchy, Saint Petersburg Orthodox Ecclesiastical Academy.

Powell, David E. 2000. "The Problem of AIDS." In *Russia's Torn Safety Nets: Health and Social Welfare during the Transition,* ed. Mark G. Field and Judyth L. Twigg. New York: St. Martin's Press.

Raikhel, Eugene A. 2006. "Governing Habits: Addiction and the Therapeutic Market in Russia." PhD dissertation, Department of Anthropology, Princeton University.

Rausing, Sigrid. 2000. "Re-constructing the 'Normal': Identity and the Consumption of Western Goods in Estonia." In *Markets and Moralities: Ethnographies of Postsocialism*, ed. Ruth Mandl and Caroline Humphrey. New York: Berg.

Redfield, Peter. 2005. "Doctors, Borders, and Life in Crisis." *Cultural Anthropology* 20(3): 328–61.

Ricoeur, Paul. 1995. *Oneself as Another*. Chicago: University of Chicago Press.

Ries, Nancy. 1997. *Russian Talk: Culture and Conversation during Perestroika*. Ithaca, NY: Cornell University Press.

Rivkin-Fish, Michele. 2001. "Personal Transitions and Moral Change after Socialism: The Politics of Remedies in Russian Public Health." *Anthropology of East Europe Review* 19(1).

———. 2005a. "Moral Science and the Management of 'Sexual Revolution' in Russia." In *Sex in Development: Science, Sexuality, and Morality in Global Perspective*, ed. Vincanne Adams and Stacy Leigh Pigg. Durham, NC: Duke University Press.

———. 2005b. *Women's Health in Post-Soviet Russia: The Politics of Intervention*. Bloomington: Indiana University Press.

Robbins, Joel. 2001. "God Is Nothing but Talk: Modernity, Language, and Prayer in a Papua New Guinea Society." *American Anthropologist* 103(4): 901–12.

———. 2004. *Becoming Sinners: Christianity and Moral Torment in a Papua New Guinea Society*. Berkeley: University of California Press.

Robins, Steven. 2006. "From 'Rights' to 'Ritual': AIDS Activism in South Africa." *American Anthropologist* 108(2): 312–23.

Rogers, Douglas J. 2004. "An Ethics of Transformation: Work, Prayer, and Moral Practice in the Russian Urals, 1861–2001." PhD dissertation, Department of Anthropology, University of Michigan.

Rose, Nikolas. 1996. "Governing 'Advanced' Liberal Democracies." In *Foucault and Political Reason: Liberalism, Neo-liberalism and Rationalities of Government*, ed. Andrew Barry, T. Osborne, and N. Rose. Chicago: University of Chicago Press.

Russian Orthodox Church. 2000. *Osnovy Sotsial'noi Kontseptsii Russkoi Pravoslavnoi Tserkvi*. Moskva.

———. 2005. *Kontseptsii Uchastiia Russkoi Pravoslavnoi Tserkvi v Bor'be s Rasprostraneniem VICH/SPIDa i Rabote s Liud'mi, Zhivushimi s VICH/SPIDom*. Moskva.

———. 2006. *Deklaratsiya o pravakh i dostoinstve cheloveka X Vsemirnovo Russkovo Narodnovo Sobora.* www.mospat.ru.

———. 2008. *Osnovy ucheniya Russkoi Pravoslavnoi Tserkvi o dostoinstve, svobode i pravakh cheloveka.* www.mospat.ru.

Shelley, Louise. 2006. "The Drug Trade in Contemporary Russia." *China and Eurasia Forum Quarterly* 4(1): 15–20.

Shweder, Richard A., and Robert A. LeVine. 1984. *Culture Theory: Essays on Mind, Self, and Emotion.* Cambridge, UK: Cambridge University Press.

Singer, Merrill. 2006. *The Face of Social Suffering: The Life History of a Street Drug Addict.* Long Grove, IL: Waveland Press.

Skoll, Geoffrey R. 1984. *Walk the Walk and Talk the Talk: An Ethnography of a Drug Abuse Treatment Facility.* Philadelphia: Temple University Press.

Sontag, Susan. 1989. *AIDS and Its Metaphors.* New York: Farrar, Straus and Giroux.

St. Theophan the Recluse. 1996. *The Path to Salvation: A Manual of Spiritual Transformation.* Platina, CA: St. Herman of Alaska Brotherhood.

Sun, An-Pyng. 2007. "Relapse among Substance-abusing Women: Components and Processes." *Substance Use and Misuse* 42: 1–21.

Swora, Maria Gabrielle. 2001. "Commemoration and the Healing of Memories in Alcoholics Anonymous." *Ethos* 29(1): 58–77.

Taylor, Charles. 1989. *Sources of the Self: The Making of the Modern Identity.* Cambridge, UK: Cambridge University Press.

Teplova, Tatyana. 2007. "Welfare State Transformation, Childcare, and Women's Work in Russia." *Social Politics* 14(3): 284–322.

Thompson, E. P. 1967. "Time, Work-Discipline, and Industrial Capitalism." *Past and Present* 38(1): 56–97.

Throop, C. Jason. 2010. *Suffering and Sentiment: Exploring the Vicissitudes of Experience and Pain in Yap.* Berkeley: University of California Press.

UNAIDS. 2006. AIDS Epidemic Update. www.unaids.org.

Vann, Elizabeth F. 2005. "Domesticating Consumer Goods in the Global Economy: Examples from Vietnam and Russia." *Ethnos* 70(4): 465–88.

Vannoy, Dana, et al. 1999. *Marriages in Russia: Couples during the Economic Transition.* Westport, CT: Praeger.

Verdejo-García, Antonio, et al. 2007. "Negative Emotion-driven Impulsivity Predicts Substance Dependence Problems." *Drug and Alcohol Dependence* 91: 213–19.

Voloshinov, V. N. 2000. *Marxism and the Philosophy of Language.* Cambridge, MA: Harvard University Press.

Wallander, Celeste A. 2006. "Russian Politics and HIV/AIDS: The Institutional and Leadership Sources of an Inadequate Policy." In *HIV/ AIDS in Russia and Eurasia*, vol. 1, ed. J. Twigg. New York: Palgrave Macmillan.

Ware, Kallistos (Timothy). 1997a. "'My Helper and My Enemy': The Body in Greek Christianity." In *Religion and the Body*, ed. Sarah Coakley. Cambridge, UK: Cambridge University Press.

———. 1997b. *The Orthodox Church*. New York: Penguin.

———. 2001. *The Orthodox Way*. Crestwood, NY: St. Vladimir's Seminary Press.

Waterston, Alisse. 1993. *Street Addicts in the Political Economy*. Philadelphia: Temple University Press.

Wierzbicka, Anna. 2003. "Russian Cultural Scripts: The Theory of Cultural Scripts and Its Application." *Ethos* 30(4): 401–32.

Wolf, Susan. 1987. "Sanity and the Metaphysics of Responsibility." In *Responsibility, Character, and the Emotions*, ed. F. Schoeman. Cambridge, UK: Cambridge University Press.

Yurchak, Alexei. 2003. "Russian Neoliberal: The Entrepreneurial Ethic and the Spirit of 'True Careerism.'" *Russian Review* 62: 72–90.

———. 2006. *Everything Was Forever Until It Was No More: The Last Soviet Generation*. Princeton: Princeton University Press.

Zigon, Jarrett. 2006. "Five Muscovites: Narratives of Moral Experience in Contemporary Russia." PhD dissertation, Department of Anthropology, City University of New York, Graduate Center.

———. 2007. "Moral Breakdown and the Ethical Demand: A Theoretical Framework for an Anthropology of Moralities." *Anthropological Theory* 7(2): 131–50.

———. 2008a. "Aleksandra Vladimirovna: Moral Narratives of a Russian Orthodox Woman." In *Religion, Morality, and Community in Post-Soviet Societies*, ed. Mark D. Steinberg and Catherine Wanner. Washington, DC: Woodrow Wilson Press.

———. 2008b. *Morality: An Anthropological Perspective*. Oxford: Berg.

———. 2009a. "Developing the Moral Person: The Concepts of Human, God-manhood, and Feelings in Some Russian Articulations of Morality." *Anthropology of Consciousness* 20(1): 1–26.

———. 2009b. "Morality within a Range of Possibilities: A Dialogue with Joel Robbins." *Ethnos* 74(2): 251–76.

———. 2009c. "Phenomenological Anthropology and Morality." *Ethnos* 74(2): 286–88.

WEBSITES

Russkaya Pravoslavnaya Tserkov'. www.patriarchia.ru

Russkaya Pravoslavnaya Tserkov': Ofitsial'nyi Sait Otdela Vneshnikh Tserkovnikh Svyazei. www.mospat.ru

AIDS.ru. www.aids.ru/aids/pravoslav.shtml

Doroga Domoi. www.dorogadomoj.com

Vatican. www.vatican.va

Text: 10/14 Palatino
Display: Univers Condensed Light, Bauer Bodoni
Compositor: Toppan Best-set Premedia Limited
Printer and binder: IBT Global